Faith and the Future

Concilium is an international theological journal begun in 1965. Inspired by the Second Vatican Council and the spirit of reform and dialogue which the Council inaugurated, *Concilium* has featured many of the world's foremost theologians. The *Concilium Series*, published by Orbis Books and SCM Press, highlights the contributions of these distinguished authors as well as selected themes that reflect the journal's concern for the mystical-political meaning of the Gospel for our age.

Already published

David Tracy, *On Naming the Present*

Edward Schillebeeckx, *The Language of Faith*

CONCILIUM SERIES

JOHANN-BAPTIST METZ

and

JÜRGEN MOLTMANN

Faith and the Future

Essays on Theology, Solidarity, and Modernity

with an Introduction by Francis Schüssler Fiorenza

ORBIS BOOKS

Maryknoll, New York 10545

Copyright © 1995 by the Concilium Foundation, Nijmegen, The Netherlands

Published by Orbis Books, Maryknoll, NY 10545-0308, U.S.A., and SCM Press, London, England

Queries regarding rights and permissions should be addressed to: Stichting Concilium, Prins Bernhardstraat 23, 6521 AB Nijmegen, The Netherlands.

Manufactured in the United States of America

Library of Congress Cataloging-in-Publication Data

Metz, Johannes Baptist, 1928–
    Faith and the future : essays on theology, solidarity, and
    modernity / Johann-Baptist Metz and Jürgen Moltmann, with an
    introduction by Francis Schüssler Fiorenza.
        p.   cm. — (Concilium series)
    Includes bibliographical references.
    ISBN 1-57075-016-5 (pbk.)
    1. Theology.   I. Moltmann, Jürgen.   II. Title.   III. Series:
    Concilium series (Maryknoll, N.Y.)
    BR50.M426   1995
    230—dc20   95-2532
                                                          CIP

ORBIS/ISBN 1-57075-016-5   SCM/ISBN 0-334-02600-8

Contents

PART II
Essays by Jürgen Moltmann

Preface

Johann-Baptist Metz

I have been involved with the periodical *Concilium* since its founding. First I directed its department of "Church and the World," which was soon rechristened Fundamental Theology. In the area of that discipline I maintained an intensive, and gratifying, collaboration with Jean-Pierre Jossua. In the early 1980s, together with Edward Schillebeeckx, I took on the directorship of the Dogma department, and I recall that collaboration with great gratitude. Thus, my work with and for *Concilium* reflects a considerable portion of my postconciliar theological biography. I gladly consented, then, to the publisher's proposal to reprint a limited selection of my theological contributions to *Concilium* and its series of publications. I should like to say something about the "internal systematics" of the texts selected.

First, however, I want to express my joy at finding myself with Jürgen Moltmann in this project. I have been bound to him for many years now by a unique ecumenical friendship—an ecumenical togetherness of a special sort. We have always called our joint enterprise, our public struggle in the matter of "God and the World," our joint endeavor in common responsibility where the broadest conflicts are concerned, "indirect ecumenism." The ecumenism that guides our friendship is no ecumenism of the least common denominator, no down-levelling ecumenism in the interest of the discovery of a minimum consensus. Our focus, despite our very different presuppositions and backgrounds, has always been the "grand consensus"—a basic consensus, an agreement on the vision of Christianity that we owe this world in season and out.

The new political theology, as I have sought to develop it over the years—precisely in conversation with Jürgen Moltmann—has a recognizable "guiding thread." It is directed by a basic impetus that I might call, with the conciseness and clarity of a Latin formulation, a *conversio ad passionem*. Accordingly, its governing category is a *memoria passionis*, which includes, and emphasizes, the sufferings of the stranger-other, thereupon to take them into consideration in determining one's own behavior. In this sense, theology, as I understand it, is first and foremost a theology sensitive to suffering. In academic language, I might call it a theology sensitive to theodicy. Finally, all of this connects with how theology became "political" for me in the first place—in a new sense of the word—and this not incidentally, but substantially, so that this designation bears on the fundamental concepts and categories of theology.

There are three challenges and crises that this political theology has sought above all to confront. All three center on the question of suffering: they are in some manner "theodicy-intensive." I have grasped the conversation with *Marxism* as a coming to grips with the dramatization, in terms of social critique, of the question of suffering. *Auschwitz*, the *Holocaust*, or better, the *Shoa*, has thrust me more and more relentlessly before the question of why we hear and see so little of this horrible suffering—or, for that matter, of any of the story of the world's suffering—in our Christian theology. And the inclusion of the non-European world, especially the hitherto so-called "third world," into the purview of theology has shifted social suffering and misery, as well as the suffering of the (culturally, racially, ethnically) "other," quite into the radius of theology's *logos*. Most of the selections published here are readily identifiable in terms of this "theodicy triad." Finally, "Time without a Finale" constitutes an attempt to indicate how, in this connection, one ought to deal with a "postmodern" Nietzsche (whose emergence from Marx's shadow had already been observed in the 1972 text, "The Future in the Memory of Suffering").

A certain random element has necessarily come into play in the selection of articles from *Concilium* to be included here. But the same would have had to be said if all of my essays from this periodical had been reprinted. And so the responsibility for each of the selections in this volume must be that of its author. I must bear responsibility for mine, Jürgen Moltmann for his, and we two for each other.

Preface

Jürgen Moltmann

I am delighted about the publication of my contributions to *Concilium*, together with those of my friend Johann-Baptist Metz. I would like to take the occasion of this preface to express my gratitude and to add a word of praise.

In 1979 I was asked to join the board of directors of *Concilium* and since then have edited together with Hans Küng the issues on ecumenism. While I have had much experience editing theological and ecclesial journals, nowhere else have I enjoyed a more friendly and constructive collaboration as in the company of Hans Küng and the committee of directors of *Concilium*. We were always able to agree quickly about the current issues within the difficult area of ecumenism, as well as in the even more complex area of interreligious dialogue. We always found suitable authors for the different articles and—this is probably unique— almost no one ever declined our invitation. Only when one knows how difficult it is to motivate authors to write something new on a pre-assigned topic can one truly appreciate this accomplishment of *Concilium*. Each issue of *Concilium* is nothing short of a new book. *Concilium* appears simultaneously in six languages and as such is the only truly ecumenical and intercontinental journal. In the company of *Concilium* I have come to know something of the worldwide community of the "catholic" (in the best sense of the word) people of God. The presence of Latin American, Asian, African and Eastern European theologians prevented both Eurocentrism and fixation on the problems of the so-called First World. As a Protestant Christian and theologian I have never had any problems with the Roman aspect of the Catholic church. Occasionally I have even had the impression that I was the only one in *Concilium* who did not have problems with Rome. The Ecumenical Movement, which is working toward community among the divided Christian churches, is the most important gift of the twentieth century. No one had expected it and it made headway more easily than all of us had thought. Part of the ecumenical community is also the theological community, from which a common theology might one day arise. All Protestant churches and theologians can learn from *Concilium* how to develop a theology which not only preserves and renews itself, but also embraces and opens itself to that which is foreign and different. Theology is not truly evangelical if it is not meant for the entire people of God, no matter how dispersed they are throughout the world. To those who want to discover the catholic breadth of the Gospel, *Concilium* is an inestimable aid and stimulus.

I am especially pleased that Orbis Books is publishing Johann-Baptist Metz's contributions and mine together. Our ecumenical friendship began in Tübingen in 1966, on the occasion of the birthday of the atheist philosopher Ernst Bloch. Our friendship grew during the important Christian-Marxist dialogue, which the Catholic Paulus Society organized together with the Czech Academy of the Sciences in 1967. In this context we developed a sort of *indirect ecumenism.* In our discussion with the representatives of what was then called Marxism "with a human face," we were confronted with problems for which neither the Catholic nor the Protestant tradition had provided ready answers. We struggled in common for new answers and discovered common responses. In this way the theological movement which was called political theology arose at the end of the 1960s. We searched for a credible theology "after Auschwitz" and engaged very soon in a lively exchange of ideas with Black theology in the United States, liberation theology in Latin America, and Minjung theology in Korea. It is as paradoxical as it is true: to the degree that we in Germany confronted our own contextual situation "after Auschwitz," we developed world-wide relations. I have come to know Johann-Baptist Metz as one of the most stimulating theologians of the present day and always listen to his words with special attentiveness. Naturally, we are not theological twins—always of the same opinion. On the contrary, since Metz is a fundamental theologian and I am a dogmatic theologian, we view theology from different perspectives. Moreover, as a Russian proverb says, when two say the same thing, one is superfluous. Until now, we have not made each other theologically superfluous. We find our differences most interesting. I hope that the reader of these contributions from *Concilium* will sense something of this interest.

Introduction

Francis Schüssler Fiorenza

Eschatology, Hope, and Political Theology

Johann B. Metz and Jürgen Moltmann belong to the post-World War II generation of German theologians. They grew up during the regime of Adolf Hitler and National Socialism. As young men—in fact, as mere teenagers—they were drafted into Hitler's army toward the end of the war when the need to replenish dwindling manpower led to younger and younger draftees. They both suffered the bitter experiences of the war and imprisonment. Metz, born in 1928 and drafted in 1944, was captured six months before the end of the war and sent to prison camps in the United States, first in Maryland and then in Virginia. Moltmann, born in 1926 and drafted in 1944, was captured by the British forces in Belgium and was then imprisoned first in Scotland and then near Nottingham, England in the Norton Prisoner of War Camp for three years.

After the war, both returned to Germany where in the 1950s they pursued their theological studies in their respective confessional traditions—Roman Catholic (Metz) and Lutheran (Moltmann). Although they would come to international prominence as theologians in the 1960s and become associated respectively with "political theology" and the "theology of hope," their new directions in theology should be seen in the context of their personal and political experiences. The German experience with National Socialism, the Holocaust, and World War II provided the stimulus for their theologies which proclaimed that the passion *for* God and *of* God is a passion for justice and peace. At the same time the rediscovery of biblical eschatology enabled them to develop a critical distance from the theologies of their predecessors.

Johann B. Metz went to study in Innsbruck, Austria, where he encountered Karl Rahner, who subsequently became a life-long mentor and friend. Metz's first writings display his early indebtedness to Heidegger's philosophy and to Rahner's transcendental theology. This influence is clearly evident in his dissertation, *Christliche Anthropozentrik*, that sketches the anthropocentric dimensions of Thomas Aquinas's theology with categories borrowed from Martin Heidegger and Karl Rahner. Metz first became known in relation to Karl Rahner. He edited Rahner's *Spirit and the World* and brought out the second and much revised edition of Rahner's *Hearers of the Word*. Though this revision reflected in part Rahner's further development of transcendental theology, it clearly displayed traces of Metz's influence. He had eliminated some polemical references to Protestant theology and he more sharply emphasized the historical in relation to the transcendental.

Metz's own voice within theology emerged in *Theology of the World* (1968, ET 1969) that ranged from the problem of secularization to that of political theology. Whereas the first essay pleaded for Christian theology to take seriously the contemporary situation of secularization, the final essay proposed a political theology pointing to the inadequacy of secularized theologies. Metz's further publications can be understood as developing his political theology. He argued in *Faith in History in Society* (1977, ET 1980) for a practical fundamental theology. In *The Emergent Church* (1980, ET 1986) Metz distinguishes between messianic and bourgeois religion and develops a vision of Christianity that requires a "Second Reformation" in order to survive as a messianic religion in a postbourgeois world.

In the early sixties Moltmann's *Theology of Hope: On the Ground and Implications of a Christian Eschatology* (1964) broke onto the theological scene as a fresh wind. It immediately established Moltmann as a new and significant voice within theology. His name and the direction of his theology became identified with the "theology of hope." Moltmann sought to reclaim Christian eschatology from its reduction into existential theology by Rudolf Bultmann or into transcendent subjectivity by Karl Barth.

Moltmann's retrieval of eschatology uncovered the social and political engagement of Christian theology and faith. His further theological development led to innumerable essays and many books. *The Crucified God: The Cross of Christ as the Foundation and Criticism of Christian Theology* (1972, ET 1974) links the theology of hope with the eschatological significance of the Cross. He then sought to deal with the church by linking ecclesiology and pneumatology within the framework of eschatology in *The Church in the Power of the Spirit: A Contribution to Messianic Ecclesiology* (1975, ET 1977). In his Gifford lectures, Moltmann takes up the problem of creation in relation to nature and the ecological crisis: *God in Creation: an Ecological Doctrine of Creation*

(1985). In addition to volumes developing the topics of systematic theology, such as *The Trinity and the Kingdom: The Doctrine of God* (1980, ET 1981) and *The Way of Jesus Christ: Christology in Messianic Dimensions* (1989, ET 1990), Moltmann has sought to deal with concrete issues such as justice, human rights, feminism, Jewish-Christian relations, and ecology.

When one follows the theological paths of Metz and Moltmann, it becomes evident that both have taken several steps in similar theological directions. Sensitive at the time of their early work to the increasing awareness within New Testament studies of the significance of "apocalyptic" as the mother of Christian theology, both sought to reclaim Christian eschatology and apocalyptic from its imprisonment in existential and transcendental interpretations. Aware of the problems of the modern market society with its privatization of faith and religion for society, both criticized modernity not by a retreating into an individualistic piety, but by advancing the Christian faith into public discourse. At the time of the cold war and in the very face of it, both seriously engaged in the dialogue with Marxism. Consequently, they were both influenced by Ernst Bloch's philosophy of hope with its revision of the determinism of vulgar Marxism and advocacy of a utopian consciousness. Both have profoundly influenced the development of Latin American liberation theology, even though the latter have gone their own way and taken issue with some aspects of Metz's and Moltmann's interpretation of modern society and Christian eschatology.

Several common themes pulsate through their work in general and in the essays collected here in particular. Two of these, as I would like to underscore, are central to the contributions of Metz and Moltmann in this volume. The first is their interpretation of modernity, especially their critical analysis of modern society and Western rationality. The second is their focus on the significance of suffering, not only politically and existentially, but religiously and theologically. In addition, I would like to point to two distinctive emphases of each, specifically, Jürgen Moltmann's development of Trinitarian theology and Johann B. Metz's elaboration of the meaning of memory and narrative.

A Critical Theory of Modern Society

As integral to the interpretation of the current situation facing Christian faith and theology today, Metz and Moltmann have elaborated a critical theory or interpretation of modern society. Long before criticisms of modernity became fashionable in much of post-modern discourse, both Metz and Moltmann have offered a critical interpretation of modernity and modern society. Such critical interpretations not only show how Metz and Moltmann interpret the current situation, but they also indicate how their theological approaches and proposals are in part a response to the situation of modernity. These critical interpretations, which permeate several of the ensuing essays, take up the tradition of the Frankfurt School and its development of Max Weber's interpretation of modernity in terms of occidental rationality.

In the title of one essay, Moltmann raises the question, "Has Modern Society a Future?" Modern society, with its conflicts and contradictions, is, as Moltmann argues, undergoing a third industrial revolution—the first and second being mechanization and electrification, with the third computerization. The accumulation of capital and the increase of hope within the modern West has gone hand in hand with increased indebtedness and lack of hope within the world at large. The peace of nuclear deterrence has come at the price of a mutually assured destruction. The production of wealth has taken its cost with the devastation of nature and the environment. Moltmann's essay on "The Liberating Feast," provides a critical and functional analysis of how the reproduction of life through work in the modern world has deprived feast days of their renewing character and explores how the liberating feast of Christ's resurrection provides a ground for affirming hope in God's new creation. His essay on "Fundamentalism and Modernity" points not only to the conflict between fundamentalism and modernity, but also to the contradictions of the modern world. Consequently, it is important to recognize a certain legitimacy to the protest of fundamentalism against modernity while also pointing to the need to liberate fundamentalism for an openness to the future of God's world.

In "Theology in the Modern Age and before Its End," Metz notes that the Enlightenment or Modernity is not merely a historical period, but is also a process and form of rationality. The increasing dominance of Enlightenment and Western or European rationality has increasingly led to a privatization of the faith and a reduction of human imagination. It has led to the spread of a technocratic rationality and to European domination. In fact, the two are linked. Industrialization goes hand in hand with an exponential growth of impoverishment. The technological rationality that dominates nature leads to a neglect of the Other. Metz's critical analysis of modern society takes particular aim at the crisis of the church posed by bourgeois religion. The bourgeois virtues of autonomy, stability, competitive struggle, and performance obscure the messianic virtues of repentance, compassion, and unconditional love for the "least of the brethren."

In Metz's diagnosis, the global processes and tendencies within our present-day world have a radical ambiguity. On the one hand, one is becoming increasingly conscious of genuine cultural polycentrism and pluralism. On the other hand, Western Eurocentric rationality with its culture, technology, and information industry is increasingly pulling all non-European peoples into a "Eurocentric whirlpool." In the face of this situation, Metz argues in his essay, "Unity and Diversity: Problems and Prospects for Inculturation," that if the Christian churches are to mature into cultural polycentrism, they will have to develop from their memory the potential for the intercultural exchange with the Other that categories of Western and Eurocentric rationality obscure. This memory of suffering that opens us to the suffering of others in other cultures is a central category underlying the theologies of both Metz and Moltmann.

Suffering

The centrality of the category of suffering in the theologies of both Metz and Moltmann gives contour to their eschatology. Their orientation to the future and their emphasis on hope does not represent an optimistic, one-directional, developmental view of history, but includes suffering and the memory of the suffering of past victims. This emphasis on suffering receives a concrete focus on the memory of Auschwitz and the Holocaust. The catastrophe and suffering of Auschwitz is a suffering that should not simply be reconstructed but should be practically remembered. Theologians should enter into this struggle for remembrance. As Metz argues in "Facing the Jews: Christian Theology after Auschwitz," Christians must understand their identity in the face of the Jews. This involves not simply overcoming the urge to forget the Holocaust (a phenomenon not mentioned in the theology of his mentor); it is also a matter of "overcoming the forced blocking out of the Jewish heritage within Christianity."

The focus on suffering and the memory of the Holocaust has long been important for both theologians. Together they had published in Germany in 1974 a small book of meditations on suffering entitled *Leidensgeschichte* that deals with the text of Mark 8:31-38. Whereas Moltmann dealt with the theme of the suffering of the Son of Man and Christian Discipleship, Metz explicated the notion of messianic history as a history of suffering. In underscoring the memory of the suffering of victims, Metz argued that progressive views of history, with their confidence that technological and scientific control can contribute to the amelioration of suffering, overlook the suffering of the victims of the past. The suffering of such victims challenges historical optimism and progressivism. Suffering, for Metz as well as Moltmann, should not pose the theodicy question as a theoretical question but rather as a practical question. For Metz, we can believe and pray because the victims of the Holocaust believed and prayed. Moltmann, for his part, asserts that the theodicy question is a question of practical reason and that the challenge of Auschwitz "is not merely a matter of revising Christian theology with regard to Judaism, but a matter of revising Christian theology altogether." Suffering poses a practical question to Christian engagement and to Christian identity.

Moltmann's essays in this volume elaborate the way he links suffering with Christ and God. In the face of an atheistic claim that the answer to suffering is the non-existence of God, Moltmann consistently asks what is the meaning of Christ's suffering for God and for the Christian belief in God. If God is incapable of suffering, then God is incapable of loving. A God who is incapable of loving is a God who is less and not more than humans. The poor, oppressed, and suffering have identified with a suffering God who has identified with them precisely in their suffering. Moltmann's interpretation of the doctrine of the Trinity explicates the very identification of God in God's very being with suffering.

Moltmann's Trinitarianism

Moltmann's interpretation of the suffering of Christ leads him to the heart of the doctrine of the Trinity. In "The 'Crucified God': God and the Trinity Today," Moltmann interprets the death of Christ not primarily as an event between God and humans, but as an event between Jesus and his Father—an event within the Trinity and from which the Spirit proceeds. Moltmann's interpretation of the Trinity seeks to overcome the distinction between the immanent and "economic Trinity," that is, between the abstract nature of God and the inner Triune life. It means that the story of Jesus and his suffering is a story of God's very being as historical. Moltmann traces the historical relation between monotheism and theocracy and points to the theocratic character of Judaism, Christianity, and Islam. The monotheistic emphasis on oneness and domination has to be counterbalanced by the Trinitarian emphasis on community. An understanding of God as a Trinitarian community rather than as a patriarchal monarchy works against the deformations of community in life and society. Moltmann's Trinitarian conception allows an understanding of suffering as that which is not foreign to God but is rather an inner Trinitarian event.

Metz's Dangerous Memory

Metz links the memory of the suffering of past victims with the meaning of history. Forgotten suffering, suppressed hopes, vanquished possibilities are allowed a meaning in a sacred and messianic history, whereas many modern idealist and post-idealist conceptions of history have neglected the value of past suffering and have overlooked the enduring significance of the suffering of individual victims. It is important to retrieve the memories of these victims, "the Others" with regard to the history of the victors. Similar to Walter Benjamin's appeal to "dialectical images" in his theses on history, Metz appeals to "dangerous memories" as a practical critique of present history. Christian faith is the *memoria passionis, mortis et resurrectionis Jesu Christi*. This memory is grounded on the promise of freedom for all. The history of human suffering does not belong to the pre-history of human freedom, but to its inner reality. Christian memory and the retelling of the narrative of suffering become "subversions" or "dangerous memories" that prevent us from becoming reconciled to the trends of modern technological society. As Metz develops in detail in his essay "The Future in the Memory of Suffering," such memory challenges positivist, Marxist, and liberal conceptions of history and political life. Such memory displays the task of history as a practical task. Such a memory poses the challenge and task to the Christian churches that they spell out the meaning of the *memoria passionis Jesu Christi* in the midst of our modern society.

In short, the essays of Johann B. Metz and Jürgen Moltmann collected in this volume span almost a full three decades of contemporary theology, bridging the landscape of the 1970s to the early 1990s. They document the contributions of two intellectual giants of contemporary German theology as they record their views on a variety of theological and religious issues, and show how these theologians analyzed diverse concrete religious issues in the context of contemporary society. Finally, they show that although each has developed a distinctive theological approach, they both nevertheless share so much in common that a joint collection of their essays appropriately highlights their shared interests and mutual concerns.

By publishing together this collection of essays, drawn from *Concilium* (an international journal established to continue the work of Vatican II), Orbis Books provides a paradigmatic sample of the work of two theologians who through their retrieval of Christian eschatology and messianic hope have re-thought the relation between religion and society, church and world, and have reformulated the political responsibility of theology.

PART I

ESSAYS BY JOHANN-BAPTIST METZ

1

The Future in the Memory of Suffering

I

Confidence in the supposed gradual evolution of technological civilization has gone. If "progress" exists at all, it is only in opposition to its naïve generalization (as in some crude futurologies). Increasingly, the warm stream of teleology that helped our way of thinking in the past is drying up. Teleological reliance on a growing reconciliation of man with nature has collapsed; with its disappearance we notice for the first time how profoundly and tenaciously it gripped us, conditioning even our philosophical and theological interpretations of the future. But now Sisyphus suddenly reappears next to Prometheus, Camus next to Teilhard, Monod next to Whitehead. . . .[1]

We are becoming ever more conscious of the dangers and antagonisms that arise when technological and economic processes are left to their "natural" suasions, and our political and social control systems break down: dying cities, ruined environmental systems, population explosions, chaotic information channels, an increasingly aggressive and vicious intensification of the North–South conflict, leading possibly to a new outcome of the East–West power struggle, and so on. In addition, there is the threat posed to man's apparent identity and freedom by the growing possibilities of psychological and genetic manipulation. One also suspects that, left to itself, the technologico-economic planning of man's future will produce the wholly adapted human being whose dreams and imagination can no longer keep up and are suppressed by the functionalism of technical systems; whose freedom degenerates into an instinctive animal adaptability to the superior power and complexity of preformed behavior patterns; and who has been deprived of the world as something over against him, in order, in fact, to rob him of the need any longer to experience it personally. The purely technologically and economically planned production of man's future would seem to fore-shadow the very disappearance of man as the being who has nourished himself on the historical substance of his freedom: on, that is, the power to find an alternative despite all need to conform. Hence, there is no lack today of voices to follow up Nietzsche's proclamation of the "death of God" with that of the "death of man": the paralysis of human sponta-neity and the burial of man in the grave of an economico-technical structuralism; and the fear that human thinking is losing its dialectical tension with the status quo and is being integrated with an all-encroaching and anonymous production process.

This situation seems to me to forbid any discussion of the future in non-subjective categories: development, progress, or even "process." Instead, we have to ask: whose development, whose progress, and whose process? and: development, progress, and process in what direc-tion? The question of the future of our technological civilization is a question not primarily of technology, but of the control and application of technology and economico-technological processes; a problem not primarily of means but of ends and of the establishment of priorities and preferences. This means, however, that it is primarily a political and fundamentally a social problem.

But how can politics become the primary *topos* in our technological society for investigation of the future? Isn't politics, as something self-sufficient, set over against technology and economics in its death throes? Isn't there a growing anonymous dictatorship of structures and processes compared with which the dictatorship of individuals and parties seems harmless? Kenneth Boulding writes: "We can conceive of a world where an invisible dictatorship is still making use of democratic forms of government." Isn't the euthanasia of politics coming closer in our technological society? Aren't we witnessing an increasing self-paralysis of political reason and its consequent degeneration into instrumental reason in the service of technological and economic pro-cesses and their anonymous "power-systems?" Where are we to find a politics capable of controlling these systems and extricating them from the contradictions and catastrophes apparent today?

Would something like a radical "scientification" of politics help here? Certainly, political life is becoming increasingly less capable of doing without the mediation and mobilization of scientific knowledge. Yet, it is not science that constitutes and guarantees the authenticity of political consciousness as opposed to technological controls. Our modern sci-ences themselves are essentially technological and not merely inciden-tally; this is, in fact, a presupposition for their success and is grounded in the mode of cognition specific to them as sciences. Admittedly, this raises a multitude of questions that cannot be pursued here. I would remark only that if a politics is to be more than a successful accommodation to the control systems of technical and economic processes, it must be grounded in something more and something other than science (as we know and understand it today).

Obviously, this kind of politics will exist only when there is a fundamental change in our political life. But not the conversion of politics into purely technological administration and a computer-politics that in its programming merely reproduces the above-mentioned dilemmas, not an old-style decision-politics, and not Machiavellianism, a kind of stone-age politics in the twentieth century. What we need in the long run is a new form of political life and new political structures. Only when that arrives will there be any humane cultures at all in the future. In this sense, "politics" is actually the new name for culture (and in this sense, too, any theology that tries to reflect on Christian traditions in the context of world problems is also a "political theology"). I now mention some aspects of this new orientation and structural pattern of political awareness.

Our situation demands a new association between politics and morals, one that refuses to remain content with the kind of trivial affluent-society morality we retain in the liberal distinction between politics and morals. As Jürgen Habermas says: "There are indications that developed social systems already accept, or are on the point of accepting, certain international imperatives of life—namely, the elimination of war as a legitimate means of settling conflicts, and the removal of mass poverty and disparities in economic development. Even where these systems do not at present offer adequate motives for the solution of such global problems, one thing is nevertheless already clear: a solution of these problems is hardly possible without the application throughout life of those universalist norms which were hitherto required only in the private sphere. Someone still tied to the old categories might call this the 'moralization' of politics. But this kind of idea ought not to be dismissed—simply on those grounds—as naïve enthusiasm."

This connection between politics and morals cannot be ordained from above, and can and should not be allowed to relapse into the political canonization of a particular moral system. It requires the mobilization of spiritual and moral forces by means of a radical democratization of the social infrastructure, a nourishing from below of freedom and effective responsibility.

The form of political life that would allow a culture of freedom in our economico-technological processes cannot, in my opinion, afford to ignore the reserves of moral and political imagination that appear in the present subcultures and countercultures of our technological society. Far more than the conventional generation conflict is expressed in this "youth culture." It is, in a certain sense, our Western form of the Cultural Revolution, the experimental quest for an alternative to the control systems of our technological society. Anyone who merely expects the escapists to return penitently like lost sheep to the established system has misunderstood both this culture and his own situation.

Of course this new political life, whose aims are not confined to what is deemed plausible by our economico-technological controls, does not intend to bypass technology and economics altogether. There is neither an alternative to technology, nor (to date) an alternative technology. What is sought for and demanded is, instead, a new form of mediation, a new instrumental control of this technology and these technical and economic processes. One thing, above all, must be avoided: the dissolution of political imagination and political action into the pure business of planning. Only the independence of the political dimension can guarantee the possibility of a humane future.

You will perhaps remember the story of the fight between the two giants. One of them is weaker and is on the brink of defeat yet manages to keep going and finally free himself from the other's grasp. He is able to do this because a tiny hunchback sits in his ear, urging him on and continually whispering new defensive ploys. This might serve as a parable for the struggle between technology and politics, between purely economico-technological planning and a political draft for the future. Political imagination will prevent itself from ultimate absorption by the restrictive grasp of technology, as long as it keeps the moral imagination and power to resist that have grown out of the memory of the suffering accumulated in history. The dwarf stands for the memory of this suffering: in our advanced social systems, suffering is pictured as insignificant, ugly, and better kept out of sight.

Political consciousness *ex memoria passionis*, political action in the memory of mankind's history of suffering: this could indicate an understanding of politics that would lead to new possibilities and new criteria for the mastering of technological and economic processes. It offers inspiration for a new form of solidarity, of responsibility toward those most distant from us, inasmuch as the history of suffering unites all men like a "second nature." It prevents a purely technical understanding of freedom and peace; it excludes any form of freedom and peace at the expense of the suppressed history of suffering of other nations and groups. It forces us to look at the public *theatrum mundi* not merely from the standpoint of the successful and the established, but from that of the conquered and the victims. This recalls the function of the court fool in the past: he represented an alternative (rejected, vanquished, or oppressed) to his master's policy; his function was strictly political and in no way "purely aesthetic." His politics was, so to speak, a politics of the memory of suffering—as against the traditional political principle of "woe to the conquered," and against the Machiavellian ruler. Today it is a question of sublating the "division of labor" in political life between the powerful on the one hand, and the "fool" with his powerless imagination of suffering on the other. Here I see the significance of a new association of politics and morals. From it there ultimately emerges a conception of political life and political responsibility for which the great moral and religious traditions of mankind could also, possibly, be mobilized, once they have been comprehended at their deepest level of meaning.

II

Christianity does not introduce God subsequently as a kind of "stop-gap" into this conflict about the future; instead, it tries to keep alive the memory of the crucified Lord, this specific *memoria passionis*, as a dangerous memory of freedom in the social systems of our technological civilization. This assertion needs more detailed development and explication. I now mention some of the most important aspects.

First, a category that I have already used quite often in the course of these reflections on the theme of the "future" requires more exact delineation: this is the category of "memory." What prevents memory from being a traditionalistic, even a reactionary category when it is used as so fundamental a characterization of the future? How is it not a bourgeois counterconception to hope, one leading us treacherously away from the risks of our future? In what sense can memory function as a practical and critical, and even dangerously emancipatory, force?

There are some very different kinds of memories. There are those in which we just do not take the past seriously enough: memories in which the past becomes a paradise without danger, a refuge from our present disappointments—the memory of the "good old days." There are memories that bathe everything from the past in a soft, conciliatory light. "Memory transfigures," we say, and, at times, we experience this in a rather drastic form; for example, when old soldiers exchange war yarns at a regimental dinner. War as an inferno is obliterated from such memories: what seems to remain is only the adventure experienced long ago. Here the past is filtered through a harmless cliché: everything dangerous, oppressive, and demanding has vanished from it: it seems deprived of all future. In this way, memory can easily become a "false consciousness" of our past and an opiate for our present.

But there is another form of memory: there are dangerous memories, memories that make demands on us. There are memories in which earlier experiences break through to the center point of our lives and reveal new and dangerous insights for the present. They illuminate for a few moments and with a harsh steady light the questionable nature of things we have apparently come to terms with, and show up the banality of our supposed "realism." They break through the canon of all that is taken as self-evident, and unmask as deception the certainty of those "whose hour is always there" (Jn. 7.6). They seem to subvert our structures of plausibility. Such memories are like dangerous and incalculable visitants from the past. They are memories we have to take into account; memories, as it were, with future content. "Remembrance of the past," says a contemporary philosopher, "can allow dangerous insights to emerge, and society as it is established would seem to fear the subversive contents of this memory." It is not by chance that the destruction of memory is a typical measure of totalitarian rule. The enslavement of men begins when their memories of the past are taken away. All forms of colonialization are based on this principle. Every rebellion against suffering is fed by the subversive power of remembered suffering. In this sense, suffering is in no way a purely passive, inactive "virtue." It is, or can be, the source of socially emancipatory action. Thus, in this sense, the memory of accumulated suffering continues to resist the cynics of modern political power.

There is an obvious danger today that everything in our consciousness that is determined by memory, everything outside the calculations of our technico-pragmatic reason, will be equated with superstition and left to the private whim of the individual. But this doesn't necessarily mean that we are freer and more "enlightened." We merely fall prey to the dominant illusions all the more easily and are deceived in another way. There are many examples. In this sense, the remembrance of accumulated suffering contradicts the contemporary prophets of the disappearance of history. This memory prevents us from understanding history either as a mere background for an occasional festive interpretation of our existence, or merely as distanced material for historical criticism. As the remembered history of suffering, history retains the form of "dangerous tradition." This subversive tradition resists any attempt to sublate and still it by means of a purely affirmative attitude to the past (as, for example, in hermeneutical theories) and by means of a wholly critical attitude to the past (as, for instance, in ideology criticism). The "mediation" of the memory of suffering is always practical.

We must confront the fact that this memory is a memory of *suffering: memoria passionis.* In our social life, there is a kind of taboo preventing or impairing insight into the essentially cognitive and practical function of suffering.

Modern scientific knowledge is marked by the model of a dominative knowledge of nature, and in this view, man understands himself anthropologically above all as the dominative subject in relation to nature. *Scientia et potentia in idem coincidunt:* Bacon's proposition characterizes the modern conception of science as dominative knowledge. Accordingly, in a society universally determined by this kind of scientific knowledge, other forms of human behavior and knowledge (such as suffering, pain, mourning, but also joy, play, and so on) enjoy only a functional and derived validity, and are largely underestimated in a cognitive and critical sense. Hence, it is significant that there should be a kind of *anti-knowledge ex memoria passionis* forming in our society, in which the existing identification of "praxis" with "domination of nature" is banished.

Our idea of history is also unilaterally affected by a screening out of the importance of suffering. We tend, consciously or unconsciously, to define history as the history of what has prevailed, as the history of the successful and the established: in historical studies, too, a kind of Darwinism in the sense of the principle of selection (*"Vae victis!"*) tends to prevail. Again, it is of decisive importance that a kind of *antihistory* should develop out of the memory of suffering—an understanding of history in which the vanquished and destroyed alternatives would also be taken into account: an understanding of history *ex memoria passionis* as a history of the vanquished.

It also seems to me important to stress the *antiteleological* and *antiontological* character of suffering—not least of all as against certain tendencies within theology itself. I should like to expand this point briefly.[2] There is a teleological and finalistic mediation between nature and man. This would seem to be confirmed by modern natural science, wherever, as in biology, it becomes anthropology. One has only to refer to Jacques Monod as opposed to Teilhard de Chardin and Whitehead. Nevertheless, the fact remains that it is suffering that resists an affirmative theory of the reconciliation of man and nature. Any attempt of that kind ultimately degenerates into a poverty-stricken kind of ontologization of human torment. Suffering emphasizes the contrast between nature and history, teleology and eschatology. There is no "objective" reconciliation between them, no obvious, manageable unity. All such attempts fall below the level of dignity of human suffering. This is especially clear in the case of the attempt to understand human suffering as a modality of a general interaction in nature between "action" and "passion." This, in both senses of the word, is nothing but a scholasticism of suffering. The least trace of meaningless suffering in the world we experience cancels all affirmative ontology and all teleology as untrue, and exposes them as a mythology of modern times (cf. Theodor Adorno).

Ultimately, human suffering resists all attempts to interpret history and historical processes in terms of nature, or to interpret nature as the subject of these historical processes. Of course, it is presupposed here that in this suffering, we have a permanent, negative revelation of a consciousness of identity that cannot be reduced to the trivial identity of chronological inertia. This consciousness of identity does not mean the anthropocentrism of power and domination over nature, but an anthropocentrism of suffering that prevails against every form of cosmocentrism. It is not idealistic pride but respect for the dignity of the suffering accumulated in history that persuades us to try to understand nature from the viewpoint of history (which means interpreting the association between nature and history dialectically and not teleologically) and to interpret the thousands of millions of years of natural time as an "inflation time" compared with the historical time of suffering humanity (cf. Ernst Bloch).

Consequently, the substrate of human history is not nature as development or as a kind of process without any subject. The natural history of man is in a certain sense the history of his passion. In this sense, the lack of reconciliation between nature and man is not suppressed but maintained—in the face of all teleological projection and all ontological generalization. This history of passion has no goal, but—at most—a future. Moreover, a continuity of this history is made available to us not by means of teleology but, at most, by the "trace of suffering." The essential dynamics of history is accordingly the memory of suffering as a negative consciousness of future freedom and as a stimulus (with this freedom in our sights) to act to conquer suffering.

Christian faith declares itself as the *memoria passionis, mortis et resurrectionis Jesu Christi.* At the midpoint of this faith is a specific *memoria passionis,* on which is grounded the promise of future freedom for all. We remember the future of our freedom in the memory of this his suffering—this is an eschatological statement that cannot be made more plausible through any subsequent accommodation, and cannot be generally verified. This statement remains controversial and controvertible: the power to scandalize is part of its communicable content. For the truth of the passion of Jesus and the history of human suffering as we remember it in the word "God" is a truth whose recollection always painfully contradicts the expectations of the individual who tries to conceive it. The eschatological truth of the *memoria passionis* cannot be derived from our historical, social, and psychological suasions. This is what makes it a liberating truth in the first place. But this also is at the root of its nature as constitutionally alien to our cognitive systems. If the eschatological truth of the *memoria passionis* is not merely to be expressed in empty tautologies and paradoxes, then it must be reflected upon within, and determined by temporal circumstances, the memory of the suffering of Jesus must be deciphered as a subversively liberating memory within the apparent plausibilities of our society, and the christological dogmas must hold good as subversive formulas of that memory.

In this sense, the Christian *memoria* insists that the history of human suffering is not merely part of the prehistory of freedom, but remains an inner aspect of *the* history of freedom. The imagination of future freedom is nourished from the memory of suffering, and freedom degenerates wherever those who suffer are treated more or less as a cliché and degraded to a faceless mass. Hence, the Christian *memoria* becomes a "subversive remembrance," which shocks us out of ever becoming prematurely reconciled to the "facts" and "trends" of our technological society. It becomes a liberating memory over against the controls and mechanisms of the dominant consciousness and its abstract ideal of emancipation. The Christian *memoria passionis* articulates itself as a memory that makes one free to suffer from the sufferings of others, and to respect the prophetic witness of others' suffering, even though the negative view of suffering in our "progressive" society makes it seem as something increasingly intolerable and even repugnant. A society that suppresses these and similar dimensions in the history of freedom, and in the understanding of freedom, pays the price of an increasing loss of all visible freedom. It is incapable of developing goals and priorities that prevent the creeping adaptation of our freedom to the anonymous, impersonal framework of a computer society.

I should like to make two explanatory additions to the foregoing interpretation.

It might well be objected that in this approach, Christian memory is unilaterally reduced to the status of remembrance of suffering, and that the *memory of the resurrection of Jesus* is put into the background, if not altogether obscured. Obviously, it is impossible to make a simple distinction between the *memoria passionis* and *memoria resurrectionis*. There is no understanding of the resurrection that does not have to be developed by way of and beyond the memory of suffering. There is no understanding of the joyousness of resurrection that is free of the shadows and threats of the human history of suffering. A *memoria resurrectionis* that would not be comprehensible as *memoria passionis* would be mythology pure and simple. But what of a *memoria passionis* that understands itself in faith as *memoria resurrectionis*? What does it mean to make "resurrection" accessible by way of the memory of suffering? Can such a resurrection faith also be expressed in socially communicable symbols that possess some critically liberating force for us? I believe that such a resurrection faith is expressed inasmuch as it acts "contra-factually" in making us free to bear in mind the sufferings and hopes of the past and the challenge of the dead. It allows not only a "forward-looking solidarity" (Walter Benjamin: with the "happiness of our grandchildren"), but a "backward-looking solidarity" (Benjamin: with the "suffering of our forefathers"). It allows not only a revolution that will change the things of tomorrow for future generations, but a revolution that will decide anew the meaning of our dead and their hopes. Resurrection mediated by way of the memory of suffering means the following: the dead, those already vanquished and forgotten, have a meaning that is as yet unrealized. The potential meaning of our history does not depend only on the survivors, the successful, and those who make it. The history that we write and study in our history books is, in contrast, almost always a "history of the victors," a history of those who made it, of the successful, of the people who got there. They never seem to mention the vanquished and the oppressed, the forgotten and suppressed hopes of our historical existence. But is that really so understandable? Why should the "right of the stronger," a kind of historical Darwinism, prevail in history too? Great literature, on the other hand, has always tried in tragedies to search out the continuity and meaning of history in precisely the suppressed and buried "traces of suffering," to inquire after the forgotten and unsuccessful ones of history, and in this way, to write a kind of antihistory. This must be taken into account by a church and a theology where the "memory of suffering" occupies a central position. Only then will they be able to prevent themselves degenerating to the level of a church or a theology of the victors, and therefore, of political religion (in something like the Constantinian sense). On the other hand, faith in the resurrection of the dead has a wholly social and social-critical significance. It enables us to insist firmly on the memory of the suffering that has accumulated in history, in order, thereby, to determine our behavior and our hopes. Such an understanding of the unity of the *memoria passionis* and *memoria resurrectionis* is also opposed to the attempt to make the conventional distinction between a this-worldly history of suffering and a supra-mundane history of glory: in fact, between world history and sacred history. World history and sacred history are neither two quantities that can be, so to speak, superficially equated by means of theological speculation, nor can they (nor ought they to) be merely formally contrasted. Sacred history is, instead, world history in which a meaning is conceded to obscured and suppressed hopes and sufferings. Sacred history is that world history in which the vanquished and forgotten possibilities of human existence that we call "death" are allowed a meaning that is not recalled or cancelled by the future course of history.

We must also determine more precisely what is actually understood as "suffering" in the context of this article. Which "suffering," then, is intended in the *memoria passionis?* Isn't it very dangerous to talk about "suffering in general?" Doesn't the "memory of suffering" lose then all its critical, and, above all, its social-critical and political force? Doesn't that mean that suffering is wholly privatized and internalized? Doesn't everyone suffer, in a certain sense, in this view? Doesn't a rich playboy in his luxury bungalow suffer? Where are the requisite differentiations, the bases of a critical awareness in the interest precisely of those who suffer and are oppressed unjustly? Doesn't this lead to the entry of political commitment into the boring, nonspecific vagueness that is, for the most part, the today of the social and political countenance of the world Church? Surely everything tends then toward that kind of consolation that ultimately consoles no one, since it intends exactly the same consolation for all. No! In the light of the Christian memory of suffering, it is clear that social power and political domination are not simply to be taken for granted, but that they continually have to justify themselves in view of actual suffering. This is perhaps the only, but the decisive, political proposition that can be derived from the New Testament and its "theology of suffering." But it suffices. The social and political power of the rich and the rulers must be open to the question of the extent to which it causes suffering. It cannot escape this reckoning by invoking the specific suffering of the rich and powerful. Moreover, this critical interrogation of domination and riches is part precisely of that consolation the Gospel would bestow upon the rich and the rulers. But this also means: I cannot overlook the suffering and oppression brought about by power and riches, and I cannot point out that the rich and powerful are also basically lonely and unhappy, and have their own form of suffering. I have, instead, the primary duty of opposing them, and this is a resistance that means that I confront them with the claim of Christian consolation and Christian redemption. The memory of suffering, in the Christian sense, does not, therefore, merge with the darkness of social and political arbitrariness, but creates a social and political conscience in the interest of others' suffering. It prevents the privatization and internalization of suffering, and the reduction of its social and political dimension.

As a kind of initial thesis, I suggested that the problem of the future was primarily political and fundamentally social. I now ask: How is the Christian *memoria passionis* to be connected at all with political life, and what justification is there for such an association? What have the two really got to do with one another? Doesn't bringing them together mean their mutual decay? As I have stressed, it is not a question here of a subsequent introduction of the Christian memory of suffering into the existing forms of political life, but of making this *memoria passionis* effective in the transformation of our political life and its structures—a transformation already shown to be the decisive requirement for tackling the question of the future. Yet, the fundamental question remains: Doesn't political life fall victim to the reactionary influence of universalist norms once it is associated with the Christian *memoria passionis?* For this Christian *memoria,* as an eschatological remembrance, does entail a particular interpretation of the meaning and subject of universal history.

But how can the question of the meaning and subject of history as a whole have anything to do with political life? Doesn't all talk of a universal meaning of history in its political application lead to totalitarianism or, anyway, to an uncritical, fanatical kind of utopianism? All *positivist* theories of social and political life insist on this danger. These theories are, of course, subject to the question of whether their rigorous rejection of the question of meaning does not eventually subject political life to a purely instrumental form of thinking, and in the long run abandon it to technocracy. Moreover, positivism is also subject to the question of whether by its rendering taboo, or just ignoring, the question of meaning, it does not close its eyes to those ideologies that constantly seek to enthrone themselves as the subject and bearer of the meaning of history as a whole, and consequently endanger our social and political action.

In contrast, *traditional Marxism* and its theory of political life wholly maintain the question of the meaning and subject of history as a whole. The intention here is essentially practical: to determine the content and goal of revolutionary praxis. For Marxism does acknowledge a politically identifiable bearer of the meaning of history: and recognizes it as the proletariat, which in its political praxis sets out to realize this meaning. But, in fact, it is difficult to see how such a fusion of the meaning of history and political praxis doesn't eventually end in a political totalitarianism behind that transformation of political life that we seek for the sake of our future.

In its *liberal* theory of political life, traditional idealism also preserves the question of the meaning and subject of history. This position, however, differs from Marxism in acknowledging no socially apparent and politically identifiable subject of history as a whole, and, indeed, in rejecting any attempt at a political identification of this subject. Hegel, for instance, calls the subject of history as a whole the "world spirit," whereas, others speak of "nature," and yet others of "universal humanity." These are all apolitical predicates. Here reference to the bearer and meaning of history remains essentially abstract. Nevertheless, it is clear that this abstract discourse about history as a whole can have an eminently practical political meaning. It makes possible and helps to bring about the liberation of political life from universal forces and universalist norms. Political life is set free to assume a wholly pragmatic orientation; politics as determined solely by the "thing itself"—what is "really at issue." But are these "factual structures" really anything other than the actual structures and tendencies of our economico-technological processes? Where are we to find a contra-factistic consciousness offering a political alternative to these processes and their anonymity, if not in a pure decision-politics? Undoubtedly its antitotalitarian effect is important in this liberal understanding of political life; nevertheless, in its positive version it seems to offer no impulsion for the transformation of political life that we are looking for.

Let us look again at the association between the Christian *memoria passionis* and political life. In the memory of this suffering, God appears in his eschatological freedom as the subject and meaning of history as a whole. This implies, first of all, that for this *memoria,* there is also no politically identifiable subject of universal history. The meaning and goal of this history as a whole are instead, to put it very summarily, under the so-called "eschatological proviso of God." The Christian *memoria* recalls the God of Jesus' passion as the subject of the universal history of suffering, and in the same movement, refuses to give political shape to this subject and enthrone it politically. Wherever a party, group, race, nation, or class—even the class of technocrats—tries to define itself as this subject, the Christian *memoria* must oppose that, and unmask this attempt as political idolatry, as political ideology with a totalitarian or—in apocalyptic terms—a "bestial" tendency. In this way, in the light of the Christian *memoria passionis,* political life is liberated as protected from totalitarianism. But, as opposed to the liberal version of idealism, this liberation is now utopian in orientation and not undefined. The Christian memory of suffering is in its theological implications an anticipatory memory: it intends the anticipation of a particular future of man as a future for the suffering, the hopeless, the oppressed, the injured, and the useless of this earth. Hence, this memory of suffering does not indifferently surrender the political life oriented by it to the play of social interests and forces, which for its own part, turns upon the presupposition of conflict, so that it always favors the powerful but not the friendly, and always acknowledges only that measure of humanity that is the estimated prerequisite for the successful pursuit of one's own interests. The memory of suffering, on the other hand, brings a new moral imagination into political life, a new vision of others' suffering that should mature into a generous, uncalculating partisanship on behalf of the weak and unrepresented. Hence, the Christian memory of suffering can become, alongside many other often subversive innovative factors in our society, the ferment for that new political life we are seeking on behalf of our future.

Finally, let us consider the situation of the Churches in our society. Clearly, the Churches are now fast ceasing to be religious establishments serving society as a whole; clearly, they are increasingly becoming minorities, whose actual and public influence is constantly decreasing. They are becoming more and more what might well be termed cognitive and emotional minorities. The question arises whether the Churches are on the way to becoming sects. If the answer is Yes, are they to be more or less irrelevant subcultures within the framework of our technological super-society? This is the focal point of a number of questions that cannot be taken further here. I shall mention only one. *If* the Church spells out the *memoria passionis Jesu Christi* in the midst of our society—that memory of suffering in which the history of human passion is made unforgettable—then it can ultimately be or become a minority without necessarily falling into false sectarian self-seclusion. Then it will remain the bearer of a dangerous and subversive memory on which much more depends than the will to self-assertion of a religious institution—and that more is the future of our humanity.

Translated by John Griffiths

NOTES

1. The present text is based on a paper given at a theological congress in New York in October 1971, involving debate and dialogue with "process theologians" and Teilhardists. Some passages arise from that confrontation.

2. The background indicated in note 1 above is especially important for the understanding of the passage.

2

Messianic or "Bourgeois" Religion?

To issue critical diagnoses of such a well-organized and internation-ally highly regarded religious community as Catholic Christianity in West Germany is in itself a delicate venture. The problem becomes more difficult when what is attempted is to show that the critical area is none other than the one in which Christians in these parts seem most at home, in the comparatively large degree of harmony between the prac-tice of religion and the experience of life in society.

The critical hypothesis we shall try to substantiate in what follows begins with this question: Is Christianity in West Germany in the end a bourgeois (*bürgerliche*) religion—with great social value but without a messianic future?[1]

Bourgeois Future—Messianic Future

When the Church in West Germany repeats the messianic sayings about the Kingdom of God and the future it represents, it is speaking in the main to people who already have a future. We could say that they bring their own futures to church with them, the strong and unshakeably optimistic to have it religiously endorsed and rounded off, the anxious to have it protected and strengthened by religion. In this way, the messianic future frequently becomes a ritual rounding off and transfiguration of a "bourgeois" future already worked out and—as death approaches—an extension of this "bourgeois" future and the ego which that thrives in it into the transcendence of eternity. *In the Chris-tianity of our time, the messianic religion of the bible has largely become "bourgeois" religion.* This observation is not intended as a denunciation of the "bourgeois"; his social role is not, as such, our subject. Nor is it primarily a criticism of the fact that the Church in Central Europe consists mainly of the so-called "petty bourgeoisie" and "bourgeoisie" who set the tone of Church life in our own country, too. It is more the expression of a worry about Christianity which, it seems to me, loses its identity if it does not realize and emphasize its difference from "bourgeois" religion.

In this "bourgeois" religion, the messianic future is in the gravest danger. Not in danger of being alienated and becoming a tranquillizer or a consolation, an opium for the have-nots, for those with no future, but of turning into an endorsement and encouragement for the haves, the propertied, for those in this world who already have plenty of prospects and future.

The messianic future of Christian faith does not just endorse and reinforce our preconceived "bourgeois" future. It does not prolong it, add anything to it, complete or transfigure it. It *disrupts* it. "The first shall be last and the last shall be first." The meaning of love cuts across the meaning of having: "Those who possess their lives will lose them, and those who despise them will win them." This form of disruption, which drops like a bomb on our complacent present, has a more familiar biblical name; "repentance," turning of hearts, *metanoia*. The direction of this turning is also marked out in advance for Christians. It is called *discipleship*. We must remember this if the future for which faith fits us is not to be interpreted in advance in terms of "bourgeois" religion—or, in other words, if we do not want simply to replace the messianic future with our own future, the one in which we are well in control.

The Change of Heart Is Not Taking Place

To change states of affairs is said not to be the concern of the Gospel and not the business of the Church, which seek to change hearts. This is true and false at once. The moving of hearts is, in fact, the first step to the messianic future. It is the most radical and most demanding form of reversal and revolution, and it is so because changing states of affairs never changes all that really needs to be changed. However, this also means that this change of heart is certainly not an invisible, or, as people like to say, "purely inward" process. If we are to trust the Gospel testimonies, it goes through people like a shock, reaches deep down into the direction of their lives, into their established system of needs, and so finally into the states of affairs which that helps to shape. It damages and disrupts one's own interests and aims at a revision of familiar practice.

I want to express the fear (again, not as a denunciation, but uncertainly and with sadness) that *this change of heart is not taking place*—at least not in the form in that it is publicly proclaimed. The crisis (or the disease) of life in the Church is not just that this change of heart is not taking place or is taking place too little, but that the absence of this change of heart is also being obscured by the appearance of a mere belief in faith. Are we Christians in this country really changing our hearts, or do we just believe in a change of heart, and under the cloak of belief in a change of heart, remain the same? Are we disciples or do we just believe in discipleship, and under the cloak of belief in discipleship, continue in our old ways, the same old ways? Do we love, or do we believe in love, and under the cloak of belief in love, remain the same egoists and conformists? Do we share the sufferings of others, or do we just believe in sharing them and remain, under the cloak of a belief in "sympathy," as apathetic as ever?

It is no theological answer to these questions to stress that, after all, repentance is grace. Theology should take particular care that this appeal to grace does not slip into that leniency we show ourselves, that it does not simply become confused with that indulgence we show to our own bourgeois hearts. The same applies to the objection that such a criticism of contemporary Christianity ignores the sin in which Christians continue to be trapped. Clearly, theological talk about sin and the forgiveness of sins must not be arbitrarily separated from the messianic call for a change of heart. And then when people insist that this change of heart is in the end a purely "inward process," that is certainly not an article of faith but entirely an ideology of our "bourgeois" religion with which we yet again conceal from ourselves our failure and refusal to change.

A "bourgeois" theology assists this concealment. For example, in its theological discussion of the last things, the messianic future was long ago freed from all apocalyptic tensions: there really are no dangers, no contradictions, no downfalls left. Everything is dominated by the idea of reconciliation. However, by taking this line, this bourgeois eschatology unconsciously gives our present a certificate of moral and political innocence, reinforces this "bourgeois" present in itself instead of pushing it beyond itself: everything will be all right in the end anyway, and all differences reconciled.

In this process, hope in "bourgeois" religion steadily loses its messianic weakness, the fact that it still expects something. But the price hope pays for being detached from expectations that could ever be disappointed is high! Hope becomes a hope without expectations, and hope without expectation is essentially hope without joy. I think this is the source of the joylessness of so much joy in "bourgeois" Christianity.

Love in "bourgeois" religion, too, it seems to me, loses more and more of its messianic character. Messianic love is partisan. There was certainly a privileged group around Jesus—those who were otherwise under-privileged. The universality of this love does not consist in a refusal to take sides, but in the way it takes sides, without hate or personal hostility—even to the folly of the cross. Is there not a concept of universal Christian love in "bourgeois" religion that is just sloppy, and one that hardly needs any longer to prove itself as love of enemies because the feeble and unpartisan way it bridges all the agonizing contradictions means that it has no opponents left at all?

Under the cloak of "bourgeois" religion there is a wide split within the Church between the messianic virtues of Christianity that are publicly proclaimed and ecclesiastically prescribed and believed in (repentance and discipleship, love and acceptance of suffering) and the actual value structures and aims of "bourgeois" practice (autonomy, property, stability, success). Among the priorities of the Gospel, the priorities of "bourgeois" life are practiced. Under the appearance of the belief in repentance and the belief in discipleship, the "bourgeois" subject is set up—with an absence of contradiction that even it finds uncomfortable—with its interests and its own future.

If I am right, Kierkegaard's critique of "Christendom" can be taken as an early form of criticism of "bourgeois" religion in Christianity. Kierkegaard claimed that "Christendom"—without attracting attention and even without noticing—had more or less identified Christian existence with the "natural" existence of the "bourgeois": the Christian practice of discipleship was covertly transformed into "bourgeois" practice. In the shape of "Christendom," Christianity had once again successfully and quasitriumphalistically come to terms with the power of the prevailing society, in this case with that of "bourgeois" society. But, at what price? No less, says Kierkegaard, than the abolition of Christianity itself, the Christianity of discipleship, as he keeps on insisting. I regard this as an early critique of Christianity as a "bourgeois" religion, which is in the full sense, prophetic and not at all obsolete today, but—for Catholics and Protestants—more urgent than ever.

Rigorism Instead of Radicalism

The bishops feel the dangers that the "bourgeois" religion as practiced contains for the life of the Church. They are aware of the danger that the Church will not so much move the hearts of the "bourgeois" as be changed by the "bourgeois" into an institution of "their" religion, a service-Church to supply their security requirements. *Nevertheless, our Church's pastoral approach to "bourgeois" religion tends, in my view, to be based on resignation,* a strategy of latent distrust, fed by the suspicion that the "bourgeois" is not to be trusted in the end, that ultimately, he would overwhelm Christianity with his priorities and preferences if there were relaxation even at one point. So the bishops react with legal rigorism in those cases in which actual or supposed truisms of "bourgeois" society come into most evident conflict with the preaching of the Church, as in the question of divorce or the readmission of divorced people to the sacraments, in questions of family and sexual morality, and lastly in the matter of compulsory celibacy, to mention only these examples. This is not an attack on the Christian ideal of monogamy or a plea for sexual libertinism or an attack on the eschatological–apocalyptic virtue of celibacy. The question is simply whether such legal rigorism is the way to overcome the contradictions of "bourgeois" religion in Christianity and make the Christian alternatives to a life that has become "bourgeois" really visible. Or, to put it an other way, whether this is the way to heal the split between the messianic virtues of the Gospel we preach and those the "bourgeoisie" practice; i.e., whether repentance for discipleship is possible.

The main fault of this rigorism with which the official Church reacts to the crisis and disease of Church life implied by "bourgeois" religion is that it seems to be no real help to the base, to the average parish. It is the parishes that have to bear the full weight of this contradiction. It is here that it is becoming clear that the rigorism of the Church offers no salvation in the battle against the distortions of "bourgeois" religion if the radicalism of repentance is not faced and risked in common.

In the local community, the contradiction between the messianic virtues of Christianity that are preached and the "bourgeois" ones that are actually lived is particularly painful. The "bourgeois" virtues of stability, the competitive struggle, and performance obscure and crush the messianic virtues of repentance, selfless, and unconditional love for the "least of the brethren," and compassion, which receive only notional assent—virtues that cannot be practiced in exchange relations, for which you get, literally, nothing, as in the love that does not insist on recompense, loyalty, gratitude, friendship, and mourning. They have a diminishing existence and are at most—under the division of labor—devoted to the family, which in turn, is coming more and more under the pressure of social exchange processes.

In the family, the sector to which the Christian virtues in their privatized form are allocated, the contradictions are becoming blatant. Here love has, as it were, to be reduced to a love that sacrifices universal justice. *But where Christian love is lived only in the family, it soon becomes impossible to live even there.* As with celibacy, the Christian family is tending too much to develop into an isolated mode of life, exactly the same tendency present in "bourgeois" society.

Of the alternative, discipleship lived in practice, there is no sign. The more difficult it becomes to conceal this contradiction with the Gospel, the more emphatic the ecclesiastical appeals seem to become that present the family and celibacy as islands of Christian virtue—and, it seems to me, the greater the danger to them from legal overloading.

The "family" model of the parish is threatened by the same fate that already seems to have overtaken the family. It is losing its young people or is no longer able to integrate them with their criticisms, their alternative attitudes, and their experiments in political emancipation. However, there *are* young people waiting for the call to discipleship, there *is* a longing for radical Christian existence, for alternatives to "bourgeois" religion. If these young people are becoming increasingly hard to reach, if they are gradually going away to other struggles, the fault is not theirs alone.

If the term "bourgeois" religion is justified, this will become particularly clear in the role that *money* plays in it. Money is, after all, a tangible symbol of "bourgeois" society, and the principle of exchange that governs it down to its foundations. An examination of the function of money in a "bourgeois" religion involves more than looking at the semi-ideological status of Church tax. The main issue is the compensatory function that money, in general, has acquired. One aspect is its use by the Church authorities, where fines are instituted as a disciplinary measure, and money becomes almost an aid to the maintenance of ecclesiastical orthodoxy. More important, however, is the salvational function of money for Christians, in general. Money, often acquired totally without compassion, becomes a substitute for compassion with the suffering of others; it serves to express solidarity and sympathy, as compensation for the neglect of a wider justice imposed by a society determined at a fundamental level by exchange. Thus, money becomes the great link between the Christian virtues, which in "bourgeois" religion are kept strictly to the private sphere, and social suffering; it becomes a *quasisacrament of solidarity and sympathy*. Even then, in its quasisacramental role, it still expressed something of what, in my view, it cannot provide— the direction and spread of our love and compassion by those messianic standards for which there are really no limits to liability. The problem of the big Church charities is not that they exist, but that, in the minds of the Christians of our country, they take the necessary help out of the wider messianic context (which includes factors such as solidarity, political education, and a desire for practical change) and reduce it to a process of mere monetary contributions.

Radicalism Instead of Rigorism

I start from the presumption that the reason for the Church's loss of appeal is not that it demands too much but that, in fact, it offers too little challenge or does not present its demands clearly enough as priorities of the Gospel itself. *If the Church were more radical in the Gospel sense, it would probably not need to be so "rigorous" in the legal sense.* Rigorism springs from fear, radicalism from freedom, from the freedom of Christ's call. For the Church's preaching and pastoral work, acting by the priorities of the Gospel should include using the all-embracing strategy of love to attack the ideal of exchange as it seeps down to the moral foundations of social life. It means overcoming the reification of interpersonal relations, their increasing interchangeability and superficiality. If it does this, the Church is radical without necessarily having to be rigorous in the legal sense. If it did this, for example, it could admit to the sacraments even those who had failed in their marriages and asked for forgiveness, without having to fear that it was opening the floodgates. Nor would the Church then need compulsory celibacy to dress up a Christianity that had lost its radicalism. There would be no danger that the apocalyptic virtue of celibacy would die out; it would constantly reemerge out of the radicalism of discipleship.

Then, too, authority in our Church would lose the bureaucratic face that everyone complains about: it would be able to take on more clearly the features of an authority for religious guidance, display its administrative and legal competence less, and its religious competence more.

Politics, Morality, Religion: The World Context

How can we bring about a shift in priorities? How can we achieve a renewal that will affect even the psychological foundations of "bourgeois" life? I see only one way: we need *a change of direction throughout the Church, throughout society, and in the whole of world politics.* This is not a detour or an escape into undemanding abstraction. What is much more of an abstraction today is the approach that "abstracts" from the worldwide connections in which our individual and social life is involved.

Our world, for the first time aware of itself as a whole, is at the same time riven with deep, agonizing *oppositions*, which threaten more and more to become an apocalyptic gulf between poor and rich, rulers and ruled. Purely political or economic strategies for ending these oppositions are either not in sight or are proving inadequate, only with difficulty covering up the apparent irreconcilability of the interests. This makes many people bewildered and apathetic and drives others into hatred and fanaticism (a much more likely result of our ubiquitous apathy than a conversion to committed love). Others take up rigid defensive attitudes and' end by adopting a strategy of self-preservation and internal security.

Everyone can see the signs of this looming social apocalypse: the atomic threat, the insanity of the arms race, the destruction of the environment, terror, the global struggle for exploitation (the North–South conflict) with its danger of a social war on a world scale. However, the catastrophe remains mostly ideas "in the head," not in our hearts. It produces depression, but not grief; apathy, but not opposition. People seem to be becoming more and more voyeurs of their own downfall. Counter-measures are scarcely to be seen, probably because the familiar strategies and prophecies are failing.

It is certainly not my intention here to mystify "the catastrophe" or to ridicule any nuance, any sign of an initiative, by some slick juggling with the idea of the totality of the disaster—quite the opposite. My only aim is to see that we appreciate the scale and nature of the action that has become necessary. Must we not start from the assumption that the oppositions that are producing hatred and despair or apathy can only be overcome without a catastrophe when there is a change in personal priorities in the rich countries of this earth (and not just among the grabbers within the oppressed nations who have grown rich through their ruthlessness), in other words, when there is a real change of heart here? Is this not the only way in which the poor and exploited can escape from their damaged lives, stunted as they are from the very beginning? *Is not moral action becoming a factor in world politics?* To put it the other way, are not economics and politics becoming part of morality in a new way?

Christians are convinced that such a moral reorientation cannot be kept up unless it is supported by religion. They start from the assumption that where religion not only disappears among the so-called enlightened elites, but even among the people the report of the existence of God is no longer abroad, man's very "soul" dies, and in the end, the apotheosis of banality or hatred dawns. The individual becomes a machine, a new sort of beast, or just an offense, to be dealt with by totalitarian means. It is precisely for these reasons, in view of the situation I have described, that Christianity with its moral reserves and its capacity for repentance is called to stand the test of history. *It is my view that nothing is more urgently needed today than a moral and political imagination springing from a messianic Christianity and capable of being more than merely a copy of accepted political and economic strategies.*

The Church's Work of Reconciliation

The Church's international character provides us with a dramatic illustration that focuses on this situation and the challenge it contains, or the call for a change of heart that rises from it. This is the relation of the rich churches to the poor churches, let us say, *of the German-speaking churches to those of the Latin American subcontinent.*

I am not placing the question of repentance in the context of the international Church in order to have an imaginary parade ground for aesthetic radicalism. This is no abstract speculation about the future, but a practical question. Have others, namely, our fellow participants at the eucharistic table in the one Church, even a present? We can forget about the future completely for the moment!

This concern with the Church internationally should also have another effect. I am convinced that there will only be a reconciliation between the traditionalist wings and the more liberal wings of our European Church if the Church's work of reconciliation makes its main task reconciliation between the poor and rich churches as a whole, and so makes a contribution to the reconciliation of our painfully torn world. In other words, the goal of sanctity must be linked with that of militant love.

These poor churches have already given us this new model of Christian life. They have given it to us in the witness of those countless Latin American Christians who have lived the messianic virtues of discipleship to the extent of sacrificing their lives. They are the productive model of sanctity for our time; sanctity, not as a strictly private ideal that one seeks for oneself and that can, therefore, easily lead into conformism toward the existing situation, but sanctity that proves itself in an alliance of mysticism and militant love, that takes the suffering of others itself. Our time certainly has a martyrology of its own. It contains the names of the lay people, priests, and bishops who have risked all and given all in the struggle for a Church with the people. With them, these allies united by messianic confidence, repentance becomes possible; the spell of "bourgeois" religion is broken. Such a perspective shows how little the current priorities in the life of the West German Church are simply the natural priorities of a church; it shows that there can be quite different pastoral priorities from those that are central in this country.

A change of direction on a massive scale is taking place in the churches of Latin America, which, in my view, has a providential significance for the whole Church and in which, in one way or another, we are all involved. In the last ten years (since Medellin) an upheaval has been going on there that could be described as the change from a Church that ministers to the people to a Church of the people. The suffering and oppressed people are finally becoming the masters of their history—not in opposition to the Church or by ignoring the Church, but through the Church and in the power of its messianic hope. It could, therefore, come about that one day not just the oppressed people, but also the victorious people, could become part of the Church! It is, of course, true that Christian hope exists even in a life under oppression. The messianic hope of Christians is, after all, much more a hope of the slaves and the damaged of this earth than a hope of the victors. However, the "successful" and prosperous Christians are the last people this entitles to argue for a strictly interiorized version of Christian hope that they then impose on the poor churches.

Moreover, it is that same Central European, "bourgeois" religion of interiority that influential cardinals, bishops, and certain working parties in my country seem to want to became the new standard for the Medellín Church in Latin America. This vision fills me with fear and prompts me to ask whether the cost to Latin America of all the alms is not, indeed, out of this world.

Sharing the fate of these churches challenges us here to change. Only if we change, will Christians here be able to show help and solidarity. The direct struggle of the poor and oppressed people there must be matched here by struggle and resistance against ourselves, against the insidious ideals of always having more, of always having to increase affluence. It must be matched by a struggle against the overdetermination of the whole of life by exchange and competition, which only permits any solidarity and sympathy as an alliance of expediency between partners of equal strength and any humanity only as a humanity of expediency. A repentance of this sort, which extends down to the affective foundations of life, is required of us not by some abstract progress of humanity, but by the Church as a eucharistic community and as a sign of messianic hope.

A Brazilian bishop—and it wasn't Dom Helder Camara—recently wrote to me, "No German can say he isn't an exploiter." A hard saying, but nevertheless, an episcopal one. We Christians in this country must live with the suspicion of being oppressors, if perhaps oppressed oppressors. The suspicion is not refuted by the fact of our willingness to give alms. The challenges of the love demanded here cannot be satisfied merely by the "sacrament" of money, particularly because the way in which that money was acquired itself increases the poverty that the same money is supposed to relieve. Clearly, something more is required here, a radical process of repentance, a new relationship to social identity, property, and affluence in general, which will be very hard to establish.

Some Rethinking—Where Should the Change of Heart We Have Described Start?

Where must we begin the change in priorities and the new approaches? Obviously, it can only be done in lengthy processes of transformation. I am quite certain that there are sufficient reserves of enthusiasm and energy for change even in our Church, but I venture to ask whether these energies are being properly approached and "harnessed." For example, do the Church organizations, which are more or less all organized according to social models of a past age, release the spiritual and social energies that are undoubtedly invested in them in a way that allows them to respond to the challenge? To put the question more sharply the other way around, why do the Church authorities want organizations of this type, and why were the new-style youth organizations of the 1960s treated by the bishops with so much suspicion? To take up an earlier idea, could not the big Church charities, which are almost our only channel for showing solidarity with the poor churches, do much more than merely collect money? Ought they not, precisely because they realize that money is far from innocent, take an active part in developing the awareness, not just of the recipient countries, but also of the givers? In this respect, I feel that these important charities, as part of a process of universal solidarity, are only in their beginnings.

There are signs that the Christians in West Germany are ready to learn and change. In recent years, a hostility, still perhaps rather vague, toward the destructive effects of capitalism has developed at the base. Ecological responsibility is becoming an issue. There is a committed, if still relatively powerless, interest in the plight of the poor churches and of the Third World in general. At the Würzburg synod, there was a new attempt, at least at the level of planning, to take up the battle for youth and, no less important, for the workers. If our general pastoral approach turns away from the defeatist attitude of a "floodgates strategy" and faces the challenges of radical repentance, the beginnings of a new sort of parochial activity, youth work, or industrial mission would not have to be given up as lost before they had seriously begun.

When I mentioned signs of a new messianic practice I did not mean merely the process in this country that could be called a "swing to religion" or "the return of society to religion." These are popular labels, and recently not only Church circles, but also political parties have been trying to cope with this phenomenon, but in my view, it is profoundly ambiguous. The "return to religion" does not necessarily mean that a society, as it were, wants to go beyond itself; it may be calling in religion to enable it to remain itself, to reinforce its own security, because it senses that religion will be its ally in defending a threatened status quo. Where Christianity in this country gives way to this social pressure, it may become more respectable, but I am afraid it will also slip even further into the role of a purely "bourgeois" religion, soothing society's conscience in the face of the worldwide challenges we have mentioned and enabling it to go on living as it does now. An authentic turning to religion, on the other hand, would have to mean a turning to repentance, to the messianic practice of love.

Discipleship as Class Treason?

It is possible that the demands of love here may seem to be treason—a betrayal of affluence, the family, and the customary patterns of life. However, it is also possible that this is just the place where we need discernment of spirits in the churches of the rich and powerful countries of this earth. Certainly, Christianity does not exist only for the brave, but we are not the ones who define the challenges of love, and we are not the ones who fix the conditions by which it is tested. So, for example, Christian love in periods of nationalism must be quite prepared to be suspected of lacking national feeling. In situations of racism, it will incur the suspicion of race treason. In periods when the social contradictions in the world cry to heaven, it will incur the suspicion of class treason for betraying the allegedly obvious interests of the propertied.

Did not Jesus Himself incur the reproach of treason? Did not His love bring Him to that state? Was He not crucified as a traitor to all the apparently worthwhile values? Must not Christians, therefore, expect, if they want to be faithful to Him, to Christ, to be regarded as traitors to "bourgeois" religion? True, His love, in which in the end everything was taken from Him, even all the authority and dignity belonging to love suffering in powerlessness, was still something other than the expression of a sharing in solidarity of the suffering of the unfortunate and oppressed. It was the expression of His obedience, with which He suffered for God and His powerlessness in our world. But must not Christian love, which imitates His, constantly strive toward that obedience?

When the practice of Christian love is placed under the sign of this obedience, which forbids us to confuse the mystery of God's will with the quite unmysterious desire of familiar ways of life for self-preservation, something of the messianic power of this love may be revealed. It strikes deep into preconceived patterns and priorities of life. It has power to move hearts, power not to increase sufferings but to take them on itself. It has the power to show unconditional solidarity, partisan and yet without the destructive hate that negates the individual, combining in itself the aims of sanctity and militant love—even to the folly of the cross. Yes, folly, for such a "change of hearts" will probably be dismissed by the experienced strategists of the class struggle as feeble or useless, and branded as treason by those who are infatuated with exchange and who reject the inhuman consequences of capitalism only verbally, if at all.

All this may seem to some a considerable exaggeration. But what would a more cautious and "balanced" discussion of the messianic practice of discipleship be like? How would caution and "balance" throw light on the crisis we have been talking about?

Translated by Francis McDonagh

NOTE

1. This is a revised version of the lecture I gave to the 1978 Catholic Congress in Freiburg entitled "Faith—the capacity for a future?" ('Glaube-Befähigung zur Zukunft?'). The emotion that I was both unable and unwilling to remove from the text is perhaps best explained by the fact that in a country in which Christianity, so to speak, has a potential majority in political and social life, critical attitudes can only be introduced in a more or less "missionary" speech.

This paper could not deal with many important matters, such as the historical process of the association of Christianity and the "bourgeoisie" and the so-called dialectic of the "bourgeois" history of freedom. This is frequently ignored, particularly in progressive liberal theologies, which allows a tacit identification of the "bourgeois" and the Christian subject. There was also no discussion of the "bourgeois" principle of individuation and the Christian principle of individuation, etc. For these and similar matters the reader is referred to J. B. Metz *Glaube in Geschichte und Gesellschaft* (2nd ed. 1978).

3

Theology in the Modern Age, and before Its End

Anyone who tries to determine the fate of theology with regard to the modern age cannot merely produce a partial synopsis of the history of theology; rather, he or she must tackle some of the theology of history.

To begin with, even in theology, we have moved a long way from working with the traditional pattern of antiquity, the middle ages, and modern times as a way of dividing up the history of theology and the Church. At the very least, the concept of modern times is taken in a much more differentiated way. The epoch labeled as the modern age no longer simply begins with the religious and secular divides of the sixteenth century and what led up to them, but with the processes of the Enlightenment, which have had persistent effects on the fields of the sciences and intellectual inquiry and of political life (thanks to the French and American revolutions), and these effects extend to the way theology sees itself. This Enlightenment is not simply a historical process but something that is still present, especially when two considerations are borne in mind. First, even socialism sees itself as the child and heir of the Enlightenment, and hence, the two major ideological blocs in the world today interpret themselves as dependent on the Enlightenment, even if for the socialist revolution, the problem remains that it itself began in a pre-bourgeois and, indeed, feudalistic society and so far has only been able to establish itself successfully in such societies. Secondly, it should not be overlooked that even the fundamental crises of the Enlightenment that have, for example, led to the formulation of the "dialectic of the Enlightenment" are still understood as aspects of these very processes of Enlightenment.

These processes of Enlightenment by which the modern age continues to be defined and determined are to be regarded as processes strictly centered on the West and Europe, if for the moment we take Europe and North America together. Max Weber coined the term "occidental rationality" to describe them, something that has meanwhile arrived at a kind of world domination by means of the spread of technology and the ideologies contained within it, as well as by means of the instrumental reason of the sciences.

These processes have led to a fundamental crisis of Christian theology. Universally recognized labels for this are the processes of secularization and of emancipation (of classes and races, and, as is now emerging, of women), of demythologization, etc. The attempt to grapple with these crises at their roots and to digest them theologically has dissolved the classical unity of theology and led to a variety of forms for theology's attempt to give an account of the hope that is in us. I list some crises whose solutions radically affect the shape of doing theology.

First, there is the disintegration of the religious and metaphysical images of the world in these processes of the Enlightenment. The crisis of theology occasioned by this disintegration applies also to the Reformation and its theologies, because the Reformation took place within the framework of an all-embracing Christian understanding of the world. This disintegration brought to an end the stage of theology's cognitive innocence. Since then, theology must grapple with the questioning of its historical innocence by the concentration on historical data and development and of its social innocence by the bourgeois and Marxist versions of the critique of ideology. No longer can it displace the questions connected with this from the center to the apologetic fringes of theology and continue undisturbed with the enterprise of theology, protected by this kind of apologetics. The *logos* of theology is itself affected by this crisis. It cannot withdraw from these questionings to a completely secure metaphysical foundation. Historical as well as social questions penetrate to the core of theology and demand an extremely differentiated treatment that can no longer be provided by the individual theological practitioner. Theological learning is hence forward conducted in a plural community of communication—or else it comes to nothing or, what ultimately comes to the same thing, falls back into the classical systemization. Thus, coming to terms with these crises compelled an internal pluralization of theological initiatives, leading, for example, to the initiatives of what is termed liberal theology concerned especially with the problems of historicism, the initiatives of a dialectical theology trying to escape from the identification of bourgeois and messianic religion, and the initiatives of recent political theologies that have above all sought to tackle the problems that arise from a postidealist critique of religion and that, for their part, fight against the identification of Christianity with the political religions of enlightened societies or the myths that provide them with legitimacy (civil religion, bourgeois religion).

The processes of the Enlightenment mean that theology itself is threatened by a twofold reduction that at the same time presents something akin to a permanent constitutional crisis for theology. In the first place, we can talk of a privatistic reduction of theology in which the *logos* of theology is entirely concentrated on religion as a private affair and, thus, is in danger of losing continuity with the messianic cause of Christianity. On the other hand, we can talk of the danger of a rationalistic reduction of theology; in other words, of a withering of the imagination, a radical renunciation of symbolism and mythology under the excessive cognitive pressure of the abstract modern world of the sciences. Of course, the processes of the Enlightenment do not mean either that society has been completely secularized or that religion and with it theology completely privatized. Indeed, one of theology's tasks in the criticism of society involved in the processes of the Enlightenment is to unmask the idea of a completely secularized society, and in this sense, one that has been completely rationalized as the specific myth which a nondialectical setting up of Enlightenment as an absolute always produces. This task of criticizing society that falls to theology will, of course, turn out differently according to the different political cultures with which theology is confronted.[1]

The processes of the Enlightenment, especially in the various forms of the critique of ideology, have also forced on theology in a new way the question of who does theology, where it is done, and the interests of those involved. Through the development of the dialectic of theory and practice, theology has been thrown back on to the practical foundation of its wisdom and its formation of theories. This point of view has far-reaching consequences. The question arises whether theology can see itself solely within the framework of the existing ecclesiastical and social division of labor, in other words, in practice, theology as part of academic education taught by professional theologians at institutions such as universities and seminaries established by secular society and the Church. At present, another form is emerging alongside this (indispensable) form of doing theology. Not without ambiguity this is labeled grassroots theology, and an initial report on it was given in *Concilium*, 1978. Productive examples can be found in the theologies of liberation, as well as in the form of the Black theologies, and in the initiatives of feminist theology.

To this must be added the fact that the profound and, indeed, catastrophic crises that emerge in the process of Enlightenment (and that may be due to its being set up as an absolute in an undialectical way) have led to an additional crisis of theology. Here I would simply refer to the catastrophe of Auschwitz. If theology wants to remain itself by not turning its back on such catastrophes and does not wish to betray its historical responsibility, then it must regard as finished that form of theological idealism not centered on a particular agent with which German theology has supplied the Christian world. A theology aware of such catastrophes can no longer be a theology locked into a concept of a system but must become one locked into a concept of the active agent, and one with a practical foundation. In the face of such catastrophes, theology is directed from history in the singular to histories of suffering in the plural. These can never be explained in an idealistic fashion but merely recalled with a practical purpose. In this sense, theology must become its own critique of ideology: it must learn to see through the high content of apathy of theological idealism and to unmask its lack of sensitivity for the discontinuous character of historical and political catastrophes. Once again, this leads precisely to giving a theological vindication of the Gospel in the face of the modern age and its catastrophes, and doing this in the framework of an internal theological pluralism.

Attention should be drawn to a specifically Catholic dilemma with regard to the modern age and the processes of scientific and political Enlightenment that have taken place in it. It is well known that the Catholic Church and the mainstream of its theology has taken up a more or less defensive attitude to the European history of the modern age. Rather than playing a genuinely creative role in the modern age's history of freedom, and particularly in the processes of bourgeois and postbourgeois Enlightenment, it has for the most part opposed this. What have been termed the Catholic ages within the modern age, and particularly since the Enlightenment, have essentially always been "anti" ages: the age of the counter-reformation, the age of the counter-Enlightenment, the age of the counter-revolution, the age of political restoration, and the romantic movement. In this one can, of course, see considerable awareness of the internal contradictions of this European modern age and its history of freedom, one can indeed recognize at least a latent feeling for its internal dialectic. But must one not also see historical omissions that, in fact, have made it so difficult for the Catholic Church and its theology to deal creatively with the history of religion and the history of freedom? Is it merely an accident that Catholics are regarded as notorious late developers and, as it were, as dyslexics in the school of freedom? How can the dilemma indicated here be overcome? Can Catholics and Catholic theology appeal to a history of freedom that was fought and suffered for, not only without them, but to a considerable extent, against them? Is there any credible way of overcoming this dilemma that affects both the credibility of theology and its applicability in practice?

The prospect I shall try to introduce in the considerations that follow may seem questionable to many in view of the problems that have accumulated. It can even seem today to be like a devious attempt to escape from theology's difficulties and dilemmas in face of the modern age. I see in it an authentic way for the Church and theology to follow. I would not mention it if it did not already exist in hints and beginnings—in the life of the Church, in the changes taking place in theology. It is a question of whether the profoundly European-centered modern age has not been overcome at the embryonic stage for the Church and for theology, and whether these new ways do not also indicate a solution for the dilemma that has been indicated and an inspiration for coping creatively with the demands made on theology by the modern age.

We shall disregard the fact that there is talk of such an "end" in the cultural and political field. In the cultural field, which is my background, there is an abundance of such indications of an end,[2] and recently the question of a new relationship between mythology and modernity has cropped up among us again.[3] I admit that, in view of the recent history of my country, I am not a little frightened by enthusiasm for the idea of myth (in the nontheological sphere). My starting point is that myth is used here to describe that uncomprehended totality of a revolutionary transformation in thought and attitude with which we are continually confronted by the global problems that have meanwhile become problems of everyday life: the relationship between rich and poor in this world, the ecological question, and underlying everything, the question of peace. Talking of myth and modernity remains acceptable if myth does not stand here for a dangerous regressive de-differentiation of all these vital questions but for awareness of a turning point, which in what follows, I can only indicate in the life of the Church and of theology.

Today, for example, we must start from the fact that the Church no longer simply "has" a third world Church outside Europe, but that it "is" a third world Church with its origins and its history in the West and Europe. To put it another way, the Church today is in transition from what culturally is a more or less monocentric Church of Europe and North America to a culturally polycentric universal Church. In this sense, it stands at the end and watershed of a modern age that is characterized in exclusively Eurocentric terms. This is of great importance not just for the life of the Church but for the fate of theology, because the Church's social history affects the intellectual history of theology.[4]

To make the theological importance of this new situation clear, I would like to divide the history of the Church and of theology so far into three epochs[5]: the epoch of Jewish Christianity, relatively short in terms of years, but fundamental for the identity of the Church and of theology; then the very long epoch within a single culture, even if one with many different strands, in other words, the epoch of Hellenism and European culture and civilization up to our own days; and finally, the epoch of a culturally polycentric, genuinely universal Church whose first hints and beginnings showed themselves at Vatican II. The end of cultural monocentrism does not mean its dissolution into an arbitrary contextual pluralism that enables Western and European theology to maintain itself unscathed against these non-European cultures and churches. Embedded in this cultural polycentrism is the history of the Church's Western origins, which in practice was also always a history of guilt (with regard to the non-European cultures). However, now it is a question of mutual inspiration and mutual creative assimilation.

In putting these ideas forward I must of course presuppose much that cannot be expounded and demonstrated in detail here; for example, the fact that in the contemporary world, such a cultural polycentrism does in fact (still) exist, in other words, that it has not already been replaced in the embryonic stage by that secular Europeanization of the world that we call technology or technological civilization, and thus, by the universal domination of occidental rationality—in which, of course, far more of Europe's history, anthropology, and politics are bidden than the technocrats of all shades of opinion would have us believe. Then we must presuppose the view strongly represented in modern theories of culture,[6] that there is something akin to a mutually inspiring creative assimilation of different cultures.

Nevertheless, if this broad diagnosis remains acceptable as a hypothesis in the theology of history, this has far-reaching consequences for the questions raised here. To elucidate this I shall confine myself in this context exclusively with the relationship with the Latin American church. The objection could perhaps be raised that this is not a suitable example to illustrate ecclesiastical and theological polycentrism in what one might term the post-modern age because the cultures of Latin America have, as it were, been projected across the Atlantic from Europe. But if we start from the idea that in Latin America's religious and political cultures, we are not only faced with a projection of Europe, then consideration of the Church and the theology of these countries is full of promise. Mutual inspiration and creative assimilation between individual cultural spheres only occurs when they are not totally alien and unrelated to each other.

In fact, in this cultural sphere, we meet an ecclesiastical and theological life from which, within the culturally polycentric educational framework of the one Church, we can obtain impulses for grappling creatively

with those problems and for overcoming that Catholic dilemma that I
have mentioned above. In this emergence of what are termed "poor"
Churches—something that we encounter in rather abstract terms with
such concepts as the grassroots Church, theologies of liberation,
etc.—we find the attempt to invoke the grace of God as man's total
liberation and the readiness to pay the price for this historical conjuga-
tion of grace and freedom. Here a start is made on overcoming the
reduction of theology, whether in its privatistic or in its rationalistic
version: what is involved is a new unity of the experience of redemption
and of liberation, a Church community that, united with its bishops
and, thus, incorporated in the apostolic succession, is struggling for a
new relationship (and one admittedly not free from conflict) between
religion and society, between mysticism and politics.

For us in our overcomplex situation in the late Western world, this
may often seem too much of an oversimplification, too pre-theological,
as it were, too much of a hermeneutical distortion, too uncritical. However, when we look more closely, we see that this hermeneutic of the
awareness of danger, in which the business of faith and of theology is
taken seriously, as result forces together in a new way things that
with us are abstractly separated and split up: theory and practice, logic
and mysticism, grace and suffering, spirit and resistance. Here we see
a "reduction" that is quite other than a wicked and deceitful emascula-
tion of the relations of theology and faith. Its stimulus must have a
retroactive effect, in a thoroughly reformist manner, on the late Western
situation of the Church and theology, so that in our situation we may
survive the damage, the thoroughly traumatic injuries inflicted by the
modern age.[7] This is, of course, not the complete answer to the question
about the fate of theology with regard to the modern age, but it is, I
hope, a prospect.

Translated by Robert Nowell

NOTES

1. On this, see F. Fiorenza 'Religion and Politik' in *Christlicher Glaube in
moderner Gesellschaft*, Teilband 27 (Freiburg) 1982. For a topical controversy in
this context see J. Moltmann 'Das Gespenst einer Zivilreligion', in *Evangelische·
Kommentare* (March) 1983.

2. On this, see J. B. Metz *Jenseits bürgerlicher Religion* (1980).

3. See *Mythos und Moderne*, ed. K. H. Bohrer (Frankfurt 1983).

4. For the social constitution of theological reason, see W. Kroh *Kirche im
gesellschaftlichen Widerspruch* (Munich 1982).

5. Where I go along with Karl Rahner: see *Schriften zur Theologie*, vol. XIV pp. 287ff.

6. For example in those of a Lévi-Strauss.

7. On this mutual creativity and assimilation, see J. B. Metz *Jenseits bürgerlicher Religion* (1980) and M. Lamb *Solidarity with Victims* (New York 1982).

4

Facing the Jews

Christian Theology after Auschwitz

I have expressed myself before about the relationship between Christians and Jews after Auschwitz.[1] In so doing, I used a shrill tone that was too radical for many Christian ears. At this time, I cannot simply repeat what I said before; but neither do I want to recant anything. I shall try to elaborate on it.

In order to experience and understand what it means to be a Christian, it is always necessary to recognize a definite historical situation. I start with the idea that Sören Kierkegaard is right (without being able to explain this in detail at this time). The situation, without the recognition of which Christian theology does not know whereof it speaks, is for us in this country first of all "after Auschwitz." I present my thoughts in a few theses.

> *First thesis:* Christian theology after Auschwitz must—at long last—be guided by the insight that Christians can form and sufficiently understand their identity only in the face of the Jews.

This brief statement is extraordinarily well backed up in the Bible (Romans 9–11) and by the echo on the part of present-day Christian theologians (during the Nazi period, there were Bonhoeffer and Barth, afterward such theologians as Eichholz, Iwand, and the grouping around the Rhenish Synod, and on the Catholic side, theologians such as Thomas, Mussner, Zenger as exegetes), and by the echo in recent Church documents.

Just the same, it seems to me that the importance of the statement is not yet completely recognized in its consequences by Christian theology. First, I want to call attention to the fact that the thesis does not say that our Christian identity has to be established and ascertained in the face of *Judaism,* but in the face of the *Jews.* I utter this differentiation intentionally. We must be on our guard against all subjectless terminology, but most of all in the case of the Jews. *Judaism,* as such, has no face and no eyes that can be remembered. *Judaism* can again and again be interpreted down and objectified by *Christianity*—interpreted down and objectified as an outdated precursor of the history of Christianity. Yes, it can be objectified, so that present-day Jews need not be seen either as partners nor even (only) as opponents. After all, even opponents have faces. For the sake of Auschwitz, they must be seen—the destroyed faces, the burned eyes, of whom we can only tell, that we can only remember, but that cannot be reconstructed in systemic concepts.

This short linguistic observation with regard to our theological language already contains a decisive demand. This demand is directed against the use of system concepts and aims at the decisive use of subject concepts in the realm of theology. This demand for a subject-based rather than a system-based kind of Christian theological concern is not the expression of a privatistic or individualistic form of theological consciousness. It is the natural consequence of *historical consciousness* in the field of theology—demanded of us, expected of us, and granted to us in the face of Auschwitz. Even this first demand may show that here, with the view toward Auschwitz, it is not a matter of a revision of Christian theology with regard to Judaism, but a matter of the revision of Christian theology itself.

To obey the historical demand for a transition from system concepts to subject concepts, Christians and especially Christian theologians must learn to say *I* in a new manner, and, thus, can no longer disguise their historical lack of sensitivity with an objective system language. To say *I* as a Christian theologian in the face of Auschwitz: this does not mean a stylization of theological individuality, but a sensitivization for a concrete crisis situation such as the one that confronts present-day Christian theology and in the midst of which it wants to find the truth of the Gospel and testify for it—after Auschwitz. This kind of saying *I* must be learned categorically; it is by no means subjectivistic or uncritical, and also not unpolitical. As far as I am concerned, it is the teaching aim of Christian theology after Auschwitz. After all, the time of situationless and subjectless systems—as privileged locations of theological truths—is no longer with us, at least not since the catastrophe of Auschwitz, which no one can ignore without being a cynic, and which no one should be permitted to forget within an objective sense system.

I would like to explain briefly in three areas what this means for me—to say *I* in the face of the Jews, in the face of the catastrophe of

Auschwitz. Let me *first* talk of the milieu from which I came. I am from the country, from an arch-Catholic, Bavarian small town. Jews were actually not seen in this town; even after the war, they remained mere shadows or clichés; our views of how Jews looked came from—Oberammergau. The catastrophe of Auschwitz, which finally became the catastrophe of Christianity, did not enter our consciousness; nothing was heard about it, although my home town was located barely 50 km from that concentration camp in which Dietrich Bonhoeffer was killed—not least because of his attitude toward the Jews. The Church milieu of the little town from which I come, and also the milieu of the neighboring town where I attended high school, never called my attention to Auschwitz.

To learn to say *I* in the face of the catastrophe of Auschwitz is, *second*, above all a job for *theology* itself. I had the good fortune to learn that Catholic theology, which in my eyes was the best of that time, and to it I owe everything that I can do theologically myself. I mean the theology taught by Karl Rahner. To be sure, gradually, much too gradually, it dawned on me that even in this theology, Auschwitz was not mentioned. Thus, in confrontation with this catastrophe, I began to ask critical questions and to look for additional viewpoints of theological identity. Were we still caught in a kind of historical idealism? Did the logos of Christian theology still have much too high a content of apathy? Too much fortitude against the abysses of historic catastrophes? This was perhaps the reason why (especially immediately after the war) we talked so much about the *historicity* of faith and theology in order to cover up the real contradictions of historical experience through this formalism. Wasn't there a too-demanding, supposedly christologically motivated historical triumphalism at work, an overly strong sense of optimism against history, which blinded us against the real threats confronting our Christian hope? Didn't we know, ahead of any Christian practice, too much about the sense of history, which makes every catastrophe merely appear to be the echo of a departing thunderstorm? It seems that we did not know that for the understanding of our own history and our own promises, we had to depend upon a non-Christian partner, on our victims, in short, on the Jews of Auschwitz.

Looking carefully at Auschwitz made it clear to me that an adequate separation between systematic theology and historical theology, between truth and history, is not possible—even with the best of wills. Moreover, this is true for both the systematic theologians and the historical theologians, each in their own way. Historical theologians, also, cannot simply and without problems submit to a scientific knowledge, which defines historical knowledge against memory knowledge. The Auschwitz catastrophe cannot simply be historically reconstructed, it must be remembered practically. For this reason our historical theologians must reintroduce the *struggle for remembrance,* the struggle for the subject-centered memory knowledge, into the general understanding of history. Historical theologians, most of all (with the accent on *theologians*), must try to see the scenario of history with the eyes of the victims; they must know that they are engaged by society as attorneys for the dead (as formulated in a similar way by H. Oberman), as intermediaries between democracy and tradition, by interpreting democracy not only as space, but also as time; in other words, that they will try to expand democracy backward, and thus, try to gain the votes of the dead (as similarly postulated by G. K. Chesterton). How would the history of our recent past look then? Historical consciousness and historical conscience are not tested only in looking at successes and victories, but in a preoccupation with defeats and catastrophes. In these, we meet what history draws from all *evolutionistic* explanations taken from nature: the discontinuity; the pain of negativity; the sufferings; and in all of them, the catastrophe, the practical challenge to one's own hope.

For me, there is no truth that I could defend with my back turned to Auschwitz. There is no sense for me that I could save with my back turned to Auschwitz. For me, there is no God to whom I could pray with my back turned to Auschwitz. When that became clear to me. I tried no longer to engage in theology with my back turned to the invisible, or forcefully made-invisible, sufferings in the world; neither with my back to the Holocaust nor with my back turned to the speechless sufferings of the poor and oppressed in the world. This probably was the starting point toward the construction of a so-called political theology.

Third, let me also briefly refer to the saying of *I* in the face of the Jews by pointing to *religion* and religious practice. In religious practice, such as that practiced as a boy during the Nazi period, the Jews did not appear. With our backs to Auschwitz, we prayed and celebrated our liturgy. Only later I began to ask myself what kind of a religion it is that can be practiced unmoved by such a catastrophe. This was one of the reasons why I began to speak of Christianity critically as a *bourgeois* religion. (Much could be said about this also, but I will continue with my next thesis.)

> *Second thesis:* Because of Auschwitz, the statement "Christians can only form and appropriately understand their identity in the face of the Jews" has been sharpened as follows: "Christians can protect their identity only in front of and together with the history of the beliefs of the Jews."

It is the task of a Christian theology after Auschwitz to make this situation publicly clear. Let us look for a moment at the renewal of the relationship between Christians and Jews in the postwar period. We can observe *different phases and dimensions of this renewal.* First, the phase of a diffuse affection, which, for its part, is not very stable or safe from crises and can easily disappear (and that is hardly aware of the fact that such a diffuse philosemitism can easily be and remain a masked form of anti-Semitism). Next, the phase of the theological discussion of the transition *from mission to dialogue.* Finally, the beginnings of a conscious theological rethinking, the development of a Christian theology of Judaism post-Christum, with a recognition of the lasting messianic dignity of Israel, the *root* significance of Israel for the Church (as was already claimed by Bonhoeffer and Barth). The fourth phase would finally be the following: the recognition on the part of Christians of their concrete faith-historical dependence on the Jews; i.e., in line with the thesis that Christians, even in their own identity, can no longer define themselves without the Jews.

Here, *Auschwitz as an end* is taken seriously theologically, not as an end for a definite phase of Jewish history, but as an end of that kind of Christianity that refuses to form its identity in the face of and together with the Jews. In the final analysis, to say it once more—with a view toward Auschwitz—it is not only a matter of revising Christian theology with regard to Judaism, but a matter of revising Christian theology altogether. I talked briefly of this in an earlier paper, and from this paper I repeat once more: What I personally mean by calling Auschwitz the end and turnaround for us Christians, I can make clearer by referring to a conversation. In 1967, there occurred a discussion in Münster between the Czech philosopher Milan Machoveć, Karl Rahner, and me. Toward the end of the conversation, Machoveć referred to Adorno's statement: "After Auschwitz there won't be any poems any more." Then he asked me whether there could still be prayers on the part of us Christians after Auschwitz. I gave the same answer I would give today: "We can pray after Auschwitz, because there were prayers in Auschwitz." We Christians can no longer go back behind Auschwitz, but neither can we go beyond Auschwitz except together with the victims of Auschwitz. This, in my eyes, is the root of Jewish–Christian ecumenism. The turnaround in the relationship between Jews and Christians corresponds to the radicality of the end brought about by Auschwitz. Only if we face it resolutely, will we know what the *new* relationship between Jews and Christians really is, or, at any rate, could be.

I would like to make this connection clearer and explain it more fully by discussing the so-called *theodicy question in the face of Auschwitz,* i.e., the *God-question* in the face of these fearful sufferings. I would like to discuss what is meant by this for us Christians and for our understanding of ourselves by reference to a book that has become very famous, because it is a unique work—I refer to Elie Wiesel's book *Night.* The text has already become prototypical; many Christian theologians are quoting from it. For this reason, I can most easily explain my intentions with its help. "The camp commanders refused to serve as hangmen. Three SS men took over the job. Three necks were put into three nooses within a short moment. 'Long live freedom!' shouted the grownups. But the child said nothing. 'Where is God? Where is he?' said someone behind me. The three chairs were tipping over. . . . We marched past. . . . The two men were no longer alive. . . . but the third rope was still moving. . . . the child was lighter and was still living. . . . Behind me I heard the same man ask: 'Where is God now?' And behind me I heard an answering voice: 'Where is he? Here he is—he hangs on the gallows.' In this night, the soup had the taste of corpses."

I would like to make comments to this text in only one regard. *Who* really has the right to give the answer to the God-question—"Where is God? Here he is—he hangs on the gallows"? Who, if anyone at all, has the right to give it? As far as I am concerned, only the Jew threatened by death with all the children in Auschwitz has the right to say it—only he alone. There is no other *identification* of God—neither as sublime, as for instance in J. Moltmann, nor as reserved and modest, as in the case of D. Sölle—here, as far as I am concerned, no Christian-theological identification of God is possible. If at all, this can be done only by the Jew imprisoned together with his God in the abyss—it can be done only by him who himself finds himself in that hell "where God and human kind full of terror look into each other's eyes" (Elie Wiesel). Only he, I think, can alone speak of a "God on the gallows," not we Christians outside of Auschwitz who sent the Jew into such a situation of despair or at least left him in it. Here, for me, there is no *sense*, to which we could testify without the Jew. Without the Jews in the hell of Auschwitz, we are condemned to non-sense, to God-lessness.

Let us not say: After all, there are for us Christians other God-experiences beside Auschwitz. That's true! But if there is no God for us in Auschwitz, how can there be a God anywhere else? Don't tell me that such an idea violates the core of Christian self-understanding, according to which the nearness of God is definitely guaranteed through Jesus Christ. There still is the question: What kind of Christianity is entitled to this guarantee? Perhaps that Christianity identifying itself as anti-judaistic, which belongs to the historical roots of Auschwitz, or a Christianity that knows it can form and understand its own identity only in the face of the Jewish history of suffering.

In the God-question itself, we should depend on the testimony of the Jewish history of sufferings: this seems to be going too far for many Christians. For me, however, the recognition of this quasisalvation historical dependence is the very criterion as to whether we Christians are ready really to acknowledge the catastrophe of Auschwitz as a catastrophe and whether we are really ready to take it seriously theologically as the challenge that we cite so frequently moralistically. I repeat that, with a view toward Auschwitz, it is not merely a matter of revising Christian theology with regard to Judaism, but a matter of revising Christian theology altogether.

Of course there are enough *symptoms* showing that we want to keep this radical challenge through Auschwitz far away from us. There is, *for instance,* the attempt to eliminate the Holocaust from specifically Christian causality altogether. It is considered a purely National Socialist crime, which, as is stressed in the Bonn Paper, was "as much anti-Jewish as anti-Christian," or one sees this catastrophe only as a result of the "German Spirit" (which idea is opposed by H. Obermann in his latest book). Or, *second,* one has resort to quick reinterpretations of the holocaust catastrophe, that is, Auschwitz is made into a type or symbol for all kinds of threatening or possible catastrophes in the world, and forgets that the overall validity of the Jewish tragedy and of the Holocaust is found exactly in its nontransferability, in its uniqueness, and its incomparability. Just as the Church once upon a time thought, by means of a dangerous substitution theory, that it could inherit or ignore the historical fate of Israel ("The church as the real Israel"), so we find today profane substitution theories for Auschwitz that run the danger of making the catastrophe of Auschwitz appear unimportant by simply transferring it to other situations of suffering. A *third* form of removing the tension in the Christian God-question posed by Auschwitz is found in the attempt to connect the name of Auschwitz with the tragedy of Jews *and Christians.* It is certainly true that there were also Christians, even heroic Christians in Auschwitz, but we must stress with all our determination the fact that Auschwitz stands for the fearful tragedy of the Jewish people. We must do this for the sake also of those Christian martyrs, who often were sent to Auschwitz because of their solidarity with the Jews. I tried to use these arguments during the joint Synod of the dioceses in the Federal Republic of Germany (1975) when I presented the paper "Our Hope," which I had preformulated within the responsible commission. My arguments were not fully accepted (the text speaks of "Jews and Christians"), but this passage of an official synod document contains the most advanced statement concerning the new relationship between Christians and Jews in the face of Auschwitz. In it we read: "We, in Germany of all places, must not deny or make appear harmless the salvific connection between God's people of the old and the new covenant which had already been seen and confessed by Paul the Apostle. Because in this sense, too, we in our country have become debtors of the Jewish people. After all, the credibility of our talk of the 'God of Hope' in the face of a hopeless error such as Auschwitz depends above all on the fact that there were innumerable people, both Christians and Jews, who in this kind of hell again and again called on God and prayed to Him."

Fourth, very briefly, I would also like to call attention to the *handoffering* of the Rhenish synod, which courageously enters upon the theodicy problem in the face of Auschwitz. To be sure, it seems to me to be a case of false modesty when it is recommended that the God-question should "be kept open," which modesty hides the dependence in the treatment of the God-question after Auschwitz on the Jewish history of sufferings. I hope I need not mention that I do not expect a speculative reply to the theodicy question. My problem is to discover whether and how we Christians can and may speak of *God after Auschwitz* in a credible constellation.

However, I would not want to overlook the fact that Auschwitz is not only a question of theodicy, but certainly also a very dramatic question of *anthropodicy* to which attention frequently has been called. It is the question of the justification of *humankind* in the face of the sufferings at Auschwitz. In this sense, the question asked by Elie Wiesel could also be formulated with a view toward anthropodicy as follows: "Where was humankind in Auschwitz?" Many survivors went to pieces exactly because this question could not be answered because they could no longer believe in humankind. How can you continue to live among men if in Auschwitz you had to find out what they are able to do? As you know, this question opens the tragedy of Auschwitz from an entirely different point of view, which I cannot discuss here. I shall go on to the next thesis.

Third thesis: Christian theology after Auschwitz must stress again the Jewish dimension in Christian beliefs and must overcome the forced blocking-out of the Jewish heritage within Christianity.

This thesis does not merely want to bring back into the memory of Christian theology the Jewish existence of Christ himself. It aims at the Jewish-originated form of the Christian faith. To say it once more: the problem, with a view toward Auschwitz, is not merely a revision of the Christian theology of Judaism, but of a revision of Christian theology altogether. The thesis speaks of a *mode of believing.* This means that I adopt a statement by Martin Buber (*two modes of believing*), without, however, simply taking over the differences outlined by him. *Modes of believing* here are intended to characterize the tying together of faith content and faith exercise; of subject and object; of faith theory and

faith practice; of theory and practice. I assume—in contrast to Buber—
that there is not only a specifically Jewish Old Testament manner of
belief and a specifically Christian New Testament manner of belief, but
that in the traditions of the New Testament, differing modes of believing
are present. Thus, it is undoubtedly possible—although I am not able at
this time to enter upon this problem in detail—to speak of a pronounced
synoptic mode of believing in contrast to a pronounced Pauline mode
of believing, but without the two manners being exclusive of each other.
Obviously, the synoptic manner of believing is influenced more strongly
and more lastingly by the Jewish Old-Testamentary manner of
believing. But just because this synoptic manner of believing stepped
into the background as against the Pauline manner of believing in
the course of Christian history—just because of this it must again be
remembered and again identified as a "Christian mode of believing."
This Jewish-formed mode of believing belongs in the basic situation of
the Christian faith. It was not taken from the Old Testament, but exactly
from the New Testament itself.

Faith as a trusting yielding to the will of God means here a being-
on-the-road, a being-underway, even a being-homeless, in brief: discipleship. Christ is truth and way. Every attempt to know him, to understand him, is always a going, a following. Only if they follow him, do
Christians know with whom they are associated and who saves them.
This kind of Christology is not primarily formed in a subjectless concept
and system, but in discipleship stories. This kind of Christology does
not bear casually, but fundamentally, narrative features. This Christology of discipleship stands against a Christianity that interprets itself
as a bourgeois religion; it opposes the idea that Christianity is totally
at home in the bourgeois world. This Christology of discipleship also
stands against that kind of Christianity that considers itself as a kind
of religion of victors—with a surplus of answers and a corresponding
lack of passionate questions in the being-on-the-way. This Christology
of discipleship makes it clear that Christianity, too, ahead of all system
knowledge contains a narrative and remembrance knowledge. Narration and remembrance correspond cognitively to a belief that understands itself as a going, as a being-underway, as a constitutional form
of homelessness. I learned the significance of *remembrance* and *narration,* if I understand it at all, mainly from Jews, believing or unbelieving
Jews, not only from G. Scholem, but also from W. Benjamin; not only
from M. Buber, but also from E. Bloch; not only from F. Rosenzweig,
but also from E. Fromm; not only from N. Sachs, but also from Fr.
Kafka. But Christianity, too, is in its roots a community of remembrance
and narration, and it is true that its center is not an entertaining, but

on the contrary, a dangerous story, and it invites not merely to reflection, but also to discipleship.

It is the Jewish-formed synoptic manner of believing that calls our attention to the fact that the Christian belief is a sensuous happening, a happening of the senses that cannot simply be spiritualized into purely a faith of attitude. Haven't we been confronted for a long time by the danger of total spiritualization and inferiorization of evangelical contents and imperatives? Hasn't discipleship become for us too much a matter of disposition for discipleship; love a matter of disposition for love; suffering a matter of disposition for suffering; exile a matter of disposition for exile; persecution a matter of disposition for persecution? How would it otherwise be possible that Christian theologians, for example, can say that we, the Christians, are the *real* religion of exile; the *real* religion of the Diaspora, of the painful dispersion in the world? Can such a statement be defended in the face of Jewish experience through the centuries? Kafka has described it in his *Letters to Milena:* "This means, to express it in an exaggerated manner, that not a single second of rest is left to me, nothing is given to me, everything must be acquired, not only the present and the future, but also the past— something which perhaps every human being has been given, even this must be acquired, which is perhaps the hardest labour. If the earth turns towards the right—I don't know whether it does so—I would have to turn left in order to catch up with the past . . . It is as though before every single stroll a person does not only have to wash and to comb himself, etc., which is a good deal of labour in itself, but—because before every stroll all that is necessary is again and again missing—the stroller would also have to sew clothing, make boots, manufacture the hat, and cut the walking stick etc. Of course all this cannot be done well, perhaps it will last through a couple of alleys . . . And finally, in the Eisengasse, he may well meet a crowd of people hunting Jews."

Still other Jewish-influenced features of a Christian manner of believing, as found above all in the synoptic gospels, must be recalled and brought back to life; for instance, faith as resistance willing to suffer against powerful social prejudices, and this in the face of a history of Christianity that as against political powers shows much too little history of resistance *in the name of God.* Rather, this history was too much a history of adaptation and obedience. Faith should also not hide its own messianic weakness and should know—unlike an expectation-less hope—that it is not already from the start armed against all historical disappointments—faith for which exactly the God Jesus Christ remains the *other one,* the uncomprehended, even the dangerous God, etc. Didn't we Christians leave behind the Jewish God-Mystic and prayer piety too soon, although we know them from the God-experience of Jesus in the synoptic gospels?

Fourth thesis: Christian theology after Auschwitz must regain the biblical-messianic concepts for its ecumenical endeavours.

Exactly in this situation *after Auschwitz,* it should become clear to us that we can only promote unity among the Christians if in this ecumenical endeavor we do not forget that partner who belongs in the eschatological situation of Christians—the Jewish partner. In this sense, Karl Barth could remind us that there really exists only one great ecumenical task—our Christian relationship with the Jews. In conclusion, I would like to add only one more thought. Only if we Christians do not push aside this messianic perspective of the ecumenical movement; in other words, if we develop the thought of Christian unity only with an eye on the Jewish partner, only then will it be possible for us to contribute productively to an ecumenism of the great religions as a whole—at least to a coalition of religions to resist the apotheosis of hatred and banality in the world. Here I am thinking above all of our attitude toward the religion of *Islam.* It seems to me that a direct approach of Christians to Islam, so-to-speak by passing Judaism, seems neither theologically nor culture-historically possible. After all is said and done, we must not forget one thing: the Jewish religion, despised and persecuted, is and remains the root religion for both Christianity and Islam. Auschwitz, therefore, is and remains a hateful attack against the roots of our common religious history. Some of you may have missed a critical statement on the present politics of the State of Israel.

However, we as Germans: we have no choice in this matter.

NOTE

1. See "Christians and Jews after Auschwitz" in my volume *Beyond Civic Religion* (Mainz-Munich 1980), 29–50 ("Christen und Juden nach Auschwitz" in *Jenseits bürgerlicher Religion,* J. B. Metz [Mainz-München 1980] pp. 29–50).

5

Theology in the Struggle for History and Society

I

Within the Catholic Church, I find three principal concurrent theological models in operation. This does not cover everything, but it does single out three representative ideal types of theology: I mean neoscholastic theology; transcendental-idealist theology; and postidealist theology. Although they are very different, all three models fall within the scope of theology in the Catholic sense. They reflect the complexity and tensions of the present state of the church.

The neoscholastic view is still predominant in the church as a whole. Indeed, given recent developments in the church, which I see as reflecting and confirming neoconservative social trends, we may even speak of a "late summer" for this paradigm. Although in no way wishing to detract from the merits of neoscholasticism in the nineteenth and early twentieth centuries, we may describe this paradigm as mainly defensive and traditional, and unable to deal fruitfully with the challenge of modern Europe. Significantly, the principal work of nineteenth century neoscholasticism is called "theology of antiquity." This fixation on (scholastic) antiquity shows how Catholicism became spiritually and socially cut off in Europe, especially in Germany. Catholics barricaded themselves in a Catholic—and political—stronghold, a pale imitation of the great Christian stronghold—*corpus christianum*—of the Middle Ages. They adopted a strictly defensive position to the challenge of the modern world, in both social and political debates and interdenominational theological controversy. Church orthodoxy was more rigorous than radical; a defensive concern with security-minded pastoral theology—until Vatican II.

The transcendental-idealist view of theology stems from the most important and influential change in present Catholic theology. This is the attempt to use the church fathers and scholastics in a productive offensive confrontation with the challenges of modern Europe: the discovery of subjectivity as a crisis in classic metaphysics; the critico-productive confrontation with Kant, German idealism, and existentialism on the one hand, and the social processes of secularization and scientific civilization on the other. This theology found its ecclesiastical and social counterpart in new forms of church life. Taken as a whole, these can in fact be regarded as the impulse for the Vatican II Council.

Meanwhile theology was faced with crises and challenges that, in my view, could not adequately be dealt with by the two theological models so far described. Hence, I should like to mention a third theological model, which seeks to test and develop the church's theological legacy as it faces these crises and challenges. Somewhat at a loss, I call this model of Catholic theology "postidealist." It is recognizable in reflections on a new political theology in Europe and in the central thrust of liberation theology. This third theological model also has its roots in the last council. I should like to name three crises and challenges on which this theological model seeks to adopt a position:

Theology comes to the end of its historical and social innocence; that is, theology engaged in a dispute about its foundations in terms of ideological and social criticism. This amounts to an attempt by theology to establish a new relationship to history and society. Theological theories of world secularization and modernization have not yet fully clarified this relationship. Moreover, the problems cannot be solved simply by the usual division of labor between systematic theology and social ethics.

Theology comes to the end of a system that took no account of the individual situation or person, that is, theology concerned itself with the "irruption" of the poor, which does not permit the poor to vanish into an impersonal theory of poverty. Moreover, the European version of postidealist theology has also been shaped by the "irruption" of the Auschwitz catastrophe. Nothing could show more plainly that the time for theological systems divorced from situation and person is over, because no one can possibly force this catastrophe into a "peopleless" system of meaning.

Theology comes to the end of cultural monocentrism; that is, theology relating to an ethnically and culturally polycentric world. Here a traditional Christian theology needs to overcome not only a great deal of social but also ethnic blindness. As well as the "option for the poor," it must adopt the "option for others in their otherness," for ethnic and cultural characteristics are not just an ideological superstructure based on economic problems, as Marxist theory and Western praxis would like to suggest.

II

History and society are and remain the place for Christian language about God; that is, for Christian theology. The crisis that has long confronted theology may also be formulated as an epistemological problem, a problem of knowing the truth. Therefore, it is a question of the relationship between knowledge and interest. From the time of the Enlightenment, religion and theology have had to deal with the axiom that all knowledge is governed by interest. This axiom is the foundation of the Enlightenment's critique of religion and theology, on the part of Voltaire, for example; religion and theology are deciphered in terms of their social interest context, but without any application of social criticism. Social criticism, of course, is applied by Karl Marx. Even if theology did not lose its innocence through the Enlightenment's critique of religion, it certainly has since Marx.

The attempt to take this situation into account and remain a proper theology capable of speaking the truth distinguishes postidealist theology's first phase of development. This tries to create the awareness that theology and church are never simply politically innocent, and therefore, one of theology's fundamental tasks is to consider political implications. However, this is still not the main problem in theology's crisis. How can theology admit the connection between knowledge and interest without either giving up or perverting the question of truth? Is the question of truth not reduced here to a mere question of relevance, along the lines of "true is what is in my interest or in the interest of a particular group of persons"? No, it is just that the question of truth now takes a different form, which may be formulated thus: Are there any interests capable of truth? Of course, interests can only be capable of truth when they are universal or universalizable; that is, when they relate without exception to all human beings or could be so related, because truth is either truth for everyone or not at all. In this sense, postidealist theology speaks of universal or universalizable interest, based on biblical tradition itself. This is "hunger and thirst for justice" and indeed, justice for all, for the living and the dead, present and past sufferings.

Thus, the question of truth and the question of justice are interrelated: *verum et bonum (iustum) convertuntur.* Interest in undivided justice belongs to the premises of the search for truth. Thus, knowledge of the truth and speaking about God acquire a practical foundation. In my view, this is the basis of the rightly understood axiom of the *primacy of praxis*, which is criticized in Rome's instruction on liberation theology. The only interest that is appropriate to theology, because it is a universal interest, is hunger and thirst for justice, undivided justice, justice for the living and the dead. Hence, questions about God and about justice, the affirmation of God and the praxis of justice, can no longer be separated. In other words, the praxis of Christian faith always has an interest in universal justice, and is, thus, both mystical and political. This is emphasized in talk about the one and undivided following of Jesus, mystically and politically understood.

Therefore, Christian theology is not political *because* it has surrendered Christianity to an alien political ideology. It is political because it tries to preserve the dangerous memory of the messianic God, the God of the resurrection of the dead and judgment. Theology's political root in this remembrance is much more than mere political rhetoric.

Christian speech about God is not subject to the *primacy of praxis* because it blindly submits to some present political praxis, but because the biblical idea of God, which it represents, is in itself a practical idea. The stories of setting out and hope, stories of suffering and persecution, stories of resistance and resignation, are at the center of the Christian understanding of God. *Remembering* and *telling* are, therefore, not just for entertainment; they are basic forms of Christian language about God. Thus, postidealist theology will always try to explain dogmas of the faith formulated under the influence of classical Greek metaphysics in terms of dangerous and liberating ideas. It treats these unhistorical and impersonal doctrinal statements as shorthand and tries to relate them back to the biblical stories of exodus, conversion, resistance, and suffering, and the synoptic stories of Jesus and his disciples. The result is that *simple believers* are now no longer merely being *talked at*; they become the active subjects of the language of faith and theology, a language in which individual life histories and faith histories are linked together.

If I am right, in its base communities, liberation theology is trying to relax the usual division of labor in the church and to overcome the model of the church as *minder*. This usual division of labor may be summed up thus: the bishops teach, the priests look after, the theologians explain and defend teaching and educate the minders. And what about the people? They are the recipients of this teaching and minding. Such a division of labor sees the church, thus, as a minding church and theology has to go along with the system willy-nilly. On the other hand, liberation theology works to change this minding church *for* the people into a church *of* the people; that is, a church with a community whose members are growing in personal awareness. It points out that besides the magisterium, the church's teaching office, there is also the authority of the faithful, to which theology (and not just theology but also the magisterium) is bound to listen. This view is the legacy of Vatican II. Finally, the church constitution of this council stresses the personal and subjective view of the church, in particular by its use of the biblical phrase *people of God* to designate the church. Hence, the council, at least in principle, underlined the active role of the faithful in the articulation and development of faith.

III

In my country, Germany, after the Second World War, there was a lot of theological talk about the "historicity" of human beings. I have a suspicion that with this general blanket term we were trying to retreat and get away as quickly as possible from the particular history of our own country, which, especially because of Auschwitz, was a catastrophic history. However, for the Judeo-Christian religion, unlike all other great religions of the world, history has a specific importance. Christianity is dominated by the vision of *God and history, God in history.* There are several reasons why this is not fully clear to us today. One reason is that Christianity and theology—at least among us in Europe at this stage of evolution and technology—is under the anonymous pressure of a historical weariness, a tendency to posthistory. The less human beings are their memory, the more they are their own experience. Everything seems to be technically reproducible, finally even the human producer. Secondly, I think in present-day theology, Christianity's indispensable Jewish legacy, which has a thoroughly historical way of thinking, is overshadowed by its Hellenistic Greek legacy, which is more inclined toward an ahistorical dualism and, therefore, constantly threatening to transform Christianity into gnosticism, in which history is without salvation and salvation outside history.

I think theological talk of "two histories," one natural and one supernatural, falls into this danger. This is another dualistic undermining of the important adventure of our historical lives. It cancels our history's final horizon, its ending in the parousia, the *Lord's Second Coming.* In fact, there is not world history and, "after it" or "above it," salvation history. The history of salvation, about which Christian theology speaks, is that same world history, shot through with a constantly threatened and disputed but unshakably promised hope: the hope of God's justice, which also includes the dead and their past sufferings, and forces the living to be interested in justice for all. Faith in the messianic God, God of the resurrection of the dead and judgment, God before whom not even the past is fixed (before whom past sufferings do not disappear into the impersonal abyss of an anonymous, eternally indifferent evolution). This faith is not opium to lull us in humanity's historical struggle; it is the guarantee and measure of the dignity of every human person.

It shares with Marxism the discovery of the world as history, historical project, in which human beings are to be the enactors of their own history, and this challenge should be taken seriously. But, this, of course, raises two important questions for a postidealist theology orientated toward history and society. First, there is the question of the status and value of past suffering in the process of history and, second, the question of individual guilt. Although it is central to postidealist theology, I pass over here the first (very important) problem, the problem known classically as that of theodicy; that is, the justification of God in the face of the world's pain. Certainly in this context Gustavo Gutiérrez's reflections of Job are especially important.

However, I shall concentrate briefly on the second question, about the status and dignity of individual moral guilt. Unlike Marxism, postidealist theology stresses that this guilt is not an assumed but an authentic phenomenon in the historical process of personal lives. It cannot be regarded as an expression of pure alienation, although theology and its preaching of guilt and sin have all too often been alienating and oppressive. Denial of this guilt is an attack on freedom, because the dignity of freedom includes the capacity for guilt. Moreover, acceptance of guilt before God does not prevent human beings from having full responsibility for their own history. On the contrary: where moral guilt is denied as an original phenomenon; that is, denounced as false consciousness, mechanisms arise to make excuses for the sufferings and contradictions in life. We get self-defense strategies for allegedly guiltless individuals. The historical responsibility of the person in history is irrationally halved, and the horror and dismay projected one-sidedly onto the historical opponent. Thus, the question of guilt and nonguilt, right and wrong, cannot be reduced to a purely political opposition between friend and foe.

If and insofar as Marxist praxis of class struggle is mistaken about the abyss of human guilt and, thus, implicitly denies human moral dignity, it cannot be taken as a fundamental principle in the historical process of salvation. If and insofar as Marxist historical and social analysis is based on this premise, it cannot be accepted by theology uncritically as it stands. Of course, this is also true of all historical and sociological theories, which see themselves as metatheories for religion and faith, for whom Christianity is a historico-culturally necessary but now superceded phase in the evolutionary history of humanity. Theology cannot justify itself with regard to these theories by producing an even more comprehensive "pure theory." It can only do so by returning to individual believers and their praxis of a single, undivided discipleship, which must take effect in historical and social life. Of course, this theological claim must question its ecclesiastical basis, and the question will be particularly demanding where the usual ecclesiastical division of labor is in force. In my view, this is shown in the exchange between theology and basic community life in the so-called poor churches.

The individual development of the believer in poor Third World churches is threatened at the moment by a danger that I think liberation theology fails to take into sufficient account. This is the threat of what I will call here *secondary colonization*, through the invasion of the Western cultural industry and its mass media, particularly television, which increasingly holds persons captive in an artificial world, alienating them from their original images, languages, and history. Does this "soft" terror of the culture industry have more dangerous effects in poor countries than in Europe? Does it not threaten to paralyze the process of liberation? Finally, is not the opium of the poor no longer religion but mass media culture, which reaches even the most miserable slums? This mass media culture makes the poor and exploited feel overloaded even before they have achieved any personal liberation: it robs them of their memory, even before they have become aware of their own history; it threatens their language even before they have acquired this language and become culturally literate. An important amount of liberation work is taking on this "new immaturity," not only in Latin America but also in Europe.

IV

To conclude, I would like to turn back to Europe. In the present intellectual culture of Europe, often described as "postmodern," the usage I have adopted here of "history" (in the singular!) and "society" has been very strongly criticized. It is regarded as a suspiciously totalizing way of talking, which threatens the individual. It is regarded as language destroying the colorful multiplicity of life and leading to the dictatorship of a monolithic praxis. The scapegoat is often biblical monotheism. It is regarded as the godfather of a predemocratic, antipower-sharing autocracy, the father of an obsolete patriarchalism, the forerunner of totalitarian ideologies of history; in short, as a mania for uniformity in religious garb. In contrast to this monotheism, mythical polytheism is praised because it is said to guarantee an innocent multi-

plicity of life. God is sacrificed to the gods. There is talk of new mytholo-
gies: a new enjoyment of myths is spreading in secularized Europe; a
new cult of innocence, deeply unpolitical, with a voyeuristic attitude
toward social and political crises, a life on a reduced scale, private nest-
feathering and new-age fantasies as a new religion. In the postmodern
manner, what is proposed is the abandonment of all universities and
single-minded reason in the name of a praxis-free, colorful multiplicity
of life and its unreconciled histories.

There are European theologians who see a chance for Christianity in
this polymythic atmosphere. There is no theologico-political perspective
I recognize here. I see only a calling into question of the substance of
the Judeo-Christian religion and the danger of atrophy to our political
culture. I distrust the promise of exoneration from the obligation to
make choices and the promise of liberation for the sake of greater
individualization. This latter is linked to the postmodern dismissal of
the idea of unity and with the esthetic-mythical birth of a new multiple
way of thinking. Will not new power settle down in a world of unrelated
and "hands-off" multiplicity? In the history of my German people was
there not a dangerous suspension of the idea of unity and equality of
all human beings? Were not the Jews, before being sent to the gas
chambers, excluded metaphysically and legally from this unity? Thus,
politically and culturally can we allow ourselves that innocence we
esthetically propose? Can we allow ourselves it in the face of the world's
misery? The "new thinking" in Europe works toward the suspension
of morality, it fascinates by its presumption of a new innocence for
humanity. Friedrich Nietzsche is regarded as the new prophet. But is
this new thinking not ultimately an excuse-making strategy, against
the individual and against history? A bit like this: the excuse for the
individual in the face of historical and social catastrophes in the world
is that the individual does not exist as an individual person capable of
guilt. If capacity for guilt belongs to the dignity of freedom, then this
"new thinking" in Europe actually withdraws from the history of freedom
that it claims to be saving. Here what is needed is Christianity's power
of social criticism and historical imagination.

This Christianity and its theology do not derive from a guilt-free polymythic "spiritual wealth," but from the gospel "poverty of spirit," which
does not take comfort in myths far removed from history and praxis.
This Christianity compels us, against the mythical ban of a posthistori-
cal world, to speak again and again of humanity and solidarity, oppression and liberation, and to protest against injustices crying to heaven.

Translated by Dinah Livingstone

6

Unity and Diversity

Problems and Prospects for Inculturation

The New Situation in the Church's History

People rightly talk today about a new phase in the history of the Church. After what was a relatively short period of time, but a period fundamental to theological and historical identity of the Church, namely that of Judaeo-Christianity, the Church was dominated for almost 2,000 years by a relatively uniform cultural sphere—that of Europe and the West. Now the Catholic Church stands before a break in its history, one that, in my view, must be seen as the most far-reaching since the time of the primitive Church. The Church is in the process of moving from being a culturally more or less uniform, that is, a culturally monocentric, European (and North American) church to becoming a world church with a diversity of cultural roots and so in this sense, polycentric.[1] The last Vatican Council can be seen as a tangible institutional expression of this.[2]

This situation confronts the Church in a totally new and dramatic form with the problem of *unity and diversity*. This issue lies at the heart both of the planned *universal catechism* and of the discussion about the meaning and scope of what is called *inculturation*, which this article discusses in detail. What will be crucial to the handling of this new situation is whether this dramatic tension between unity and diversity is met by purely defensive safety-first mentality or whether an offensive loyalty to the Church's mission ultimately prevails, something like what Karl Rahner called *prudent risk-taking*.

Problems of a Polycentric Inculturation

In this section, I concentrate on two difficulties created by the bold move to a polycentric world church. The first difficulty has to do with the situation of our present-day world, and the global processes and tendencies visible in it. Talk of a culturally polycentric world church presupposes that real cultural polycentrism exists in today's world. However, this is far less obvious than it may appear at first sight. It seems to me increasingly hard to avoid asking whether macrocultural diversity in our world is not gradually disappearing; is not, slowly but surely, being broken down or absorbed by the secular Europeanization of the whole world that we call *science* and *technology* or *technological civilization.* This Western rationality increasingly rings the world with its technology and its culture and information industry, and it changes, not only the way people act, but, clearly, also the way they think. It is as though non-European peoples and cultures were being pulled into a *Eurocentric whirlpool.*

> What makes one's heart sink is not the fact that the population of a poor country should press, with gentle but elemental force, for an improvement in their living conditions, but the process of compulsory imitation which this sets off . . . The stereotype of progress is increasingly questioned by Europeans and North Americans; it reigns unchallenged now only in the "developing countries" of Asia, Africa, and Latin America. Other people are the real Eurocentrics.[3]

Even if such language may be thought exaggerated, it can hardly be denied that non-Western peoples and cultures have already come under intense pressure to conform to the secular Europeanization of the world. This fact raises the question whether cultural polycentrism in our world is not already rotten at the core. Is there really enough cultural identity and resistance left to fight this worldwide movement of European civilization, which diffuses its myths of progress as well as its undeniable advances? It is not only theologians today who are worried by the question of how ethnic and cultural diversification in our world, that is, its cultural polycentrism, can be preserved in the face of a uniform world civilization with no substance.[4]

If we reply by suggesting that there still exists a living and resistant cultural polycentrism, this brings us to the real theological question, and our second difficulty. If this is the case, how does the Church, in the process of becoming a real world church, connect with these non-European cultures if it clearly cannot treat the plans of a universal technological civilization, the secular Europeanization of the world, as an innocent vehicle for the universal propagation of its message? As is well known, this central question is dealt with in current theological discussion under the heading of *inculturation.* I cannot go into all the implications of this concept here as it is used in the Church and in theology, but I am anxious to remove in advance one misunderstanding that is very frequently associated with the idea of the implantation of Christianity in non-Western countries. It is impossible not to mention this misunderstanding, although doing so makes the problem of inculturation more difficult rather than less so.

Many well-meaning attempts are made these days to preserve the Church from ethnocentric fallacies and, for the sake of cultural polycentrism, to prevent a second seizure of power in the universal Church by Europe. These attempts are often accompanied by suggestions such as these: Christianity must at last remove its European garb, strip off its European and Western skin, and so on. What evidently underlies this language is the idea of an historical Christianity, a Christianity distinct from culture and innocent of ethnic ties. Another way of putting this is to say that the underlying idea is that of a *pure* or *naked* Christianity, which begins with nothing but itself and only clothes itself in the garments of different cultures in a subsequent act, when it already has its fixed identity, distinct from culture and history. This idea is a fiction; it feeds on unexamined metaphorical talk about naked facts of *pure truth.* There is no such thing as a Christianity existing prior to culture and history, a culturally free or naked Christianity. That is why the constantly implied parallel between inculturation and incarnation is only partially correct. Even the distinction that has grown up within (*sic*) European Christianity between religion and culture does not get us much further here, because it too is a culturally specific formulation.

The culture that ecclesial Christianity cannot simply take off like a garment is the European and Western culture formed from Jewish and Hellenistic Greek traditions. With regard to inculturation, this raises the explosive question: if the Church cannot merely strip off this historically contingent clothing and slip into some other new cultural garb, how can there ever be such a thing as a culturally polycentric world church? On these assumptions how can there be an inculturation of the gospel that is not Western expansion merely disguised for tactical reasons? In other words, is what we call cultural polycentrism in the last resort anything other than the continuation of a monocultural colonization of the souls of foreign peoples and cultures by less drastic means than in previous epochs of church history?

This brings out the whole explosive and dramatic nature of the issue of *unity and diversity* in the present ecclesiastical and ecumenical situation. It contains within itself a variety of dangers: the danger of an intensified official centralism as a defensive protection for unity, the speculative danger of a gnosis remote from history offered as a transcendental basis for the culturally polycentric diversity of Christianity, and the associated danger that the fixed and unchangeable *deposit* of doctrinal and moral teaching will be envisaged as akin to Plato's ideas,[5] and the parallel *liberal* danger of envisaging cultural polycentrism as a neutral and innocent coexistence of cultural contexts.

Conditions for a Successful Polycentrism

I would like to offer the following tentative answer to the questions outlined above as a starting point for discussion. A culturally polycentric world church, which nevertheless must not and cannot step out of its Western European history, is possible on condition that, within the domain of European culture, this church remembers and acts on two basic features of its biblical inheritance. First, it must see itself as, and prove itself, in terms of its biblical inheritance, to be a religion committed by its mission to seeking freedom and justice for all. Second, it must see itself as, and prove itself to be, a religion that derives from its biblical inheritance a particular culture, a culture based on the acknowledgment of the other in their otherness; in other words, on the creative acknowledgment of ethnic and cultural plurality, such as ought to be familiar to us from the primitive history of Christianity.

The two basic principles are indivisible. Nevertheless, in this chapter, I do not wish to devote any more attention to the question of how far the Church must translate the biblical inheritance into the basis of a political culture that seeks freedom and justice for all. Discussion about political theology and the theology of liberation had made important advances here in recent years. My main concern here is to stress that a church that is maturing into a universal cultural polycentrism must treat and implement the biblical inheritance primarily as the basis of a hermeneutical culture; that is, a culture that acknowledges the other in their otherness. This is particularly important because the European mentality as formed over the last 2,000 years, while it has internalized the biblical universalism whose limit is the *ends of the earth* (see Acts 1:8), has been guided in this far more by the principle of domination than by that of acknowledgment. In his book *Die Eroberung Amerikas. Das Problem des Anderen*,[6] T. Todorov shows that this conquest succeeded because the Europeans were superior to the indigenous peoples in hermeneutics. While, for example, the Aztec could only understand and locate Cortes' tiny group within their own "world picture," and therefore, evaluated it wrongly, the Europeans were in a position to understand, evaluate, and outwit these alien others in their otherness, almost in terms of their own "system." However, this understanding of others in their otherness was, as we know, no acknowledgment: it was primarily the expression of a hermeneutics of domination, not of a hermeneutics of acknowledgment.

In Christianity's biblical origins, the encounter with strangers and the acknowledgment of others in their otherness was central. The welcoming approach to strangers who are different from oneself is a fundamental biblical attitude, which is constantly remarked on in the stories about Jesus. Furthermore, many of Jesus' parables point to the dimension of promise present in the acknowledgment of the other, the one who is different. In other words, the origins of Christianity contain the seeds of a hermeneutical culture based on acknowledgment, which in the history of Europe was grossly obscured and fell into the background, and has never in the course of church history won that universal significance that might have been expected from its biblical origins. The Church seems constantly to have fallen victim to the temptation to confuse its own universalism, the universality given to it with its mission, with the universality of the kingdom of God, and to neglect or ignore the eschatological difference between the Church and the kingdom of God.

The last Vatican Council is a prime example of moves toward a culture promoted by the Church itself, which is based on the acknowledgment of the other in their otherness. In the declaration on the relationship of the Church to non-Christian religions, previous purely apologetic and defensive attitude to these religions and their cultures was for the first time replaced by a recommendation to see them in a positive light, although it would have been good to have more detailed guidance about whether and how far the Church itself must listen to the alien prophecy of these religions. In the decree on religious freedom, the Church defines itself as the institutionalization of a religion of freedom, which in the proclamation and propagation of its convictions rejects any means of coercion that circumvents that freedom. It does so because it seeks to be guided, not by an abstract right of truth, but by the right of the (other) person in their truth.

In language that is familiar today both in theology and in the Church at large, we might say that the Church must develop two options in order to meet the challenge of cultural polycentrism without denying its own cultural background. It must let itself be led by an option for the poor and an option for others in their otherness. It must translate this culture into practice in a political culture of freedom and complete justice and in a hermeneutical culture based on the acknowledgment of others in their otherness; and it must constantly keep in mind the link between these two options. This leaves us not only with many social barriers to overcome, but also much ethnic blindness in our traditional Christianity and the ethnic deficit of traditional Christian anthropology. The two options are often seen as two sides of a coin, but in my opinion, ethnic and cultural diversity and social class differences cannot be simply identified. Ethnic and cultural particularities are not just an ideological superstructure generated by underlying economic problems, as both Western practice and Marxist theory might imply.

A culture based on the acknowledgment of others in their otherness, rooted in Judaism and Christianity but not seeking world unity by conquering others who are alien or weak and forcing them to pay the price for our European progress, would make it possible for the tendency to universality that has become a part of the European outlook to combine with the wisdom and sufferings of other cultures as promise. A coalition seems to me completely possible between two elements. Non-European cultures have resisted the abstract European logic of evolution in which history is finally replaced by natural economic laws and memory by computers. The European partners would be those who are also searching today—not seeking to abolish our scientific and technological world and its achievements, but certainly looking for new ways of interacting with that world. They are aware of the cultural background of our technological rationality and its increasingly automatic and anonymous processes of modernization, in which human beings are less and less their own memories and more and more their own guinea-pigs.[7]

Unless I am making a mistake, one of the main obstacles to the development of a culture of acknowledgment in Church and theology is the predominance of an epistemological principle that entered Christianity through Plotinus. I mean the epistemological principle according to which like is always known by like. If we follow the biblical traditions, if we follow Paul (for example, in his conflict with Peter), we must formulate a different principle of knowledge for the Church and theology, one that states that only unlike can know unlike—in mutual acknowledgment. This remark leads to the next stage in our discussion.

Tasks for Theology

The process of developing cultural polycentrism in the Church confronts theology with new tasks. First, we must realize that the concept of theology current in the Church and the distinction it presupposes between theology and the living of religion is itself culture-specific and marked by ethnocentricity: this concept of theology itself derives from European and Western tradition. This must be firmly realized before we talk today about non-European theologies. If traditional theology is to take account of the conditions and assumptions under which the Church is maturing into cultural polycentrism, then it must on its side attempt to develop what I would tentatively call bridging categories in intercultural exchange.

One such category for promising intercultural mediation is, it seems to me, that of memory, and especially in the form of remembering suffering. The Church, of course, from its beginnings, is a remembering and retelling community gathered around the eucharist to devote itself to following Jesus. This characteristic gives it potential for intercultural communication and inculturation. I would propose the hypothesis, which I believe could be firmed up with empirical evidence, that memory and retelling should be regarded as more valuable for productive interchange between different cultures than the anonymous argumentation of classical metaphysics or the scientific language of Western rationality, which must both be regarded as specifically Eurocentric: indeed Western rationality cannot lead to cultural polycentrism, but only to an acceleration of the secular Europeanization of the world through technology and the culture industry.

If this is correct, it is the task of theology today to protect remembering and retelling from suspicion of reductionism and homogenization and to develop their communicative value, indeed superiority, for intercultural exchange. It is true that the category of remembrance and the associated basic anamnetic structure of Christianity are not exactly the focal point of theological attention at present. Indeed, Christian theology's reasoning has difficulty in coming to terms with this category. Under the influence of the categories of classical Greek idealist metaphysics, remembrance has been split off from theological reasoning: memory appears only in the liturgy, and is regarded as primarily a part of worship and not strictly belonging to theo-logy or thinking about God. In my view, this exclusion of the basic anamnetic structure of Christianity is connected to the fact that very early in the history of Christianity something like an attack of schizophrenia occurred. More and more the view gained ground in Christian theology that, while the faith of Christians might have its roots in Israel, their ideas derived— exclusively—from Athens, from Hellenism. Although it would be wrong to minimize or underestimate the importance of Greek ideas for Christianity, there remains a question to be faced which is particularly urgent today: has Israel on its own no intellectual contribution to make to Christianity and Europe? Indeed it has, and Israel's intellectual and rational contribution to Christianity is an original one. It is the conception of thought as remembering, as historical remembrance, as that memory that is of crucial importance, especially in intercultural exchange. This is something I feel must be taken very seriously in present-day theology with an eye to the beginnings of polycentrism.[8]

In the face of this new situation in church history, theology is left with an important hermeneutical task in the interpretation of dogma. Although the dogmas of the faith have been formulated with an over-reliance on Greek metaphysics, the need is not to dilute them, and certainly not to deny them; however, there is a need to try to make them intelligible and to decode them as formulations of a dangerous memory,[9] as abbreviated formulas, shorthand *dangerous stories* in which the substance of the faith can be communicated between cultures.

There are, of course, many dimensions to the claim of memory to be a privileged category of intercultural exchange. For the indigenous peoples of Latin America, for example, land and the soil is not simply a potential means of production, but the living space of their collective memory, the locus of their history. When this soil is taken from them, this land stolen, their memory is destroyed, and with it the organ they need to be genuinely evangelized. The current campaign of the Brazilian bishops against such land theft is, therefore, an example of a battle for a noncolonialist evangelization.[10]

This brings our discussion into the sphere of ecclesiology and pastoral theology. The main question for theology here is: who are the agents of a polycentric inculturation? Guided by the suggestions of the last Council, theology here must develop and establish the idea that the regional particular churches and the local churches must be given an important role in the development of a successful inculturation, and that the authority and responsibility of believers stressed by the Council, that is, their participation in the life of the Church in their own right is of crucial importance to the process of polycentric inculturation. This, however, opens another chapter of this discussion.

Translated by Francis McDonagh

NOTES

1. On this, see the relevant essays of mine in: Franz-Xaver Kaufmann and Johann-Baptist Metz, *Zukunftsfähigkeit, Suchbewegungen im Christentum* (1987).

2. On the signs and Vatican II statements that point in this direction see, in addition to the texts cited in note 1 above, Karl Rahner's essays in his *Schriften zur Theologie* XIV (1980).

3. Hans Magnus Enzenzberger, "Eurozentrismus wider Willen," in: Enzenzberger, *Politische Brosamen* (1982), pp. 40,42.

4. On these issues, see also the article by Peter Rottländer in *Concilium* #204 (1989).

5. For a criticism of this approach, see Herbert Vorgrimler, "The Adventure of a 'New World Catechism' ", *Concilium* 192 (Edinburgh 1987), 103–109.

6. French edition 1982, German 1985.

7. The hermeneutical culture of acknowledgment sketched out here is not only important for the new situation of the Church on the road to cultural polycentrism; it is also important for the situation of our world as a whole. Only if such a culture of acknowledgment becomes established can the emerging *one world* become something other than the expression of an undifferentiated and empty or a repressive uniform world civilization.

8. This aspect reveals the ecumenical significance of this new, culturally polycentric phase of church history. On the one hand, in the perspective of a culturally polycentric world church, the sixteenth-century split in the Church appears as primarily an internal European event. This does not make it less important, but gives it a new place among the new priorities of the ecumenical consciousness: the gradual superseding of a narrow, Eurocentric image of the Church may indirectly bring the histories of the European churches closer together and lead them to a new unity. On the other hand, one important—and long overdue—result of the move toward a culturally polycentric world church may be to bring about a more productive ecumenical relationship between Christians and Jews, between Church and synagogue. In practice, the European gentile Christianity that grew up on Hellenistic soil was too heavily marked and defined by a contrast with its Jewish origins, and this is one of the reasons why antisemitism has lain so near the surface for most of past church history. If particular churches now work through their distinctive cultural identities to rediscover their origin and common past, the fundamental Jewish component will become clearer.

9. On this, see my thoughts in J.-B. Metz, *Faith in History and Society* (London 1980).

10. On this, see Alberto Moreira, "Orthodoxy for the Protection of the Poor?," *Concilium* 192 (Edinburgh 1987), 110–115.

7

1492—Through the Eyes
of a European Theologian

I

"Come right up to the balustrade," said Bishop Murelli during a liturgy in Caxia. "Come up so that you can see the faces." They were above all, time and again, small faces, black faces, faces that shone—for moments, for a song, for the duration of a cry, a shout. And there were dreams, there were desires in these eyes—or also tears.

Then I saw the other faces, the other eyes: among the *campesinos* eking out the most wretched of existences around the edges of Lima, above all, time and again, among the poor women, and above all— particularly at night—among the street children of São Paulo. I saw the eyes without dreams, the faces without tears, as it were the unhappiness beyond wishing. I saw children's faces, deadened as a result of sniffing a disgusting glue as a substitute for opium, the substitute for dreams in a life that is truly forced below the level of dreams, below the limits of tears: poverty, that ends up in the wretchedness of being without dreams or tears! Those of whom I am speaking are not sixty or seventy years old, with burnt out, used up dreams; they are three, five years of age, street children with no parents and no one to care for them, and how many of these hundreds of thousands would still be alive if I were to go back?

Finally, I kept seeing the faces of the Indians, faces shaped by the dark shadows of what is called the mysticism of the Andes; in any event, I, the European, would call it a kind of mysticism of mourning. There is constitutional mourning in the Andes. However, among these Indians, faces have long been in process of modernization. If you spend too long looking at television, your face changes. Will this mourning prove capable of being combined with our Western civilization? Or will we simply develop the Indians out of their mourning? In my view, were that to happen, humankind would be poorer by a hope. I don't want to romanticize. There is nothing romantic about these mourning faces of the Indians, and in any case "romantic" is far too European a category: it is, in fact, a favorite term of disparagement used by those who do not want to concede our own inability to mourn. In my view, these mourning faces are shaped by a distinctive strength, a secret resistance. Against what? Against the hectic acceleration of time, which we have brought about and to which we ourselves have long been subjected? Against the forgetfulness that nests in our modern consciousness? These faces seem to be missing something that we have long forgotten in the name of "progress" and "development." Christian hope is certainly no kind of superficial optimism. The substance of Christian hope is not simply remote from mourning, stripped of any kind of mourning. With the inability to mourn, there ultimately develops an inability to allow oneself to be comforted and to understand or experience any comfort other than mere postponement.

II

Can we Christians here in Europe, can the churches of our country, bear to look at these faces? Can we, do we want to, risk the change of perspective and see our lives as Christians, in the churches—at least for a moment—from the perspective of these faces? Or do we experience and define ourselves exclusively with our backs to such faces? The temptation to do that is great and, unless I am mistaken, it is growing. 1992: who among us does not think primarily of the Single European Market and the new possibilities for trading that have meanwhile opened up to it in Central and Eastern Europe? If we in Europe associate 1992 with Columbus, with the quincentenary of his discovery (1492–1992), do we not do so exclusively from our perspective? Does not a crypto-triumphalism prevent us honestly from adopting any other perspective?

Such questions become more acute when we note the mentality that (in my view) is at present to be found in Europe (and in North America) and is spreading. By way of a definition, I might venture to call it the "everyday postmodernism" of our hearts, which is again putting the so-called Third World at a faceless distance. Is there not at present something akin to cultural and spiritual strategy of immunizing Europe, a tendency toward a mental isolationism, the cult of a new innocence, an attempt intellectually to avoid the global demands made on us, a new variant of what I once called "tactical provincialism"? What can be described philosophically as postmodern thought—the repudiation of universalist categories, thinking "in differences," in diminished numbers, in colorful fragments—has a parallel in everyday life. Is there not a new mood among us that is again putting the distress and wretchedness of the poor peoples at a greater existential distance from us? Is not a new provincialism spreading among us, a new form of privatization of our lives, the mentality of an onlooker without any obligation to critical perception, a voyeuristic approach to the great situations of crisis and suffering in the world? In our Enlightened European world, are there not increasing indications of a new, as it were, secondary, innocence that is nourished by the impression that while nowadays we are more informed than ever about everything, above all about what threatens us, and about all the crises and terrors in the world, the move from knowledge to action, from information to support, was never so great and so unlikely as it is today? Does not such an impression dispose one to resignation? Or to a flight into myth and its dreams of innocence, remote from action? Is not an over-familiarity with crises and misery rife among us? In the end, we get used to the crises over poverty in the world that seem increasingly to be a permanent part of the scene, so that we shrug our shoulders and delegate them to an anonymous social evolution that has no subjects.

However, for the church, the sorry reality of these poor lands that cries out to heaven has long been a fateful question, a touchstone of its character as a world church. In the end of the day, the church does not only *have* a Third World church; by now it *is* largely a Third World church, with an indispensable history of European origins. In view of the mass misery that cries out to heaven (or no longer cries out because its language and dreams have long been shattered), the church cannot reassure itself that here it is experiencing the tragedies of a time shift in a world that is coming together with increasing rapidity. Nor can it tell itself that these poor are the victims or even the hostages of their own heartless oligarchies. The world church needs to spell out and take seriously what was said biblically in the language of an archaic itinerant Christianity preached around the villages: "What you did to the least . . ." The European church may not, therefore, as it were, in a postmodern way, allow its criteria to be talked out or belittled under the pressure of circumstances and mentalities. It may not withdraw from the tension between mysticism and politics into a thinking in terms of myths that is remote from history. In the end, with its creed "suffered under Pontius Pilate," it is and remains attached to concrete history, to that history in which there is crucifixion, torture, suffering, hatred, weeping—and loving. No myth can give it back that innocence it loses in such a history.

Certainly, the church is not primarily a moral institution, but the bearer of a hope. Its theology is not primarily an ethic but an eschatology. But the roots of its power lie precisely in the helplessness of not giving up the criteria of responsibility and solidarity and leaving the preferential option to the poor only to the poor churches. All this has to do with the greatness and the burden that is laid on us with the biblical word *God*. It does not remove us from social and political life, but simply takes away the basis of hatred and violence from this life. It calls on all men and women to walk upright, so that all can kneel voluntarily and give thanks with gladness.

III

Once again, the faces, and even more the eyes. With what eyes was Latin America, was this "Catholic continent," discovered? At the beginning of the times we in Europe call *modern*, at the beginning of the modern period, an anthropology of domination was developing—secretly, and overlaid by many religious and cultural symbols. Man understood himself increasingly as a dominant subject, there to put nature under his control. His identity was formed by this lordly subjection, this seizing of power over nature. His eyes looked downward. His logic became a logic of domination, not of recognition: a logic of assimilation and not of otherness. All virtues that did not contribute to domination—friendliness and gratitude, a capacity for suffering and sympathy, mourning and tenderness—faded into the background, were cognitively depotentiated, or entrusted to the world of women in a treacherous "division of labor." We may have long failed to notice the features of this anthropology and logic of domination because the pressure toward subjection very soon shifted outward—against alien minorities, alien races, and alien cultures. Obviously, the history of European colonization has its roots here. Who would venture to dispute that this mechanism of domination continually made its way through into the history of Christian mission as well?

Certainly, the project of European modernity contributed, and continues to contribute, quite different features. Thus, within it—in the processes of political Enlightenment—there developed a reason that seeks to be practical in achieving freedom and justice. For a long time, it was encoded in European terms. So what came about in the meanwhile was a developing *secular* Europeanization of the world—by way of science, technology, and economics; in short, by way of the world-domination of Western rationality. However, this caught up the whole world in a tremendous frenzy of acceleration. The dawn of the industrial age already brought with it great impoverishment and misery in Europe, especially in the last century. Although the pace of this European industrial development has been quite rapid, and Europe has changed more in the last 150 years than in the whole of the past 2000, among us, the development, nevertheless, took place in slow motion as compared with the pace of the process of industrialization that can be noted, for example, in Brazil. The growing acceleration of this modernization, this industrial and technical development—above all, in posturban metropolises such as São Paulo—seems to be matched by an increase in impoverishment that has grown exponentially. The development has no time to develop. It destroys the time of human beings, who seem to be crushed between premodern conditions of life and rule and postmodern technology.

The political culture that seeks freedom and justice for all can be established only if among us and in those Latin American countries it is combined with another culture that, for want of a better term, I might call a new hermeneutical culture: the culture of the recognition of others in their otherness, with the way in which they form a social and cultural identity, with their own images of hope and recollection. It is imperative that supposedly neutral economic and technological forces which are allegedly free of political and moral pressures should be tested by them. Only such a culture of recognition makes possible a respectable and redemptive interchange between Europe and these countries. Indeed, in the end, the European spirit is itself endangered by the process of modernization that it has set in motion: it increasingly acts as an automatic process, and increasingly, human beings in these processes are merely their own experiments, and less and less their memories.

IV

From the very beginning, with its consciousness of mission Christianity struggled for a culture of the recognition of the other. What was to be normative for this consciousness of mission was not Hellenistic thinking in terms of identity and assimilation, but the biblical notion of the covenant, according to which, like is not known by like, rather, unlikes know one another by recognizing one another. One example of this is the dispute between Peter and Paul along with the dispute at the Apostolic Council over the question of whether gentile Christians were to be circumcised. This recognition of the others in their otherness is expressed in the refusal of the Jewish Christian Paul to subject the gentile Christians to circumcision. So, at the roots of the biblical tradition lie the impulses to a new hermeneutical culture: any "will to power" is really alien to it, in the recognition of the others in their otherness. This hermeneutical culture was again obscured in the history of Europe; it also faded into the background in the history of the Church. So, with what eyes was the Latin American continent "discovered"? Did this early Christian hermeneutic of recognition play a normative role? Or was the process of the Christianization of America not far more (if not exclusively) accompanied by a questionable hermeneutic of assimilation, a hermeneutic of domination, that had no eyes for the trace of God in the otherness of the others and that, therefore, continually also violated the culture of these others it did not understand, and made them victims? At any rate we must use this question to measure all the ceremonial words spoken on the occasion of the quincentenary.

V

The church does not hope for itself. Therefore, it does not need to split its own history—in a suspiciously ideological fashion—in order only to display the sunny side of this history, as those must do who "have no hope." To concede failure does not mean falling into a neurotically arrogant cult of self-accusation. It is quite simply a matter of honoring our eschatological hope and venturing conversion and new ways in the light of it.

That also applies, *mutatis mutandis,* to our Christian theology. I have often asked myself why so little attention is paid to the history of human suffering. Is that the sign of a particularly strong faith? Or is it perhaps just the expression of a historical way of thinking, detached from any situation and empty of humanity, a kind of idealism equipped with a high degree of apathy in the face of the catastrophes and downfalls of others? The new political theology in Europe developed, among other things, out of the attempt to make the cry of the victims of Auschwitz unforgettable in the *logos* of theology. And the theological impetus of liberation theology, as I understand it, comes from the attempt to make it possible to hear the cry of the poor in the *logos* of theology and make the face of strange other men and women recognizable in it; i.e., to interrupt the flood of ideas and the closed character of systematic argumentation with this cry and with these faces. That may make the language of theology small, poor, and completely unsolemn. But if it becomes that, it will come close to its original task. In the end, the mysticism Jesus lived out and taught, which should also have directed the *logos* of Christian theology, is not a narrow mysticism of closed eyes, but an empathetic mysticism of opened eyes (cf. e.g., Luke 10.25–37). The God of Jesus cannot be found either here or there if we ignore its perceptions.

8

Freedom in Solidarity

The Rescue of Reason

THE TWO SIDES OF THE EUROPEAN SPIRIT

"Eurocentrism?"

Eurocentrism is the main charge continually leveled against the European spirit, in the wider world and in Europe itself, especially today. The Europeans are constantly criticized for being too Eurocentric. But what does Eurocentric mean? Where is the Eurocentrism of the European spirit rooted? My answer is brief and to the point; it is rooted, not in the fact that we Europeans have *exported* too much of Europe to the world, but in the fact that we have exported too little, or, more precisely, that we have always sought to disseminate only half of Europe, half of the European spirit throughout the world. I know that this answer sounds provocative, and is open to possible misunderstandings, but I hope that it will take on clearer contours in the remarks that follow.

European Rationality—Type I

By means of science and technology, or the so-called technological civilization, Europe has, to some degree, come to dominate the world and, thus, has created the one world we now experience, with all its contradictions, open and latent. With its information and communications industry, it moves like a bulldozer all over the globe. Everywhere brains are being Europeanized as a result of this technical modernization. So-called occidental rationality is bringing about the secular Europeanizing of the world. As is well known, this type of rationality, which has its roots in Europe, is governed by a will to have power over untamed nature. Its knowledge is a form of the knowledge for ruling. The logic inherent in it is a logic of domination, not of recognition; it is, at any rate, a logic of assimilation and transformation, not a logic of otherness.

European Rationality—Type II

However, is the message of the European spirit exhausted in this secular Europeanizing of the world? If the answer is yes, what might the consequences be? In the course of this secular Europeanizing, would not all other cultures increasingly be marginalized and turned into folklore? Would not their alien prophecies ultimately fall silent—even and particularly for Europeans themselves? A new type of rationality is developing, above all in the processes of the European Enlightenment. It is directed by a reason that wants to be effective and achieve itself as freedom—also and specifically as the freedom of others, and thus, as justice. This type of rationality is the basis for a new political culture that has in view the subjective freedom and worth of all human beings. This universal message, which is native to the European spirit, is strictly anti-Eurocentric. Without its dissemination throughout the world, the secular Europeanizing of the world would be simply a contribution to its downfall. Not all universalism is an expression of the will to power. Certainly this kind of "European universalism," this "universalism of human rights" (as one might well also call it), can only come about if it is disseminated in a readiness to recognize the otherness of others; i.e., only if the age of European insensitivity, which has already cost so many victims, is not repeated in the age of human rights.

The Crisis

But what about this "good" and promising half of the European spirit in Europe itself? In answering this question we should not be too self-confident, too uncritical. Here we will do well to resort to a bit of ideological criticism, an approach that seems little heeded or even neglected today. Here I would mention just one prominent instance of the currently all too self-confident and uncritical approach to the basic European situation—and I see that situation not only in continental Europe but in North America as well. In summer 1989, an article appeared in the United States entitled "The End of History?" It was written by Francis Fukuyama, head of the planning staff in the State Department. Briefly, Fukuyama's thesis is that the West has now finally won the Cold War, and therefore, the United States has become the apotheosis of everything that was to be expected in history from Western European modernity. Does this completely ignore the dangers inherent in the West, in the European spirit? It seems to me particularly important to point to them in view of the fundamental changes in Europe, the "new Europe." Has it been demonstrated, for example, that the type of rationality stamped by the will to power, the type of reality that believes it can do anything, has not also swallowed up the type of reality I described as a type of reason seeking culture and justice, and thus, as the basis for a new political culture? Is there not a danger that the "good" European spirit only acts as compensation and has no substance? In Europe, too, the so-called processes of modernization are increasingly running by themselves, with no subjective control over them. What about this "good" spirit of Europe? Let me mention some symptoms of its crisis or its threatening collapse, and I hope I can do this without being too pessimistic about our culture.

Technology and the Information Industry

There is such a thing as the death of the freedom-seeking spirit, extrapolated by technology. A freedom based on the subject and on solidarity seems long since to have been overdetermined by technology. Increasingly, we have techniques for reproducing everything, ultimately even reproducing human beings who themselves reproduce. Human beings are increasingly just their own experiment and less and less their own memory. Has not the model long been a computerized intelligence that cannot remember itself because it also cannot forget anything; in other words an intelligence without history, without passion, and without morality?

Is this development aimed at heightened independence or does it lead to a new, to some degree secondary, bondage, a bondage far harder to overcome than the first bondage at the time of the Enlightenment, because those who are the victims of secondary bondage do not even suffer as a result of the bondage they suffer? How compatible with the media and with sources of information is that spirit in search of itself, as the freedom of the subject in solidarity? In recent years, North American scientists, in particular, have pointed to the ambiguities in our modern culture and information industry. The mass media do not merely result in richer subjectivity with more intense perception; they also encourage a kind of lassitude in the subject, by making increasingly unnecessary the effort of creating language that we have imagined ourselves and history that we have experienced ourselves. The flood of information apparently serves not only to enlighten, but also to some degree to bring a new secondary form of bondage, because it increasingly detaches people from the possibilities, and even the consequences, of their concrete actions. So, is the spirit of European modernity, the spirit of the Enlightenment, slowly but surely turning into a second bondage?

Scientific Theory

There is such a thing as the death of the freedom-seeking type of rationality, extrapolated by scientific theory. At the moment, our modern scientific knowledge is not orientated on the subject as the basis of knowledge. "Subject," and "freedom," "liberation," and so on are, in strict scientific terms, anthropomorphisms. In terms of scientific theory, if I understand it rightly, talk of freedom of the subject in solidarity is an anachronism. To know what is the case, one must begin from the death of the subject. There are no subjects, only self-referential systems. The spontaneity of the spirit does not rule in them. That would be an idea left over from the old Europe. Rather, what rules is the coldness of space, the coldness of an infinitely indifferent evolution, a history of evolution without a subject.

Neomyths

In my view, the new delight in myths that is springing up, the neomythic cult of European postmodernity, points to the death of that type of rationality that seeks expression in the freedom of the subject in solidarity. In the farewell to European modernity, which is so often celebrated, a new cult is being disseminated, a cult of shedding obligations, a new cult of innocence, praise of myth because of the ethical suspension it contains, because of the supposition of human innocence grounded in it. Now only qualified options are available. Commitment, if there is any, is commitment with the right of exchange: "Here I stand, but I can also do other things. I am never merely my own opinion. Anything goes, including the opposite."

As we know, in the background here we have Nietzsche, the prophet of farewell to European modernity. However, we should note that this Nietzsche is not just the herald of the death of God in the heart of Europe, the passionate critic of Christian *monotono-theism* in favor of a Dionysian polymythy, but also the herald of the death of human beings as we have so far known and been familiar with them. As is well known, Nietzsche himself speaks of the death of the subject; he regards the subject as a mere *fiction*, and talk of *I* as an anthropomorphism. He already describes the collapse of truth-seeking language in the intoxication of metaphors and subjectless discourse. He prophesies and calls for the end of normative-moral consciousness in a life *beyond good and evil* in which the successor to man, super-elevated man, is none other than his own infinite experiment. Certainly, for the sake of Nietzsche, we ought to differentiate more closely here. However, I am simply challenging the stereotype Nietzsche himself comes across as. Does his *new* man, the exalted Dionysian man, reflect the future of the European spirit? A freedom *beyond good and evil*, remote from memory, suffering, and mourning, above all, an innocent freedom? This self-realization of the European spirit in a Dionysian mode is not necessarily utopian. Its most trivial realization is obvious: human beings as gently functioning machines.

Safeguarding Theological Traces

It may be that I have exaggerated this crisis of the European spirit. I will not deny a degree of one-sidedness. It may be useful in due course to seek correctives. Are there any? Be that as it may, many people nowadays are in search of such correctives, as resources for resistance. They turn directly to cultures outside Europe and their wisdoms.

Here I would like to suggest taking note of the depths of European culture itself; in particular, where they go back to the biblical traditions. From them, it is possible to derive themes for the spirit and culture of a freedom in solidarity, which seem to me indispensable in the situation of crisis that I have described. Certainly, these motives and perspectives have been obscured, not least by the way in which Christianity became theology. That makes all the more urgent the task of rescuing them from oblivion or even that oblivion of oblivion that prevails in theological discourse. What follows can be no more than a safeguarding of their traces in the crisis of the European spirit.

Anamnetic Rationality

The kind of perception of the world that was at work in original Christianity takes the form of anamnetic reason. The type of rationality in the biblical traditions, if I may put it that way, is, thus, basically anamnetic. It resorts to the indissoluble unity of reason and memory— and precisely this seems to me to be repressed or forgotten in the Enlightenment type of rationality in search of freedom. There is good reason for the Enlightenment criticism of dogmatism and traditionalism. However, has it not overlooked the fact that there is a particular form of memory in that critical reason that does not want to be pure criticism? Has it not overlooked the fact that, not only faith, but also that reason which seeks to be effective as freedom needs such memory? Over against the world of our scientific and technological systems this memory takes the form of a dangerous memory, a dangerous memory without which human beings increasingly lose themselves as subjects seeking freedom in solidarity. In remembering this, reason seeks to assure itself of the semantic content on which not only the substance of faith but also interest in subjective freedom and freedom in solidarity feeds. Now, Christianity has indeed preserved the anamnetic character of its identity in worship ("Do this in remembrance of me"). However, it has largely neglected to develop this anamnetic constitution culturally and to defend it against an abstract modern reason. Only where Christianity succeeds in doing that can it also enter into the crisis of the European spirit with saving criticism.

A Memory of God That Is Critical of Myth

The European spirit as manifested in the processes of the Enlightenment sought above all to break out of the anxieties of a mythically bewitched world in the interest of human freedom. This concern also governed the radical Enlightenment criticism of religion. However, one question here cannot either be answered or excluded; namely, the question of consolation. Therefore, the freedom-seeking spirit of the Enlightenment constantly produced new irrationalisms by suppressing this question—against its declared intent: new myths, say, as clandestine ways out of the straits of historical life, as ways of shedding the concrete experiences of suffering and catastrophe, and of absorbing anxiety and guilt.

The memory of God in the biblical traditions is more radically aware than the Enlightenment type of rationality of a criticism of all myths, or at any rate, of a proviso that is critical of myths. In the earliest biblical traditions, the name *God* was applied for the first time and uniquely in the history of humankind to human beings. Israel's capacity for God here is evidently rooted in a remarkable incapacity; namely, the incapacity really to find comfort in myths or ideas remote from history. Biblical monotheism is accompanied by a pathos critical of myth. However, at present, even Christian theology is often distancing itself from this monotheism. It is seeking, for example, through depth psychology, to go behind it to a polymythic primal history of humankind or to see through it in trinitarian theology to a history within God. However, in my view, such attempts reflect a world with a mystical and polytheistic character that has lost the power to be critical of myth. The new praise of myth in the postmodern spirit of Europe makes me suspicious: is not the ethical suspension sought in myth, the assumption of a radical human innocence given by myth, a disguised form of despair at freedom, above all at thoughts of freedom in solidarity in the face of the injustice in our world, which cries out to heaven?

A Culture of Acknowledgment

The Enlightenment type of rationality on which our political culture in search of freedom and justice is based was always threatened by the dangers of ethnocentric and culturally monocentric shortcuts. Time and again, it seems, this new political culture came to grief on the others, whom it had to recognize and acknowledge in their otherness. In the face of this crisis, I want to refer to a third impulse that is indebted to biblical traditions. Within them lies the impulse to a hermeneutical culture that acknowledges others in their otherness. The neighbors in the central biblical commandment to love thy neighbor are not primarily those who are near, but the others, the alien others. Does Christianity still have the power to cultivate this biblical knowledge of the traces of God in the otherness of others? Only if it does, can it offer support in the crisis of the European spirit and its universalist morality. Certainly, the idea of acknowledgment here is not aimed at transforming the others in their otherness. Nor is otherness in itself already a matter of being "in the truth." Otherwise, everything would end up in a vague relativism of cultural worlds, a relativism already bearing within itself the germ of a new uncomprehended violence. Consequently, the hermeneutical culture sought here may not abandon the tension between the authenticity of cultural worlds and the universalism of human rights developed in the European tradition. Nowadays, there is almost everything still to be done in this direction, not only in politics but also in the Church.

Translated by John Bowden

9

Time without a Finale

The Background to the Debate on "Resurrection or Reincarnation"

In my view, the problem of time stands in the background of the debate on "resurrection or reincarnation" carried on in this volume. Two "messages" about time confront each other: that of Friedrich Nietzsche, with its Dionysian tone, about time without a finale, as it were, the eternity of time, and the biblical, apocalyptic message of time that is limited.

The Divinity of Time

We know Friedrich Nietzsche as the one who proclaimed the death of God in the heart of Europe. "God is dead" is the message of the "madman" in Nietzsche's *Gay Science*. God is dead, and the churches are simply the "tombs and monuments of God."[1] What *is*, if God is dead? Looked at closely, Nietzsche's message about the death of God is a message about time. His revocation of the rule of God is the announcement of the rule of time, the elementary, inexorable, and impenetrable sovereignty of time. God is dead. What now remains in all passing away is time itself: more eternal than God, more immortal than all gods. This is time without a finale; indeed, as Nietzsche explicitly emphasizes, "without a finale in nothingness."[2] It is time that does not begin and does not end, time that knows no deadlines and no purposes, whether heavenly or earthly, whether purposes seen speculatively, as by Hegel, or purposes to be realized politically, as with Marx. It is time that wills nothing but itself, time as the last remaining monarch after all the metaphysically built thrones have been overthrown; time as the only postmetaphysical fascination. For millennia, we had tried to form a concept of the incomprehensible God. Now, in ever-new attempts, we are attempting a definition of undefinable time—spurred on or irritated by Nietzsche, Heidegger, and others. It is one of the most remarkable signs of the time that at present nothing is so puzzled over and reflected on, written about and argued over, than time itself.[3]

Under the Spell of Unfettered Time

We are increasingly exposed to an anonymous pressure of acceleration, an obscure mobilization of the world in which we live. We are living under the mythical spell of time that has been released, unfettered, and left to itself. Anxiety is going the rounds that in this we could even lose ourselves. "Romanticism" is questioned in intellectual culture, and the nervous cry for a "homeland" is in the ascendant. Nietzsche, for his part, knew very well in what almost apocalyptic-seeming turbulences humanity ends up if it finally wants to bid farewell to the apocalypse; i.e., to thinking of time with a definite finale:

> Where are we going? Away from all the suns? Are we not for ever falling down? And falling backwards, sideways, forwards, to all sides? Is there even an above and a below? Are we not wandering as if through endless nothingness? Is not empty space breathing upon us? Has it not become colder? Is not the night and more night coming constantly? Do not lanterns have to be lit in the mornings?[4]

Perhaps we are getting used to the diffuse atmosphere of dislocations and accelerations, used to the self-running processes in which the medium is more important than the message, and ever more rapid communication is more important than what is to be communicated. Perhaps we are getting used to the prohibitions that no one has put up publicly, but that stick all the more firmly in our heads: the prohibitions against demobilization, against lingering, against delaying. Perhaps we are becoming more insensitive to the circumstances that while we can discover more and more, we can be familiar with less and less.

The Eternal Recurrence of the Same

Nietzsche made a proposal about doing justice to the sovereignty of time, which he proclaimed.[5] To break "the will's aversion to time," as he himself confesses, he musters his "most abysmal ideas": the idea of the eternal recurrence of the same. The character of being is to be stamped on coming-to-be, as the supreme expression of the will to power. That is how he puts it in a note from 1885 entitled "Recapitulation." So, passing away should be presented as constant becoming in the eternal return of the same, and thus, be made "permanent." Nietzsche's formula for Heidegger's *Being and Time* runs: "That everything returns is the most extreme approximation of a world of becoming to that of being—a culmination of contemplation."[6] That may sound abstract at first, and far removed from the everyday experience of the domination of time. But what about ideas of the migration of souls, which are again preoccupying many people today? What above all about the notion of reincarnation, which is finding an increasing number of adherents? Is there not a reflection here of the suggestive power of this early Greek myth of the recurrence of the same, to which Nietzsche refers? The recent book of the German writer Botho Strauss has the displeasing title *Beginninglessness*.[7] It is a literary-aesthetic attempt at a cosmology for which the world has neither a beginning nor an end; in other words, a paraphrase of the so-called steady-state cosmology[8] and the exercise of a thought and vision that forbids itself the idea of beginning and end. Evidently, the theses of the beginninglessness and endlessness of the world age correspond.

Kierkegaard's Protest

Kierkegaard energetically opposed the notion of the recurrence of the same. He encountered it with the idea of repetitive memory. In his book on Nietzsche, Karl Löwith reports an attempt by Kierkegaard to see whether something can be repeated in such a way that the same thing recurs.

> He (Kierkegaard) had once been in Berlin and now repeats this journey to test what significance the repetition can have. He remembers how this and that had been and looked the first time; however, precisely because of his memory, he is forced to discover that nothing repeats itself but everything has changed from what it was before. The landlord and the lodging, the theatre and the whole atmosphere of the city on his first visit—everything has changed with time, and so in the new situation even the little that has remained physically the same no longer fits the different environment and so is also different from what it was before. To the extent that there is a repetition of details, it is a "false" one, because the whole, which determines the direction of all individual

details, has not remained the same. Precisely the memory of things past teaches him the impossibility of a recurrence of the same.[9]

Memory robs the notion of the recurrence of the same of its force. So, at a time in which we live less and less by memories and more and more from our reproductions, and understand them as our own experiment, we should recall the power of memory that opposes recurrence. We should resist a special kind of forgetting, that forgetting of forgetting through which the reign of a time without beginning and end establishes itself in our souls.[10]

God and Time

At the heart of the biblical message there is also a message about time, a message about the end of time. All biblical statements carry a time stamp, a stamp of the end of time. In the biblical Israel, we encounter a people who seems incapable of consoling and calming itself by myths or ideas. Myth ultimately seems as remote from it as metaphysics.[11] Again and again, Israel turned into a landscape of cries. Israel, so talented for the here and now, so caught up in the world, did not, according to all the important evidence, believe in and think of its savior God as outside the world, as that which is beyond time, but as the limiting end of time. This experience of God applies to the traditions of Abraham: "I will be with you as the one who will be with you"; it applies to the prophets' message of crisis and conversion in which the landscape of Israel turns into an eschatological landscape; it applies to Job and his cry "How long?," and finally, it applies to late Old Testament apocalyptic and its theodicy that reaches deep into the New Testament. Certainly, statements about the apocalyptic traditions have to be made with great care (and here I can do no more than refer to the articles about them in the present issue). Here I emphasize just one point: in its approach this apocalyptic is not, as critics have often suggested, a speculation remote from history, a catastrophe-driven assumption about the moment when the world comes to an end. In essence, it is, rather, an attempt to disclose the limited nature of world time, an attempt to temporalize the world against the horizon of temporally limited time.

That is now also and particularly true of the history of the founding of Christianity. What theologians were later to call "the expectation of the imminent end of the world" spans the whole New Testament scene. Jesus lived and suffered against this background, and Paul formulated his Christology and carried on his mission under the horizon of its understanding of time. Here for Paul, the idea of time as having a limit does not mean, say, an emptying and devaluation of time and the world that appears on its horizon. For Paul, time is in no way an insignificant transitional period; it is not time in the waiting room. The horizon of limited time does not mean any devaluation of the present (as is frequently suggested even in theology); on the contrary, only in it can the "present" be experienced in that emphatic way characteristic of Paul. His final and irrevocable *nun*, "now," can only be uttered against the background of limited time; under the horizon of inductively infinite time there is nothing ultimately valid, but only the hypothetical!

The apocalyptist Paul is a missionary. Without him and his missionary activity, the historical project of Europe, what was later called the Christian West, is unthinkable. Against the horizon of limited time, the world moves toward being a world of history; this specific experience of time becomes the root of the understanding of the world as history and, thus, the start of historical consciousness.

Paul the apocalyptist is also evidently in no way a fanatic about the end of the world. He does not pass over and poison the political landscape with fantasies of decline as pointed as those of the Zealots. One only has to read his sober plea for the Roman state in Romans 13 (which tends to irritate us today). The horizon of limited time does not make those who consciously live in it either voyeurs or terrorists of their own decline. Christianity became prone to totalitarianism and aggression only when it sought completely to detemporalize the apocalyptic legacy, for example by strict moralizing. That led to an apocalyptic overstraining of moral action: and it is here that the danger of fanaticism and undistanced practice lurks.

Escapism from Time in Theology

The way in which Christianity became theology increasingly blurred the dramatic connection between God and time, as we find it in the original texts. For reasons I shall not discuss here,[12] Christian theology has forgotten, halved, eased the tension in the temporal expression of limited time that its biblical heritage has forced on it. In the meantime, it has come to live on alien, borrowed conceptions of time that make it questionable how the God of the Christian tradition could still be spoken and thought of at all in their context. Of the hidden understandings of time found in theology, I would mention these: cyclical time, time framed by the pre-established cosmos; linear-teleological time, the progressive continuum to the degree that it either grows into infinity evolutionistically empty or else is dialectically delayed and interrupted; psychologized time that, as strictly biographical, has been detached from world time and natural time—and neomythical conceptions of time generally. Even in theology itself, Nietzsche seems to have more opportunities than the legacy of apocalyptic, in so far as it has to serve as a program of temporalization.

Since the days of Marcion and his dualistic axiom of the banefulness of time and the timelessness of salvation, there has been something akin to a permanent Gnostic temptation for Christian theology. It is accentuated today in the dualism between our lifetimes and world time. Can we still connect talk of God in any way with world time? Are we not here reverencing a secret dualism? We abandon world time to an empty, anonymous evolutionary time and seek to bring only individual lifetimes into a relationship with God. But in doing this have we not—in good Gnostic fashion—long since abandoned the creator God, and are we not exclusively venerating a redeemer God who is presupposed as being in the depths of our souls? Can a theology that holds fast to the confession of the creator God avoid the tension between cosmology and psychology, between the cosmological and the psychological conceptions of time? To say the least, it is not the individual lifetime but the time of the others, not the period up to one's own death but the experience of the death of others, which keeps eschatological unrest alive.

The Anxiety in the Anxieties

The mortal illness of the Christian religion is not naivety but banality. The Christian religion can become banal when, in its commentary on life, it only duplicates what has, in any case, become the modern consensus without it—and quite often against it. The naivety of biblical religion, on the other hand, lies in wait for those things that have been taken for granted. It does this, for example, by dwelling a moment longer on the texts and images of the biblical apocalypse and by enduring or holding out in their presence a little bit longer than modern consensus allows. When Christian religion returns to apocalyptic wisdom and its message of time and suspects elements of a dangerous memory here, it does not do so in order to comment on the cause of time with a *Schadenfreude* tuned to apocalypticism; rather, it does it in order to detect the sources of our anxiety.

What are we anxious about? There are many alleged sources of our individual anxieties—not least also in the life of religion and the church. The advice and criticism of psychology can be helpful in detecting them and providing reassurance; it can help in making such anxieties disappear, anxieties that paralyze and intimidate, make us look small and insincere, unfree and easy to dominate . . . but is there not something similar to a deeper anxiety in all our individual anxieties, an anxiety that determines all of us? If we had less anxiety about our anxiety, we would presumably know more closely what really made us anxious.

It may be that archaic human beings were always made anxious by the feeling of the near end of their lives and their world; and that this mythical anxiety paralyzed their work in the world. Some of this mythical anxiety also shows through in the present anxieties about catastrophes. For modern human beings, however, there is an anxiety that has become more radical—not the anxiety that everything could be ending and that, for example, the planet could be doomed but, more deeply rooted, the anxiety that nothing is ever going to end any more, that there is no end. There is an anxiety that all and everything is being dragged into the surging wave of a faceless and merciless time that ultimately rolls over everyone from behind like the grains of sand on the beach and that makes everything equal in the way that death does. Even a nuclear exploding planet would ultimately be delivered over to the endless death of a time "without a finale in nothingness." This kind of domination of time drives out any substantial expectation and gives rise to that hidden anxiety about identity that eats away the souls of modern human beings. It is difficult to decipher because it has been successfully practiced for a long time under the figures of progress and development until we discover it for a few moments in the depths of our souls.

Worstward Ho!

One of Samuel Beckett's famous plays is called *Endgame.* In it, one of those in the dialogue, Hamm, asks in great anxiety: "What's happening? What's actually going on?" The other, Clov, answers "Something or other is running its course." These are shreds of dialogue from the tragedy of the quenching of life—the silent quenching of life without any apocalyptic cry. "Something is running its course." At this time, without a finale human beings, human beings as we have known them so far, are dying. The majesty of time proclaimed by Nietzsche as the death of God is claiming its victims. The domination of time without end is claiming the end of human beings. No one knew that better than Nietzsche himself. So he often talks about the "abolition of mankind"; at any rate, he speaks about the death of the subject, regards the subject as a mere fiction and the *I* as well as the whole human being right up to the present as the real anthropomorphism.[13] And what about Nietzsche's dream of the new man, the exalted man, the Superman who is to be born from his message of time without a finale? Only the vision of man completely insensitive to time occurs to me, man as a smoothly running machine, man as a computerized intelligence, who does not need to remember himself because he is not threatened by any forgetting, man as a digital intelligence without history and without passion. Certainly, that too would be a triumph of time over God—over God and over human beings. No finale could ever be as bad as no finale at all.

In Samuel Beckett's *Worstward Ho!* we read, "Longing that all go. Dim go. Void go. Longing go. Vain longing that vain longing go."[14]

NOTES

1. Friedrich Nietzsche, *Werke in 3 Bänden*, Darmstadt [2]1960 = ed. Schlechta I–III, here II, 126ff.

2. Schlechta III, 853 (posthumous).

3. Cf., e.g., the bibliography on time in H. Lübbe, *Im Zug der Zeit*, Berlin 1992, 25–35.

4. Schlechta II, 127.

5. For the following quotations from Nietzsche cf. J. B. Metz, 'Theologie versus Polymythie oder Kleine Apologie des biblischen Monotheismus,' in O. Marquard (ed.), *Einheit und Veilheit, XIV Deutscher Kongress für Philosophie*, Hamburg 1990, 170–86, esp. 175f.; abbreviated version in *Herder Korrespondenz*, April 1988.

6. Schlechta III, 853 (posthumous).

7. Munich 1992.

8. It recalls the doctrine of the "eternity of the world" which Augustine declared to be incompatible with the doctrine of creation. Cf., e.g., E. Behler, 'Ewigkeit der Welt', in *Historisches Wörterbuch der Philosophie*, Vol. 2, 844–8.

9. K. Löwith, *Nietzsches Philosophie der ewigen Wiederkehr des Gleichen*, Stuttgart 1956, 177.

10. Cf., e.g., J. B. Metz, 'Für eine anamnetische Kultur', in II. Loewy (ed.), *Holocaust: Die Grenzen des Versteheus*, Reinbek and Hamburg 1992, 35ff.

11. For details, see J. B. Metz and T. R. Peters, *Gottespassion*, Freiburg 1991.

12. Cf. my text in n.5. above.

13. For the relevant passages from Nietzsche's work cf. again n.5.

14. Samuel Beckett, *Worstward Ho*, London 1983, 36.

PART II

ESSAYS BY JÜRGEN MOLTMANN

10

The "Crucified God"

God and the Trinity Today

The debate about the existence of God and the function of faith has given rise in recent years to a feeling of uncertainty among Christians, who are moving, without much sense of direction, between the two poles of "God is dead" and "God cannot die." In struggling to renew the Church and to recreate society, many Christians have simply excluded the God question. Behind this political and social crisis in the Church, however, is the christological crisis—to whom do Christians ultimately refer their faith?—and the whole question of God—on which God is Christianity ultimately based, the crucified God or the idols of religion, class, and race? The Church cannot be credible unless the Christian faith is certain. One of the consequences of this debate, however, has been a new convergence in theological thinking in the different Christian confessions, especially in the sphere of the doctrine of God.[1] I discuss some aspects of this tendency in this chapter.

I

Theological thinking about the God question has, of course, followed the suffering experienced by Christians because of injustice in the world and isolation in that suffering. History has concentrated for the most part on man's struggles for power and on class and racial struggles. If we are to find a universal history of man, we must look beyond these to the "history of suffering in the world."[2] Men are separated from their fellow men in possessing, in the positive aspects of life, but they are equal in poverty, in the negative aspects. Man's experience of suffering in the world goes beyond theism and atheism. It makes it impossible for him to believe in the existence of an omnipotent God who is good to all men and who "rules the world splendidly." A faith in God that justifies suffering and injustice in the world and does not protest against it is inhuman and even satanic in its effects. On the other hand, however, any protest against injustice tends to lose its impetus when it is based on atheism and a conviction that this world is the ultimate reality. The angry cry of protest is sustained by man's longing for the One who is completely different. As Max Horkheimer said, this is a "longing that the murderer will not triumph over the innocent victim."[3] It is a longing for justice in the world and for the One who ultimately guarantees it, and without this longing there can be no conscious suffering because of injustice. If man, suffering because of injustice, calls the existence of a just God into question, then the reverse also happens, and his longing for justice and for the One who guarantees it causes him to question his suffering, so that it becomes a conscious pain. Suffering and protest go beyond theism and atheism to the question of theodicy: if God is just, what is the origin of evil? If the sting in the question "Why is there suffering?" is "God," then the sting in the question "Is there a God?" is, of course, "suffering."

The traditional theistic answer to this twofold question is that this world is "God's world," a reflection of the deity, but the mirror is broken; the answer is no longer satisfying and strikes men as purely idolatrous. The traditional atheistic answer to this question simply deprives it of its foundation—as Stendhal and Nietzsche observed, "the only excuse for God is that he does not exist." What is ironical is that the nonexistence of God is made into an excuse for God on the basis of a failed creation, which in practice amounts to this: if man loses the habit of asking about justice, he will become adapted to and satisfied with bad relationships.

Critical Christians and critical atheists do, however, achieve a measure of agreement in the practical struggle against injustice within the context of the question of justice in the history of suffering in the world. But what does our recollection of the suffering of Christ mean for us in this context? Before we can answer this question, we have to find out the meaning of Christ's suffering first for God himself and then for the Christian believer. Because a God who reigns in a state of impartial blessedness in heaven cannot be accepted today, Christian theologians may have to reconsider the old theopaschitic questions. Did God suffer himself? Would a God who was incapable of suffering not be a God incapable of love and, therefore, poorer than any man? What meaning can a suffering God have for suffering men, on the other hand, apart from a religious confirmation of their suffering?

Theologians have to confront Christ's suffering and recognize God's being in Christ's crucifixion before they can deal with the question of suffering in the world without falling into Christian illusions on the one hand and atheistic resignation on the other. It is only when they are clear about what took place between the dying Jesus and "his" God that they will learn what this God means for those who suffer and are abandoned in the world.

II

Of what did Jesus die? The Jews sentenced him on a charge of blasphemy because of his message of God's justice and unity with those deprived of all rights. The Romans crucified him because he threatened the *Pax Romana* and its gods. He died abandoned by the God and Father to whose coming he bore such striking witness in word and deed. Ultimately, then, Jesus died of his God and Father, who abandoned him. It is on this point, at which the Son of God is abandoned by the Father, that the question of God and suffering is concentrated.

One of the earliest testimonies is provided by Mark; according to this gospel, Jesus did not die bravely and beautifully, but crying out and weeping (Mark 15:37). According to Mark 15:34, he uttered the opening words of Ps. 22 ("My God, my God, why hast thou forsaken me?") and to complete the paradox, the centurion who had witnessed Jesus' death replied to this cry of abandonment by God by confessing that Jesus was the Son of God. How are we to interpret this? Obviously, the later tradition was offended by Mark's interpretation and reproduced Jesus' dying cry with more pious words. Various Western texts contain the version: "My God, with what do you reproach me?" and Luke has replaced the expression of Jesus' abandonment by words from the Jewish evening prayer from Ps. 31:5: "Into thy hands I commend my spirit." For theological reasons, John said: "It is finished" (John 19:30). We may, I think, assume that Mark's difficult version comes closest to the historical reality.

If two texts say the same thing, it does not have to mean the same in each case. It would, therefore, be wrong to interpret Jesus' cry from the cross in the sense of Ps. 22, but right to interpret the psalm in Jesus' sense.[4] "My God" in Ps. 22 is the God of the covenant with Israel and "I" is the suffering righteous man who presses God for his legal right of faithfulness under the covenant. In Jesus' use of "my God," on the other hand, there is the whole content of his new message of the approaching kingdom of God and of his own life led in closeness to God, which has enabled him to speak so exclusively about "my Father."

This gives Jesus' abandonment a very distinctive aspect—the one who has abandoned him is not simply the God of the covenant with Israel, but his God and Father. Consequently the "I" who is abandoned is not simply the partner in the covenant, but the Son.

All the same, the legal nature of the complaint is fully preserved. Jesus' cry from the cross has, as the psalmist's cry, nothing to do with despair—it is a call for God's faithfulness. Whereas the psalmist claims the righteous man's legal right to God's faithfulness under the covenant, Jesus claims his legal right as the Son to unity with his Father. Jesus' death means that not only God's faithfulness, but also the very deity of God, whose closeness and fatherhood Jesus had proclaimed, are at stake. This is why Jesus, in using these words, is claiming his right to be in a special relationship with the Father, a relationship in which he is the Son. He is, in other words, saying: "My God, my God, why hast thou forsaken yourself?" This abandonment on the cross has, therefore, to be seen as something taking place between Jesus and his God and, there consequently, as taking place between God and God.

Why was Jesus' abandonment by God on the cross traditionally handed down at all after the Easter event? Clearly, there was an initial enthusiasm in the early Church, in which the cross represented no more than a transitional stage on the way to the glory which the primitive Christians experienced in the presence of the Spirit. Paul and Mark corrected this early Christian enthusiasm for the glorified Lord by calling to mind the lasting significance of the cross of Christ. They were convinced that, by penetrating further and further into the suffering of the unredeemed world, faith would discover more and more the real meaning of the crucifixion of the eschatological person of Christ. The resurrection of Christ did not reduce the cross to the level of a purely transitional stage. On the contrary, it raised it to the level of a saving event. The cross can be seen as a theological mystery not in the light of history, but only in the light of faith in the resurrection. In the history of man, after all, many prophets ended in the same way as Jesus. The Pauline and Marcan theology of the cross presupposes, in other words, faith in the Easter event. But how is it possible for God himself to be abandoned in his Son, to suffer and die in him?

III

This poses a great dilemma for Christian theologians; indeed, both Catholics and Protestants who have specialized in the history of dogma are agreed that the *derelictio Jesu*, the abandonment of Jesus, was the central difficulty in the Christology of the early Church. There was, it is true, a "religion of the cross" in the early Church's veneration of the crucified Christ. Ignatius was able to speak of the "sufferings of my God" (Rom. 6:3) and to imitate them in his martyrdom. The theologians of the period were not, however, capable of identifying God's being with the suffering and death of Jesus, because of their fundamentally ancient concept of God, according to which God was incapable of suffering and dying, in contrast with man, who could suffer and die. Again, according to the ancient world, salvation was to be found in deification, which in turn meant immortality. Even Cyril of Alexandria, the early Christian Father who stressed most strongly the unity of divinity and humanity in Christ, felt bound to interpret the suffering and abandonment of Jesus as man's distress, not his own. Anyone who claims that Christ himself was overcome by fear and weakness is denying his divinity.[5] But was it really not possible in the early Church to relate Jesus' suffering to God's being?

The Council of Nicaea rightly declared, in opposition to Arius, that God was not so changeable as his creature. This is not an absolute statement about God, but a comparative statement. God is not subject to compulsion by what is not divine. This does not mean, however, that God is not free to change himself or to be changed by something else. We cannot deduce from the relative statement of Nicaea that God is unchangeable that he is absolutely unchangeable.

The early Fathers insisted on God's inability to suffer in opposition to the Syrian Monophysite heresy. An essential inability to suffer was the only contrast to passive suffering recognized in the early Church. There is, however, a third form of suffering—active suffering, the suffering of love, a voluntary openness to the possibility of being affected by outside influences. If God were really incapable of suffering, he would also be as incapable of loving as the God of Aristotle, who was loved by all, but could not love. Whoever is capable of love is also capable of suffering, because he is open to the suffering that love brings with it, although he is always able to surmount that suffering because of love. God does not suffer, like his creature, because his being is incomplete. He loves from the fullness of his being and suffers because of his full and free love.

The distinctions that have been made in theology between God's and man's being are externally important, but they tell us nothing about the inner relationship between God the Father and God the Son, and therefore, cannot be applied to the event of the cross, which took place between God and God. Christian humanists also find this a profound *aporia*. In regarding Jesus as God's perfect man, and in taking his exemplary sinlessness as proof of his "permanently powerful consciousness of God," they interpret Jesus' death as the fulfillment of his obedience or faith, not as his being abandoned by God. God's incapacity, because of his divine nature, to suffer (*apatheia*) is replaced by the unshakeable steadfastness (*ataraxia*) of Jesus' consciousness of God. The ancient teaching that God is unchangeable is, thus, transferred to Jesus' "inner life," but the *aporia* is not overcome. Finally, atheistic humanists who are interested in Jesus but do not accept the existence of God find it impossible to think of Jesus as dying abandoned by God, and therefore, regard his cry to God from the cross as superfluous.

All Christian theologians of every period and inclination try to answer the question of Jesus' cry from the cross and to say, consciously or unconsciously, why God abandoned him. Atheists also attempt to answer this question in such a way that, by depriving it of its foundation, they can easily dismiss it. But Jesus' cry from the cross is greater than even the most convincing Christian answer. Theologians can only point to the coming of God, who is the only answer to this question.

IV

Christians have to speak about God in the presence of Jesus' abandonment by God on the cross, which can provide the only complete justification of their theology. The cross is either the Christian end of all theology, or it is the beginning of a specifically Christian theology. When theologians speak about God on the cross of Christ, this inevitably becomes a trinitarian debate about the "story of God," which is quite distinct from all monotheism, polytheism, or pantheism. The central position occupied by the crucified Christ is the specifically Christian element in the history of the world and the doctrine of the Trinity is the specifically Christian element in the doctrine of God. Both are very closely connected. "It is not the bare trinitarian formulas in the New Testament, but the constant testimony of the cross which provides the basis for Christian faith in the Trinity. The most concise expression of the Trinity is God's action on the cross, in which God allowed the Son to sacrifice himself through the Spirit."[6]

It is informative to examine Paul's statements about Jesus' abandonment on the cross in this context. The Greek word for "abandon" (*paradidomi*) has a decidedly negative connotation in the gospel stories of the passion, meaning betray, deliver, "give up," and even kill. In Paul (Rom. 1:18 ff.), this negative meaning of *paredōken* is apparent in his presentation of God's abandonment of ungodly men. Guilt and punishment are closely connected and men who abandon God are abandoned by him and "given" up to the way they have chosen for themselves—Jews to their law, Gentiles to the worship of their idols, and both to death.

Paul introduced a new meaning into the term *paredōken* when he presented Jesus' abandonment by God not in the historical context of his life, but in the eschatological context of faith. God "did not spare his own Son, but gave him up for us all; will he not also give us all things with him?" (Rom. 8:32). In the historical abandonment of the crucified Christ by the Father, Paul perceived the eschatological abandonment or "giving up" of the Son by the Father for the sake of "ungodly" men who had abandoned and been abandoned by God. In stressing that God had given up "his own Son," Paul extended the abandonment of the Son to the Father, although not in the same way, as the Patripassian heretics had done, insisting that the Son's sufferings could be predicated of the Father. In the Pauline view, Jesus suffered death abandoned by God. The Father, on the other hand, suffered the death of his Son in the pain of his love. The Son was "given up" by the Father, and the Father suffered his abandonment from the Son. Kazoh Kitamori has called this "the pain of God."[7]

The death of the Son is different from this "pain of God" the Father, and for this reason it is not possible to speak, as the Theopaschites did, of the "death of God." If we are to understand the story of Jesus' death abandoned by God as an event taking place between the Father and the Son, we must speak in terms of the Trinity and leave the universal concept of God aside, at least to begin with. In Gal. 2: 20, the word *paredōken* appears with Christ as the subject: " . . . the Son of God, who loved me and gave himself for me." According to this statement, then, it is not only the Father who gives the Son up, but the Son who gives himself up. This indicates that Jesus' will and that of the Father were the same at the point where Jesus was abandoned on the cross, and they were completely separated. Paul himself interpreted Christ's being abandoned by God as love, and the same interpretation is found in John (John 3:16). The author of I John regarded this event of love on the cross as the very existence of God himself; "God is love" (I John 4:16). This is why it was possible at a later period to speak, with reference to the cross, of *homoousia*, the Son and the Father being of one substance. In the cross, Jesus and his God are in the deepest sense separated by the Son's abandonment by the Father, yet at the same time they are in the most intimate sense united in this abandonment or "giving up." This is because this "giving up" proceeds from the event of the cross that takes place between the Father who abandons and the Son who is abandoned, and this "giving up" is none other than the Holy Spirit.

Any attempt to interpret the event of Jesus' crucifixion according to the doctrine of the two natures would result in a paradox, because of the concept of the one God and the one nature of God. On the cross,

God calls to God and dies to God. Only in this place is God "dead" and yet not "dead." If all we have is the concept of one God, we are inevitably inclined to apply it to the Father and to relate the death exclusively to the human person of Jesus, so that the cross is "emptied" of its divinity. If, on the other hand, this concept of God is left aside, we have at once to speak of persons in the special relationship of this particular event, the Father as the one who abandons and "gives up" the Son, and the Son who is abandoned by the Father and who gives himself up. What proceeds from this event is the Spirit of abandonment and self-giving love who raises up abandoned men.

My interpretation of the death of Christ, then, is not as an event between God and man, but primarily as an event within the Trinity between Jesus and his Father, an event from which the Spirit proceeds. This interpretation opens up a number of perspectives. In the first place, it is possible to understand the crucifixion of Christ nontheistically. Second, the old dichotomy between the universal nature of God and the inner triune nature of God is overcome and, third, the distinction between the immanent and the "economic" Trinity becomes superfluous.[8] It makes it necessary to speak about the Trinity in the context of the cross, and re-establishes it as a traditional doctrine. Seen in this light, this doctrine no longer has to be regarded as a divine mystery that is better venerated with silent respect than investigated too closely. It can be seen as the tersest way of expressing the story of Christ's passion. It preserves faith from monotheism and from atheism, because it keeps it close to the crucified Christ. It reveals the cross in God's being and God's being in the cross. The material principle of the trinitarian doctrine is the cross; the formal principle of the theology of the cross is the trinitarian doctrine. The unity of the Father, the Son, and the Holy Spirit can be designated as "God." If we are to speak as Christians about God, then, we have to tell the story of Jesus as the story of God and to proclaim it as the historical event that took place between the Father, the Son, and the Holy Spirit and that revealed who and what God is, not only for man, but in his very existence. This also means that God's being is historical and that he exists in history. The "story of God," then, is the story of the history of man.

V

In the history of Christianity, the God of the poor, the sick, and the oppressed has always been the suffering, persecuted, and oppressed Christ; whereas, the God of the rich and ruling classes is and always has been the Pantokrator.[9] But what does the God who appears as the suffering servant, the suffering and crucified Son of Man mean for the history of human suffering in the world?

Anyone who suffers without apparent reason always thinks, at least at first, that he has been abandoned by God. If he calls out in suffering, he is calling out with Jesus on the cross. God is, in this case, not the one who is facing him but hidden from him, to whom he is calling, but the human God who is calling out with him and in him and who champions him with his cross at the point where he is silent in anguish. The suffering man does not simply protest against his fate. He suffers because he is alive and he is alive because he loves. The man who no longer loves no longer suffers. He has become indifferent to life. The more a man loves, the more vulnerable he becomes. The extent to which he is vulnerable depends on the extent to which he is capable of happiness and vice versa. This is a process which can be called the dialectic of human life. Love makes man alive and mortal. The aliveness of life and the mortality of death are qualities that man experiences in his interest in life, and this interest is what we call love.

The theistic God is poor. He cannot suffer because he cannot love. The protesting atheist loves, but in a despairing way. He is made to suffer because he loves, but he protests against his suffering, and therefore, against love, which caused him to suffer. How can a man continue to love despite disappointment and death? The faith that comes about as a result of the event of the cross does not answer the question of suffering either by giving a theistic explanation that it has to be like that or by making a gesture of protest against its being like that. On the contrary, the answer of faith is to lead despairing love back to its origin—"He who abides in love abides in God and God abides in him" (I John 4:16).

Wherever men suffer because they love, God suffers in them. God suffered Jesus' death and proved the strength of his love in that suffering. This same suffering enables men to find the strength to endure what threatens to annihilate them and to "seize death." Hegel called this seizing death "the life of the spirit, which is not a life that recoils from death and protects itself from devastation, but a life which endures death and preserves itself in it."[10] The man who loves and is made to suffer because of that love and therefore experiences the mortality of death inevitably enters the "story of God." If he recognizes that his abandonment is made to cease in Christ's abandonment by God, he can "abide in love" in communion with Christ's giving himself up.

Hegel believed that only a conscious knowledge of God as a Trinity made it possible for Christians to regard the cross of Christ as the "story of God": "This is for the community the story of God's appearance. This story is a divine story, through which the community has reached a conscious knowledge of the truth. This conscious knowledge that God is three in one has resulted from this. The reconciliation which Christians accept in Christ is meaningless if God is not known as the triune God."[11]

The event of the cross, thus, becomes, for the believer who loves, the story of God that reveals the future. In the present, this means reconciliation with the pain of love. In the future, it means love in a free world without anxiety and power. The history of suffering in the world is included in the "story of God" because of the story of Christ's suffering. As Whitehead has said, "In this sense, God is the great companion—the fellow sufferer, who understands." In the Trinity, God is both immanent in human history and transcendent. To use inadequate figurative language, he is transcendent as the Father, immanent as the Son, and as the Spirit of history, he reveals the future. If we understand God in this way, we shall be able to understand our own history, the history of man's suffering and hope, as the "story of the history of God." The history of life goes beyond theistic resignation and atheistic protest, because it is the history of man's interest in life, love.

Translated by David Smith

NOTES

1. H. Urs von Balthasar, "Mysterium Paschale", in *Mysterium Salutis* III, 2, pp. 133 ff.; H. Küng, *Menschwerdung Gottes, Eine Einführung in Hegels theologisches Denken als Prolegomena zu einer zukünftigen Christologie*, 1970; H. Mühlen, *Die Veränderlichkeit Gottes als Horizont einer zukünftigen Christologie*, 1969; E. Jüngel, "Vom Tod des lebendigen Gottes", in *ZThK* (1968), pp. 93–110; H. C. Geyer, "Atheismus und Christentum", in *EvTh* (1970), pp. 255–74.

2. W. Benjamin, *Ursprung des deutschen Trauerspiels* (1963), p. 183.

3. M. Horkheimer, *Die Sehnsucht nach dem ganz Anderen. Ein Interview mit Kommentar von H. Gumnior* (1970), pp. 56 ff.

4. See H. Gese, "Psalm 22 und das Neue Testament", *ZthK* (1968), pp. 1–22.

5. W. Elert, *Der Ausgang der altkirchlichen Christologie* (1957), p. 95.

6. B. Steffen, *Das Dogma vom Kreuz. Beitrag zu einer staurozentrischen Theologie* (1920), p. 152.

7. Kazoh Kitamori, *Theology of the Pain of God* (1965).

8. K. Rahner, "Bemerkungen zum dogmatischen Traktat *De Trinitate*", in *Schriften zur Theologie*, IV, pp. 103–36.

9. See, for example, N. Gorodeckaja, *The Humiliated Christ in Modern Russian Thought* (1938); J. Cone, "Singend mit dem Schwert in der Hand. Eine theologische Interpretation schwarzer Spirituals", *Ev. Komm.* (1971), pp. 442–7; H. Lüning, *Mit Maschinengewehr und Kreuz—oder wie kann das Christentum überleben?* (1971). These authors show how the piety of impotent and oppressed

people, slaves, serfs, and Indians, has been concentrated on the passion of Christ and the figure of the suffering God. Any theology of liberation has to begin with this form of christology.

10. Hegel, *Phänomenologie des Geistes, Werke* (ed. Glockner), 2, 34.

11. Hegel, *Philosophie der Religion, Werke* (ed. Glockner), 16, 2, 308.

11

The Liberating Feast[1]

In Europe, feasts were driven out of public life by the Reformation, puritanism, and industrialization. The modern world of work required life to be rationalized in terms of its goal, means, and success.[2] For men who adapted and accepted the discipline, the games in feasts seemed childish.[3] The more they came to see the meaning of their lives in calculated ends, the less meaning they saw in the purposelessness and uselessness of feasts. For these modern men, the Protestantism of the Enlightenment reduced the liturgies of Christian worship to doctrinal and moral instruction, and excluded hymns and doxologies as superfluous.[4] In this respect, feasts, games, and the liturgies of Christian worship are today in the same position. However meaningful they may be in themselves, outwardly they seem purposeless.

Today, however, with growing criticism of this world of goals, performance, and success, which increasingly seems to impoverish human life, the question of a rebirth of feasts in culture, of a capacity for play in life and of a capacity for liturgy in the representation of Christian freedom is acquiring a new importance.[5] Industrial society directed men's interests exclusively to the conquest and control of the world. As long as there existed a shortage of necessities that could be overcome by work, economy and industry were all-important. But once it becomes possible to satisfy elementary needs, there is room for a shift of interest from the production of life to its representation, and so to a rebirth of festivity in culture and religion.[6] The path of the total liberation of man from want, oppression, and abstinence is different from that of life enacting itself in freedom, but this path cannot reach its goal without being itself a foretaste and anticipation of that freedom.[7] Only the means justify the end—not the other way round—and the goal is only made credible by the path to it. This is why struggles for freedom must constantly be accompanied by the feast of freedom so that the feasts do not become remote from the world and the struggles obsessed with it.

To discover the liberating feast we need: (1) a functional and critical analysis of the present-day social significance of the feast; (2) a theological description of the event of divine liberation that is to be celebrated in and as the feast; and (3) an assessment in terms of practical theology of its liberating effect.

Functional Analysis

From the earliest times, religious celebrations have belonged to the category of ritual.[8] Functional analysis shows that rituals provide historical continuity amid changing periods and generations. Rituals also integrate individuals into groups and groups into larger associations. They also give an order to historical time and the social environment. They heal breaches and settle conflicts. Even today, rituals give life order, and in crises, give it meaning. In addition to these practical functions, religious rituals and forms of worship also have the gratuitous function of representing existence and its experiences. For this reason, functional analysis cannot fully explain its "demonstrative, existential value" (J. Buytendijk).

In pre-Christian and non-Christian cultures, worship is the feast of the gods.[9] In this feast, the pure origin of the world returns and renews life. As a symbol of the world center, the cultic place turns chaos into an ordered cosmos. The cultic times turn the flowing time of impermanence into the cycle of the "eternal return of the same." Gods and men come together in sacred places and at sacred times, as in the primal event. The myth tells the story of the primal event; the cultic liturgy enacts it. The feast catches men up in the origin, where everything is "as on the first day." In this way, the feast is a renewal. It celebrates the *restitutio in integrum.*

The modern world of work deprived the feast of its character as a renewal of the origin. The reproduction of life through work put a stop to the festive renewal of life from a transcendental source. Feasts, arts, and holidays were given new functions in the service of the world of work. Formally, they became a suspension of the laws and attitudes that regulate daily life.[10] This suspension is often held to perform a useful political and psychological function by providing outlets.[11] All forms of repressive authority must provide outlets from time to time so that the aggressions they build up can be safely worked off. Oppressed people need "bread and circuses" to enable them to endure their oppression. The same applies in psychology to forced abstinence. Without the opening of outlets from time to time the psychological balance that constitutes self-control cannot be maintained. But where feasts, games, and leisure act as outlets, they are the instruments of a domination that is incompatible with freedom. The second function of this suspension may be described as "release." Because everyday life is dominated by tension, responsibility, and pressure for achievement, there is a need for periodic release and relaxation. "Holidays" are needed to restore energy. Many people expect Sunday worship to do this for them, and that is one reason why provocative experiments with liturgy are rarely accepted. Both these functions are open to the suspicion that feasts, games, and acts of worship do more than compensate for the inadequacies and failures of regulated life by creating an unreal dream-world of freedom: "Freedom exists only in dreams and beauty blooms only in poems" (Schiller).

Today this "opium of the people" is only rarely produced by religions. The manufacturers of dreams and ideologies are much better at it. Contact with freedom in the form of outlets, relaxation, and compensation is certainly an alienated contact with freedom, but even unfree contact with freedom is nevertheless contact with freedom, and this should not be forgotten.

The alienation of the sort of contact with freedom I have described can be broken with feasts, games, and acts of worship as alternatives to the everyday world of work and make them accessible. They then come to have a similar function to the technique that sets up an unusual "counter-culture" (McLuhan) in opposition to the usual human environment in order to stimulate creative freedom by deliberate confrontation. They are no longer merely instruments of the reproductive imagination, working off the boredom of everyday life, but of the productive imagination that investigates and explores the limits of future freedom. They are now no longer dealing with the unreal possibilities of the present, but with the real possibilities of the future. They do not make up for present unfreedom with a dream of freedom, but lift the ban of the unalterability of life by encouraging people to think of real liberation. Release, outlets, and compensation have a stabilizing effect on the world of work and domination. By providing anticipation and room for alternatives and experiment, feasts and acts of worship bring a hitherto unknown freedom into unfree life. When feasts and worship make it possible to experience quite new possibilities and powers of liberation, the ban of fate and the feeling of individual impotence are lifted.

A functional theory normally starts from the present world of work and sees only the service function feast and worship perform for that world. In so doing, it supports the forces working for the stabilization of that world. In contrast, a critical theory must start from the freedom experienced in feasts and worship and investigate its liberating action on men and situations. The two approaches complement each other in that critical reflection has become essential to reveal the mostly unconscious context of feasts and worship in modern life, if the feast of freedom is to have a liberating and not a stabilizing effect. But both theories must go further and provide a material description of the actual experience of freedom in question. Only on the basis of such a description can the functions appropriate to this freedom be found and defined. What is the freedom that is celebrated in Christian worship and that gives us the right to call that worship a "liberating feast"?

Theology of Liberation

Christian worship is and always has been in essence the feast of Christ's resurrection from the dead.[12] For this reason, it was celebrated on the first day of the week, Sunday, at sunrise. It was a eucharistic celebration with bread and wine. Worship and eucharist combine in a special way past and eschatological future, recollection, and hope.[13] In the language of Ernst Bloch, the representation of the suffering and death of Jesus is hope in the mode of recollection, and the representation of the future of the Lord is recollection in the mode of hope. He who was crucified by this world is expected to come as the liberator of this world, and the liberation he brings about is already experienced in the powers of the Spirit. In the combination of past and future, recollection and hope, the present is lived as the enjoyment of this freedom. The raising of the crucified into the coming glory of God is recalled as the source of this freedom, and its effects are experienced in faith. The coming of Christ is looked for to bring the perfection of freedom to the whole of enslaved creation (Rom. 8.19). In worship and in the eucharist, men are taken up into this eschatological process of the setting free of the world to be the kingdom of glory. They celebrate this freedom in eschatological rejoicing and bring it into the world by taking up their crosses. The recollection of the suffering of the crucified rules out a view of the feast as an escape from the painful conditions of earthly life. It is more like the silent suffering of mankind and creation made audible in the groaning of the Spirit. Hope in the risen Christ rules out mere lamentation over this suffering without hope or denouncing its causes without joy. Faith in the raising of Christ from the dead leads to a firm solidarity with the unredeemed world. With freedom so near, the chains begin to rub. But at the same time, it releases us from the law and fate of this world into a new creative life. Joy at the presence of freedom through reconciliation is, thus, mixed with pain at the presence of unfreedom and hope of the world's release from it.

In the perspective of ordinary history, the resurrection of Christ cannot be proved and makes no sense. To prove something always means to add something new to the system of what is already known. But if the resurrection of Christ presents a challenge to the familiar system of the ordinary world, with its cycle of law, guilt, and death, it cannot be proved in terms of that system. But the position becomes quite different when we look at ordinary history in terms of the resurrection of Christ.[14] Then, what is ordinary makes no sense. The old law is annulled. The inescapability of history is destroyed. From this point of view, faith means recognizing the creative freedom of the God who makes the impossible possible, calls into existence what does not exist (Rom. 4.17), and exalts what is despised in the world (1 Cor. 1. 26–31), and sharing in this creative power of his. Freedom is now no longer "the understanding of necessity," but creative power for a new life. It follows from this that the raising of the crucified reveals the eschatological alternative to the system of this world and society. As this alternative, it is celebrated with feasting and introduced into unfree life as an anticipation of freedom. It is impossible to talk about the resurrection of Christ unless one has experienced the Spirit of the resurrection in faith and obtained the freedom of this Spirit. The process of the new creation of the world begins with the resurrection of Christ through this experience of freedom in faith. It will be completed when the dead, too, receive justice, and "every rule and every authority and power," and death itself, is destroyed, "that God may be everything to everyone" (1 Cor. 15.28).

The experience of freedom acquired through faith in the resurrection of Christ mocks "the world with its great wrath" (P. Gerhard). From the earliest times, Easter hymns have celebrated the victory of life in an exorcism of mockery, ridiculing death, pouring scorn on hell, and facing the lords of this world without fear.[15] This can be seen as early as the first surviving Easter hymn in 1 Cor. 15.55–57: "Death is swallowed up in victory. O death, where is thy victory? O death, where is thy sting? . . . But thanks be to God, who gives us the victory through our Lord Jesus Christ." Easter sermons in the Middle Ages and even later are said to have begun with a joke. Laughter takes away the seriousness of a threat, disarms it. It shows unassailable freedom where the enemy had expected fear and guilt. And when the foundation of all threats against man is death, Easter is really the beginning of the liberation of the oppressed. The liberating feast of the resurrection of Christ stands between the slavery of the past and the coming life in freedom. It manifests the joy of freedom, because there is no other way in which the experience of freedom can be comprehended.

Falling at the beginning of the week, the liberating feast points symbolically back to the creation at the beginning (2 Cor. 4.6), and for this reason, faith regards the creation of all things as a liberation. Called by the creator's word out of nonexistence into existence and out of chaos into order, all things are created in freedom and destined for freedom. Seen as the creation of God's freedom, the existence of the world is not necessary. No purpose is served by the existence of something where once there was nothing. Theology has described this freedom of the world by saying that if creation had been necessary to God he would not have been the creator. If it had been simply an accident, the creator would not have been God but an unpredictable demon. Nor is creation a necessary surrender of anything by God, or an outflow from the fullness of his essence. God is free, but he does not act arbitrarily. When he creates something that is not divine but also not nothingness, that thing has its origin not in itself but in God's pleasure. God freely creates a creation that corresponds to him. Between arbitrariness and necessity, theology has taught us to see the world as a creative game of his pleasure, which is undetermined but nevertheless in the deepest possible way corresponds to him. Hugo Rahner has remarked that when we say that the creating God is at play, what is concealed in this image is the metaphysical insight that the creation of the world and man was an action that made sense for God but was in no way necessary for him.[16]

The liberating feast of the resurrection of Christ points back to the creative mystery of God and stresses that creation had the unforced gratuitousness of a game. Pleasure in the experience of liberation combines with the pleasure of the whole creation in existence. The demonstrative value of being that exists in all forms of life is given a voice in man's joy in his liberation, or, put the other way round, that experience of freedom discovers its cosmic dimensions. It is for this reason that the Easter liturgy of the Orthodox Church has always consciously taken the form of a cosmic as well as a human liturgy. The status of a child of God, which is a symbol of man's liberation, has a counterpart in the free creation and "play as a world symbol."[17] The discovery of these cosmic dimensions in the liberating feast implies an alternative for everyday dealings with the world. Where these dealings are dominated in our society by the exploitation of nature as an object, the feast reveals possibilities of harmony and cooperation that recognize nature as a partner.

The celebration of the resurrection of Christ in the liberating feast as an anticipation of the universal resurrection from the dead points forward to the creation of the last times, to the new creation of all things, the kingdom of God, the kingdom of glory. Christian eschatology has never represented this end of history as the result of historical struggles or the goal of human moral efforts. It has regarded it as the end of the history of domination and work, and described it in aesthetic categories—as a song of endless joy, the dance of the redeemed, with infinitely varied patterns, the perfect harmony of body and soul, nature and man, in the revealed glory of God. It has never painted the joy of redeemed existence in the colors of this life, stained as it is with weariness, toil, and guilt, but with what Ernst Bloch called "everyone's childhood vision," unforced laughter, total admiration, and new innocence. The visions of redeemed existence are not taken from the world of struggle and work, but from the world of basic childish trust. The game of glory will put a stop to the suffering of struggle and the boast of victories. The risen one whose feast is celebrated is "the leader of the mystical dance" (Hippolytus) and his Church is his "bride and partner."[18] What is called "the end of history" is, for a Christian understanding, not an end in the sense of a goal, but release from a life subordinated by the law to goals and achievements into the joy of God. In this joy, according to Luther, man will "play with heaven and earth and the sun and all creatures. All creatures will live, love and rejoice, and will laugh with you and you with them, even in the body."[19] The liberating feast is a foretaste, a glimmering, but also a real beginning, of this new world of joy in total freedom. The liberating feast is the anticipation of the festive, free world of God. This discovery in it of the eschatological dimensions of freedom reveals another alternative to daily life, and this life is seen not so much a long march as a prelude, not as a preparation but a foreshadowing of the coming life of joy. What is left in eternity out of the flow of time depends on grace, the luck of love, and the experiences of liberation, but not on proud achievement or effort. That freedom already shows itself here and now in the flesh, in the natural grace, spirit, and loveliness of the life Dostoievski depicted in the prostitute Sonia. "Beauty will redeem the world."[20] In the experience of the faith of the resurrection God himself, as the essence of freedom, appears "beautiful" because he radiates joy (Karl Barth). Because the "kingdom of God" has been so moralized that it no longer seems to require freedom, but only obedience, it is time to rediscover the glory of God that makes us free to be happy.[21] Without this discovery there can be no liberating feast.

Practical Effects of Liberation

If we now try to investigate the action of the feast of the resurrection of Christ, the first thing we find is the influence of aesthetic categories on moral ones. The moral seriousness of liberation and improving the world has a tendency to totalitarianism. It leaves no time for festive joy and spoils the sense of beauty. When Christian faith bows to the moral law, it feels compelled to balance the law of the old world against the law of the new. The result of this, however, is not freedom but a new unfreedom. The Christian Church then becomes obsessed with the need to make itself useful all over the place in order to justify its existence, and so loses the alternative it has to offer. If, instead, it could see the liberating feast as the expression of its experience of freedom, it could break through the moral and political seriousness of history making by a relaxed joy in existence itself. This would not in any way make such determination to struggle superfluous. Far from that, it would preserve it and protect it from its totalitarian frenzy on the one hand and its temptation to despair on the other. By being freed from its obsession with achievement, the revolutionary spirit would be preserved from giving up before the unachievable. Aesthetic pleasure in freedom has a liberating effect on the liberation struggles that have to be fought. It removes the alienations always created in such struggles. It works like the gospel on the law or the indicative of new existence on the imperative of the renewal of life.

In the light of the resurrection hope, freedom has two sides. It lives in liberating protest and it lives on the superabundance of the future.[22] Because resurrection overcomes death, its protest resists death and the power of death in the midst of life. It resists the private death of apathy, the social death of the abandoned, and the noisy death of bombs. It protests against all power based on the threat of death. Freedom lives in resistance to inward and outward denial of freedom. But freedom does not live on this protest, but on the hope of a greater fulfillment. "Much more," says Paul again and again when talking about the difference between "freedom from" and "freedom for" (Rom. 5.15–20). God's grace is greater than men's sins. His freedom is more than freedom from oppression. His new creation is greater than man's past. This has been called the "economy of unearned fulfillment" (P. Ricoeur). The "but" with which we resist oppression is only the dark side of the hope in the "much more." Resistance must be rooted in hope if it is not to decay into hate and revenge. Hope must lead to this resistance if it wants to avoid turning into the opium of the people. The superabundance of hope can be celebrated only in festive ecstasies. These constantly produce new forms of opposition to all the forms of unfree life. Even if the liberating feast cannot be given a complete historical equivalent in liberation movements, it is still not meaningless, because it enables us to see better opportunities in the future. Seen as a liberating feast, Christian worship becomes a "messianic intermezzo."[23]

Translated by Francis McDonagh

NOTES

1. The ideas discussed in this article are set out in more detail in J. Moltmann, *Die ersten Freigelassenen der Schöopfung* (Munich, [3]1972).
2. See Max Weber, *The Protestant Ethic and the Spirit of Capitalism.*

3. J. Huizinga, *Homo Ludens. Vom Ursprung der Kultur* (1956).

4. P. Graff, *Die Geschichte der Auflösung der alten gottesdienstlichen Formen in der ev. Kirche Deutschlands* I (1921), II (1939).

5. On this see Harvey Cox, *The Feast of Fools. A Theological Essay on Festivity and Fantasy* (Cambridge, 1969); D. L. Miller, *Gods and Games: Towards a Theology of Play* (New York, 1970); R. E. Neale, *In Praise of Play, Toward a Psychology of Religion* (New York, 1969); G. M. Martin, *Wir wollen hier auf Erden schon . . .* (Stuttgart, 1970).

6. This distinction between production and representation (reproduction) has been developed with particular subtlety by H. Plessner, *Zwischen Philosophie und Gesellschaft* (Bern, 1953).

7. The connection between liberating feast and liberation struggle is demonstrated by J. H. Cone, *The Spirituals and the Blues. An Interpretation* (New York, 1972).

8. For a functional investigation of ritual see Emile Durkheim, *Grundformen des religiösen lebens* (1970).

9. See, for example, E. Hornung, *Geschichte als Fest* (Darmstadt, 1966); K. Kerényi, "Vom Wesen des Festes", *Antike Religion* (Munich, 1971), pp. 43–67; M. Eliade, *The Myth of the Eternal Return* (London, 1955).

10. György Lukacs, *Aesthetik*, Teil 1, 2 (Neuwied, 1963), pp. 577 ff. discusses this "role of the aesthetic sphere as suspension." In the aesthetic act, man rests from the pressure of action.

11. See F. Flögel, *Geschichte des Groteskekomischen Ein Beitrag zur Geschichte der Menschheit* (Liegnitz and Leipzig, 1788).

12. For more details of this understanding of the resurrection of Christ, see J. Moltmann, *Der gekreuzigte Gott* (Munich, 1972).

13. Thomas Aquinas, *Summa Theol.* III, q. 60, ad 3: "Sacramentum est et signum rememorativum ejus quod praecessit, scilicet passionis Christi, et demonstrativum ejus quod nobis efficitur per Christi passionem, scilicet gratiae, et prognosticum, id est praenuntiantem futurae gloriae"; "A sacrament is a sign which recalls a past event, the passion of Christ, indicates the effect of Christ's passion in us, i.e., grace, and foretells, that is, heralds, the glory that is to come."

14. See the discussion of the "theology of hope", in R. Garaudy, *L'Alternative* (Paris, 1972).

15. Flögel, *op. cit.*, gives many examples of the *risus paschalis*.

16. Hugo Rahner, *Man at Play* (London and New York, 1965).

17. Fink, *Spiel als Weltsymbol* (Stuttgart, 1960).

18. Quoted in Rahner, *op. cit.*

19. Martin Luther, *Weimarer Ausgabe* 39, I, 48.

20. J. Moltmann, "Dostoiewski und die Theologie der Hoffnung", in *Entscheidung und Solidarität Festschrift für Joh. Harder* (Wuppertal, 1973), pp. 163–78.

21. An inspiration in this task is provided by Hans Urs von Balthasar's great work, *Herrlichkeit, eine theologische Asthetik* I (1961).

22. P. Ricoeur, "La liberté selon l'espérance", in *Le Conflit des interprétations* (Paris, 1969), pp. 393–415.

23. A. A. van Ruler, *Droom en Gestalte* (Amsterdam, 1947); *Gestaltwerdung Christi in der Welt* (Neukirchen, 1956).

12

Messianic Hope in Christianity

"Are You He Who Is to Come?"

The messianic question about the "one who is to come" shows the close kinship between Judaism and Christianity. The answers that each hears seem to show them irrevocably divided. "The one who is to come" is a cipher concealing the identity of the promised Messiah and the expected Son of man.[1] The Messiah is the king of the last times who restores Israel and through Sion brings justice and peace to the nations. Christian scholars often describe him too narrowly as "an exponent of Jewish national eschatology."[2] According to Daniel 7 the Son of man is a pre-existent heavenly being. After the fall of the bestial world kingdoms, he brings the universal kingdom "of man" from God.[3] Scholars often make the Messiah responsible for historical redemption and the Son of man for redemption from history. In Jewish apocalyptic, however, the two symbols of hope were so firmly fused that a two-tier doctrine of the Messiah arose in which the Messiah represented the immanent side of the realization of the kingdom of God and the Son of man its transcendent side.[4] Both symbols of hope, however, are schematic and lack identifiable detail, for they must be transparent of him whose future they are meant to mediate. The cipher of the "coming one" was also applied in prophecy to God himself, as in Isaiah 35.4–5: "God himself will come and save you. Then the eyes of the blind shall be opened, and the ears of the deaf unstopped; then shall the lame man leap like a hart, and the tongue of the dumb sing for joy."

The enquiry about the "coming one" was put by the Jews to Jesus of Nazareth. According to Matthew 11.4, his answer was indirect: "Go and tell John what you hear and see: the blind receive their sight and the lame walk, lepers are cleansed and the deaf hear, and the dead are

raised up and the poor have the good news preached to them." Luke
sums up the mission of Jesus as the fulfillment of the promise of Isaiah
61.1–2: "to preach good news to the poor . . . to proclaim release to the
captives and recovering of sight to the blind, to set at liberty those who
are oppressed, to proclaim the acceptable year of the Lord" (4.18–19).
The liberations that take place through the action and preaching of
Jesus speak for him. They are signs of the messianic age. To those who
experience and believe in them, he reveals himself as "the one who is
to come."[5] Jesus' answer to the Baptist's question is indirect because
awareness of the messianic time depends on faith. But Jesus connects
the awakening of this messianic faith with his human person and his
sufferings: "blessed is he who takes no offence at me." The question,
"Are you he who is to come, or shall we look for another?" is thus
returned to the liberating experience of sufferers with Jesus, and
their faith.

Jewish Objections

The objections of those who "look for another" begin here. "The Jew
has a keen sense of the world's lack of redemption, and within this
absence of redemption he recognises no enclaves of redemption. The
idea of a redeemed soul within an unredeemed world is essentially,
basically alien to him; the primordial ground of his existence makes it
inadmissible. This is the heart of Jesus' rejection by Israel, not in a
merely external, merely national understanding of messianism."[6] As a
comment on later Church doctrine, this may be correct, but did the
poor to whom he preached the good news, the sick he healed, or the
outcasts he accepted regard themselves as "redeemed souls" in an unredeemed world? "Judaism in every shape and form has always maintained a concept of redemption which it treated as a process taking
place in the public world, on the stage of history and in the context of
a community, in short, definitely taking place in the visible world . . .
In contrast, there is in Christianity a view which treats redemption as
a process in the spiritual and invisible realm, unfolding in the soul and
the world of each individual and bringing about a secret transformation
which need have no external correlate in the world . . . The reinterpreta-
tion of the prophetic promises of the Bible in terms of a realm of
inwardness . . . was always regarded by the religious thinkers of Judaism as an illegitimate anticipation of something which could at best
only appear as the interior of a process whose decisive elements took
place in the external world and never without this process."[7]

Was the original faith of the healed and the liberated really this sort of interiorization of salvation? It is true that in the history of Christianity the realistic messianic hope has often been replaced by spiritualizing and individualizing representations of salvation.[8] Not only Christianity, however, but Judaism had to struggle in order to assert the realism and universalism of their hope in the face of gnosis. There cannot therefore be "completely different concepts of redemption underlying the attitude to messianism in Judaism and in Christianity."[9] In my view, the difference depends on the eschatological experience of time that takes place or does not take place in Jesus. The Baptist's question is the question about the messianic "hour." It is a "temporal" question, but in addition, what decides the validity of the hope that grows out of it is the form of the messianic anticipation of redemption in the still unredeemed world. Is it the Mosaic Torah or the gospel of Jesus? Who has the Torah on their side, and who has the Gospel? In their dispute about the messiahship of Jesus, Christianity and Judaism have grown far apart, to the detriment of both: "For Jews the Messiah is in danger of disappearing into the kingdom of God, and for the Christian Church the kingdom of God is in danger of disappearing into the figure of the Messiah."[10] A hope for the kingdom of God without a messianic present in history must lead to the expectation of a world catastrophe, because "this world cannot support the righteousness of the kingdom." On the other hand, a messianic present without a hope for the kingdom of God that is to fulfill it inevitably becomes an illusion and ignores the "mystery of evil." Christian Christology must stop making Judaism suspicious of the hope for the Messiah, and the Jewish expectation of the kingdom must stop making Christians suspicious of an eschatology of the real future.

The Messiah as a Figure of Suffering

Jewish teaching about the Messiah is not limited to revanchist or utopian hopes in "the one who is to come" as the one who will either restore the "life with the Fathers" or establish the new Jerusalem. The apocalyptic traditions also make the point that his coming cannot be calculated or deserved. He comes unexpectedly, and in the case of many, when all hope has been extinguished in suffering. He also comes in concealment and may already be present unrecognized. Legend has him born on the day of the destruction of the Temple and in preparation for his Day wandering ever since unrecognized through all the nations of the earth. His primary shape is ultimately one of suffering. He lives among beggars and lepers. He suffers with the persecuted children of

Israel. Similarly, the day of messianic liberation will be inaugurated by apocalyptic tribulations and the terrors of downfall. Recognition of the Messiahship of Jesus, not only in his mission and the signs and wonders that accompany it, but even more in his sufferings, his vulnerability, and powerlessness, and finally in his death as an outcast, is not a distinctive mark of Christianity, but one it shares with Judaism. Though there are few Jewish references to a suffering and dying Messiah, and none to one rejected by the Law, the Job figure of the Jewish people and its history of suffering sufficiently meets the description.[11]

The suffering and death of Jesus are treated by the Gospels as the suffering and death of "the one who is to come" and, therefore, painted in apocalyptic colors. Because they regarded him as an eschatological person, the New Testament writers saw in his fate the anticipation of the last judgment. But if the judgment that is to fall on all has already been executed on this individual, he has suffered vicariously and for the benefit of all. Understanding Jesus' death in terms of the messianic categories in which it appeared and is understood in the light of Easter means regarding it as an act of suffering performed by the prevenient love of God for the "dead."[12]

Through the sufferings of the Messiah, sufferers obtain messianic hope. Through the Messiah's self-giving, those who have been "given up" (Rom. 1.26)—Jews and Greeks—obtain the freedom to choose eternal life. Through his undergoing judgment *for them*, sinners are justified *in him*. This is why the Christian faith has regarded the impotent suffering death in abandonment of Jesus not as a refutation of his messianic hope, but as its deepest realization in the conditions of a Godless and inhuman world that stands under the coming judgment. That is why it has discovered the hope of sufferers in the sufferings of this one who was "to come." It has found the liberation of the guilty in the death of this innocent victim.

Messianic Christology

Must the Christian faith cut off the Jewish Messiah figure from its connections with the greater kingdom of God when it applies messianic language to Jesus? If the faith does this, it will be totally unable to tolerate any open Jewish hope alongside itself.[13] But if it does not do this, how can it hope in Jesus with any assurance? Jesus has "unmistakeable and unforgettable traits, which is just what the Jewish image of the Messiah by its very nature cannot have. In it all personal characteristics can only be seen as completely abstract because it is not based on any lived experience."[14] Does Jesus really possess these features?

In, fact his "form" destroys the religious longing for hope to take a definite shape: "He had no form or comeliness . . . as one from whom men hide their faces he was despised, and we esteemed him not," say the gospels along with Isaiah 53.

His "personality" is defined by his fate: "crucified and raised up," as the oldest creeds say. This indeed makes him unmistakeable and unforgettable, but his "living experience" is also a "deadly" one. The "double result of his life" (M. Kahler) reveals the eschatological transcendence of God. He does not let himself be fixed in an image, but frees us from the images of idols of experience and hope to await the God who is to come. Because of this, Christology cannot be the end of messianic eschatology. This euphoria of fulfillment has constantly deified Jesus and tried to destroy Jewish discontent. Instead, Christology must lead much more to open eschatological hope. The cross and resurrection leave their mark on the present and future in God's anticipatory action. Anyone who engages in uncontrolled anticipation here loses the future along with the present. An eschatology based on Christianity must, therefore, start from an eschatologically open Christology.[15] Christianity can only treat Jesus as the confirmation and fulfillment of the messianic hope if it discovers within this person the messianic future of God himself. Only when it recognizes the difference and the connection between the rule of the Son of man and the rule of God himself can it recognize its own eschatological impermanence. The Pauline idea that the Son will hand over rule to the Father, so that God may be all in all (1 Cor. 15.28) points in this direction on the theological level. If it is taken seriously, it means the end of Christian absolutism. The Church will see itself as provisionally final and hope, with the Jews and for the poor, for the completion of the kingdom in the history of God.

The Sufferings of Those Who Hope and the Hope of Those Who Suffer

I have examined the question of the Messiahship of Jesus in so much detail because there can be no new convergence between Christianity and Judaism without a revision of the Christological foundations of Christianity. Jewish criticisms of historical formations in Christianity are often accurate. We are now beginning to see, however, that these historical forms, the spiritualization and individualization of salvation and the deification of Jesus before his cross in a spirit of triumphalist clericalism cannot survive. Jewish criticisms must lead Christianity to a deeper and better understanding of Jesus, his mission, his sufferings, and his future. But this means that the factual existence of the Jews is a constant question against the messianic hope in Christ. The pres-

ence of the Jews constantly forces Christians to see that they are not
yet at their goal, and that their Church too is not the goal; instead,
eschatological and also provisional, and in brotherly openness, they
are still on the way.

Franz Rosenzweig rightly said that the most profound reason for
Christian hatred of the Jews was the hatred of Christians for themselves, "hatred of their own imperfection, of their own falling short."[16]
But the more Christianity frees itself from clerical and political intoxication with fulfillment, the more it will be able to live with the messianic
hope and recognize the permanent incompleteness of the Jewish hope
for the Messiah. Intoxication with fulfillment without an acceptance of
the cross was the fate of Christian triumphalism in the past. This temer-
ity leads to resignation and the death of hope. The most important
requirement to keep alive the messianic hope in Christianity is for the
suffering Jesus and his fellowship with the outcasts to be brought into
the foreground. Gershom Scholem records a "truly powerful 'rabbinic
fable' of the second century": the Messiah will sit among the lepers and
beggars at the gates of Rome. "This symbolic contrast between the true
Messiah sitting at the gates of Rome and the head of Christianity in
power there accompanied the Jewish doctrine of the Messiah through
the centuries."[17] Will not those who "beseech you, on behalf of Christ,
be reconciled" (2 Cor. 5.20) one day be found among those whom the Son
of man calls the least of his brethren (Matt. 25) and declares blessed?

The messianic hope that Jews and Christians received together but
have experienced differently was given to them not for their benefit, but
for abandoned humanity. Consequently, the Messiah will not appear
in Jerusalem, nor in Rome, nor in Geneva. He will come among the
poor, the mourners, those who hunger for righteousness and are persecuted for it. He will appear among the "beggars and lepers" in Jerusalem,
Rome, Geneva, and other places. Only when the suffering of those who
have the messianic hope becomes the hope of those who suffer in this
world will Jews and Christians really understand their provisional final-
ity and honor god-forsaken mankind's Messiah.

Translated by Francis McDonagh

NOTES

1. S. Mowinkel, *He That Cometh. The Messianic Concept of the Old Testament
and Later Judaism* (1956); G. Scholem, 'Zum Verständnis der messianischen
Idee im Judentum', *Judaica* I (1963), pp. 7–74.

2. R. Bultmann, *Gluaben und Verstehen* II (1952), p. 242; P. Vielhauer, *Aufsätze zum Neuen Testament* (1965), pp. 55ff. and others.

3. P. Vielhauer, 'Jesus und der Menschensohn', *Aufsätze*, pp. 92ff.; J. M. Schmidt, *Die jüdische Apokalyptik* (1969).

4. Cf. the traditional formula used by Paul, Rom. 1.3, and Scholem, 'Messianische Idee', p. 21.

5. H. J. Iwand, *Die Gegenwart des Kommenden* (1957).

6. S. Ben-Chorin, *Die Gegenwart des Kommenden (1957)*.

7. Scholem, pp. 7–8; F. Rosenzweig, *Der Stern der Erlösung* (1954³), III, pp. 97ff., 178–9.

8. R. Bultmann, *History and Eschatology* (1962) shows this and is also an example of the process. Scholem, p. 74, rightly says, "We may perhaps say that the messianic idea is the authentic anti-existentialist idea."

9. Scholem, p. 7.

10. Ben-Chorin, *Die Antwort des Jona*, p. 5.

11. M. Susman, *Das Buch Hiob und das Schicksal des jüdischen Volkes* (1948²).

12. J. Moltmann, *Der gekreuzigte Gott* (1973²).

13. Cf. A. Schwarz-Bart, *Der Letzte der Gerechten* (1960).

14. Scholem, pp. 38–9.

15. Cf. Moltmann, *Theology of Hope* (London and Richmond, Va., 1969).

16. Rosenzweig, III, p. 197.

17. Scholem, p. 28.

13

The Confession of Jesus Christ

A Biblical Theological Consideration

I

Christian faith has from the very beginning been a confessing faith. The confession of Jesus Christ forms a constitutive part of this faith. Without this confession, it ceases to be Christian faith. The public confession of Jesus Christ is the divine definition of this faith. That is why a denial of Jesus Christ is the sign of an absence of faith. Confession or denial point to the being or non-being of faith.

Christ has also from the very beginning been confessed with constantly new words, images, and gestures. He has been confessed in many different ways and forms, some of them mutually contradictory, in the different periods of history, in the many and varied civilizations on earth and on the hostile fronts of social and political conflicts. Where is the common ground between all these different confessions? What safeguards the community of those confessing the same faith? At every period of history, these questions confront Christians: Who is Christ for us in truth? Who are we for him? What challenges us? How can we confess him?

It is possible to safeguard the community in the confession of faith by preserving the unchangeable nature of the formulae so that it can at once be known what is confessed by all Christians everywhere and at all times. The Apostles' Creed has, for example, been repeated again and again in Christian services for centuries and has acted as a safeguard for the continuity of the confession of faith in time and the community of believers in space. But do modern industrial workers mean the same as mediaeval kings when they say this creed? Apart from the sound of the words, what connection is there between the starving slum-dweller in a basic community in São Paulo and the rich Christian in a European city church? The shared ritual points to a community of faith, but it does not necessarily bring it about.

With all due respect for the Sunday confession of faith together with all Christians on earth, we are bound to question what this means today. It is precisely for this reason that Christians have everywhere and at all times developed new confessions of faith. The Apostles' Creed, for example, has often been "modernized," not necessarily to fit in with fashion, but rather to give a contemporary character to the confession of faith as a response to the challenges of the period. The contemporary character of the confession of faith is as important as its continuity, because otherwise the decision of faith is no longer obligatory.

It would seem that it is only possible to have one at the expense of the other. Continuity is found in unchanging formulae and a contemporary character is only found in changing formulae. Community in the confession of faith with all Christians everywhere and at all times can only be achieved at the price of abstraction. An actual community of all believers united in the decisive questions in a contemporary situation can only be achieved at the price of partiality.

This gives rise to a real dilemma that cannot simply be suppressed. The average universality of Church statements helps no one. They frequently aim to do justice to everyone and end by doing justice to no one. Christian faith must be confessed communally and in common with all Christians everywhere and at all times. It must also be confessed here and now in an unrepeatable way concretely and with individual decision. The uniquely contemporary confession *in statu confessionis* cannot be universal. This universal confession *in communione ecclesiae* cannot be contemporary.

It is certainly possible to combine the universal and the contemporary in a suitable way in those statements that are halfway between the common confession and the contemporary confession, but the dilemma can only be overcome if the subject changes in the confession of Jesus Christ, in other words, if it is not simply believers who are confessing universally and contemporarily Christ in community and as individuals, but if it is first and foremost Christ himself who is confessing his own to his heavenly Father.

This confession of Jesus Christ means in the first place his confession to us and only then, in the second place, our confession to him. He is our witness before we can become his witnesses. Without his confession before God, our confession in the presence of our fellow-men will continue to be empty and vague. Christ is our divine confessor: "Everyone who confesses me before men, I will confess before my Father who is in heaven, but whoever denies me before men, I will also deny before my Father who is in heaven" (Mt. 10:32, 33; Lk. 12:8; cf. Rev. 3:5).

Our confession of Christ must, therefore, be orientated toward the confessing Christ. The strength and the community of our confessing faith is to be found in his confession to us. In the different periods of history, in the many and varied civilizations on earth and on the hostile fronts of social and political conflicts, only he forms the common link. This is clear from the fact that, in the history of Christian faith and its confession, only the name of Jesus has stood firm. The titles expressing his dignity, effects, person, and significance—all these are variable. Titles such as Son of Joseph or Son of David have disappeared and new titles have emerged—Logos, Representative, Liberator, and so on. The name of Jesus is not translatable, whereas the titles of Jesus can be translated into any language. With regard to Jesus, confessions of faith are unchangeable. With regard to the titles of Christ, they are open and changeable. Nonetheless, the old titles and the new ones must be related to the person and his unique history—the person who is called by the name of Jesus—and they must be understood in the light of that person. The Christ, the Lord, the Liberator is Jesus. What hope, lordship, and liberation are in truth are therefore revealed through him, his life, and his death, not through our dreams. The subject determines the predicates that we give him on the basis of our experience of faith and our hope. With our predicates and titles, we anticipate the kingdom in which Jesus is the truth and the life for all men and in which "every tongue will confess that Jesus Christ is Lord, to the glory of God the Father" (Phil. 2:11). Through their structure, their fixed point in the name of Jesus, and their openness to new titles of Christ and predicates of the future, our confessions of faith reveal the eschatological tension between the cross and the kingdom in which we now exist and believe.

II

Witness, confession, and denial—these are terms used in litigation. Witness is not borne to feelings and cordial expressions are not confessed. If witness is borne to the great acts of God and God's lordship over the world is confessed in the stories of the Old Testament, this means that the history of Israel was seen to take place in the great court of justice of the world. The God of Israel was believed by the Old Testament authors to have been engaged in a lawsuit with the gods of other peoples for his property, the earth, which he created, and man, who was his image. The Second Isaiah developed this understanding of history as a lawsuit between God and the gods in his court speeches (Is. 43:9–13; 44:7–11). The peoples bear witness to their gods, but "You are my witnesses, says the Lord" (Is. 43:10, 12; 44:8). Yahweh asks: "Is there a God besides me?" (Is. 44:8). Israel should bear witness to their God by telling the peoples about his faithfulness and proclaiming what is to come and the fulfillment of their God's promises. Israel's call to bear witness to the peoples in their God's fight against the gods for lordship over the world was in principle unlimited: "I will give you as a light to the nations, that my salvation may reach to the end of the earth" (Is. 49:6; cf. 42:6). The confession of the one true God (true because of his faithfulness) by Israel bearing witness is present in God's fight in the history of the world against the gods. This fight for lordship over the world is conducted by God's people bearing witness in their lives to their God's faithfulness and his promise. They have experienced his faithfulness, and they believe in his promise and can therefore bear witness to them. Through this witness borne by the people of Israel, other people were set free from gods and demons and led to the truth of the one God.

It is against this Old Testament background that Jesus is called the "faithful witness" or the "true witness" (Rev. 1:5; 3:14). He was sent into the world "to bear witness to the truth" (Jn. 18:37) and was for this reason called the true witness in the New Testament. In this vocation, he proved to be reliable, because he fulfilled it in his suffering and death. It was for this reason, that he was called the faithful witness. Finally, Jesus was the divine witness to the truth that sets men free from godless laws and powers. By bearing witness to this liberating truth of God, Jesus, in fact, sets captives free.

In the Second Isaiah, there is a difference between God and the people, between the one to whom witness is borne and the witnesses. In the New Testament, however, the witness and that to which he bears witness are so closely united that Jesus bears witness to the Father by revealing himself as the Son (Jn. 8:12 ff). It is for this reason, that he is called the one witness in the Gospel of John. He comes from the truth to which he bears witness, so that his witness is the truth itself. His witness for God's truth is his witness to himself and his self-witness is the witness of the one who sent him. The Holy Spirit also bears witness to him, as do those who confess him in the Spirit (Jn. 15:26).

There was another difference present in Deutero-Isaiah. The difference between the witness borne before the court and the judgment of the court ceases to exist. Henceforth the witness borne for God's truth before the court of justice of the world becomes the court of justice of the world on the basis of the divine truth of the witness borne. The witness borne and the court of law, thus, coincide. The divine witness becomes the judge, and the judges become the accused and the acquitted. The messianic time that, according to Isaiah, begins with the lawsuit between God and the gods, becomes the last hour. According to John, the last judgment has already taken place in the witness borne by Jesus Christ—whoever believes is not condemned, but whoever does not believe is already condemned. This is a vast trinitarian view of the witness borne and the confession made by the Father, the Son, and the Holy Spirit. The world and all men are involved in this trinitarian process of bearing witness by God himself.

The synoptic gospels and Paul's letters provide us with other ideas of bearing witness and confession of faith. These ideas are, as it were, halfway between the difference between God and the people of his witnesses in Isaiah and the identity between the Father to whom witness is borne and the Son who bears witness in John. In the synoptics and Paul, the object of the witness borne by Jesus is the kingdom of God. As the Messiah, Jesus bears witness to the kingdom of God and, by preaching the gospel to the poor, eating with sinners, and healing the sick, also brings it about. He calls disciples, who share in his messianic mission and proclaim the gospel of the kingdom to the whole world "as a testimony to all nations" (Mt. 24:14). Jesus also completes his messianic witness by his good confession before Pilate and the witness that he bears by his death (Mk. 14:63; Mt. 26:65). His disciples are accused and tortured, similarly to bear witness to the people (Mt. 10:18). Like Jesus' own witness, that of the disciples also has the power to set believers free and the opposite effect on nonbelievers, who are to be condemned at the last judgment. This is a messianic view of the historical process of bearing witness to the future of God. The gospel is a mediating witness. In the gospel, God's kingdom and judgment are present in history. Man's salvation and disaster are therefore decided in the gospel. Christian faith, we may conclude from this brief survey, is a faith that confesses and bears witness. The confession of the gospel constitutes its eschatological structure.

III

Whichever line is followed in the New Testament—the identification in the fourth gospel of the divine witness with the God to whom witness is borne or the mediation of both by the gospel in the synoptic and Pauline traditions—the witness borne by the witnesses of Christ always gains ground by the witness of Christ himself.

Christ's witness is a public witness of liberating truth. The witness of this truth, therefore, also takes place in public, in order to set men free from public lies and public fear. The faith of Nicodemus, who believed secretly, privately and "by night" is not Christian faith. Calvin pointed this out clearly enough to the humanist sympathizers of the Reformation. An obstacle to the public and witness-bearing character and, therefore, to the very substance of Christian faith is raised by modern political science, with its emphasis on religion as a purely private affair. Christian faith, therefore, is bound to insist on its right to be a public religion. If it is denied that right, it suffers. Then it can only bear public witness to the truth that sets men free by suffering and resistance.

The witness borne by Christ is an undivided witness of healing truth. In the same way, the witness borne by Christians is also undivided. It can, moreover, leave out no aspect of life. The restriction of this Christian witness to a purely religious, a private or an interior sphere is a reduction that has a harmful effect on the witness of salvation. If the witness is divided, Christ is divided. This is a "pious" denial of the whole Christ. Christ is the "true witness" because he bore witness to the truth. He is the "faithful witness" because he bore witness to the truth to the point of death. In the same way, the witness borne by Christians is not only a witness in words, but also a witness of their entire lives and faithfulness to the point of death. There can be no living witness without life and death bearing witness. Confessing and imitating Christ are inseparable: this was the message of the Conference of the World Council of Churches at Nairobi, 1975 (Section 1). They are two sides of the coin of the same Christian life. It is only in imitating Christ that one can really know him personally. It is only in confessing him that one can imitate him and deny oneself.

Where, then, is Christ confessed today? The theological answer to this question is: Christ is confessed in the Holy Spirit and by him. This is an extremely practical answer, because the Holy Spirit is the power in history of the new creation. He is the spirit of liberation from slavery and the power of resurrection from sin and death.

Christ is, therefore, confessed where the power of the new creation is active. He is confessed where prisoners liberate themselves from oppression. He is confessed where men no longer give themselves over to death, but hope for the victory of life. This is not a purely polemical answer, because where the power of the new creation is active, the resistance offered by the power of the old world stiffens. Where the oppressed try to set themselves free, the power of the oppressors becomes harder. Where men rise again to life, the shadow of death grows in size. This clearly means that Christ is confessed today and witness is borne to him in the struggle of the power of the kingdom of God against the godless power of death. Isaiah had this in mind when he called on the people of God to bear witness in the legal battle between

God and the gods. Witnesses are only used in battle. In the struggle between truth and lie, freedom and oppression, life and death, these witnesses should stand up for truth, freedom, and life. The "gods," against whom Isaiah's witnesses testified and whose nothingness has to be revealed today if Christ is to be confessed as truth, freedom, and life, are not only the religious idols and demons, but the deified powers of race, sex, the state, and capital. It is the demon of power itself that terrorizes men and to which millions are sacrificed. Where the Spirit of the Lord is, however, witness is borne to freedom from fear and aggression.

How is Christ confessed today? It is clear from the history of Israel and the apostles that Christ has always been confessed in word and deed, in deed and suffering, in suffering and silence, and in silence and dying. The unity of word and deed is self-evident when the whole of life is called to witness. The unity of deed and suffering results from this. The suffering and silence of those who bear witness to Christ is a surprising experience throughout the entire history of the Christian martyrs. The blood of the martyrs is the seed of the Church.

It is, therefore, essential to trust in the Holy Spirit as the divine witness to the truth of Christ, because it is God who uses the word and the deed, the deed and the suffering, the suffering and the silence and the silence and the dying as a witness to convince others. Christians are not alone with their bearing of witness in a hostile world. They are situated, with all their possibilities and also their difficulties, within the history of God who is three in one and who bears witness to himself. The Holy Spirit is their witness in their speaking and silence, acting and suffering. That is why witness can be borne without fear and very frankly: "Do not be anxious how you are to speak or what you are to say, for what you are to say will be given to you in that hour" (Mt. 10:19); "the Holy Spirit will teach you in that very hour what you ought to say" (Lk. 12:12). The confession of Christians to Jesus Christ is borne up by his confession to them and it is fundamentally only a little human response. The confession of Jesus Christ to them is accepted by the witness borne by the Holy Spirit, who brings about the new creation.

Translated by David Smith

14

The Motherly Father

*Is Trinitarian Patripassianism Replacing
Theological Patriarchalism?*

Whose Father Is God?

The use of the name "Father" for God has two different backgrounds:
(1) the patriarchal world-view; and (2) the trinitarian understanding
of Christ. In the biblical traditions, God is called "Father" both in a
metaphorical sense, to express the goodness and the kindness of his
rule, and also in a literal sense, to indicate his relationship to his "only"
and "first-born" Son. The Apostles' Creed calls God "Father" twice: the
first time where he is described as "the Almighty, Maker of heaven and
earth," and the second time where it speaks of the exaltation of the
crucified Son, Jesus Christ, to "the right hand of God, the Father
Almighty." The twofold use of the name "Father" in the Bible, and the
double reference to the Father in the Apostles' Creed, have led to a
theological ambiguity in the concept of God the Father. Is God to be
called "Father" because he is the almighty creator and lord of all things?
Or is he to be called "Father" because he produced his "only Son," who,
as the "first-born," was brother of us all? In the first instance, the
creature or the servant is looking up from a state of dependence and
hoping to find encouraging features of the "Universal Father" in the
face of the dreaded Lord-God. The name "Father" is used here not in
a literal but in a metaphorical sense. In the second instance, we are
looking at the first-born in the midst of many brothers and sisters.
Because he is our brother, his Father becomes "our Father." In fellowship with him, we experience what it means to be children of God. The
name "Father" is used literally here, because the relationship with God
is understood as a generative one. In the first case, the name "Father"

is a way of expressing kindly rule; in the second, we are concerned with a fundamental relationship of love. When he is understood as "Lord-God," the Father cannot suffer, because all things have come from him and he is dependent on no one. On the other hand, when he is understood as "Father of the Son," the Father is passionately involved in what happens to the Son: if the Son suffers, the Father suffers with him. The Son is dependent on him, but he is also dependent on the Son, because they are one in their love. Thus, neither can exist without the other. Whose Father, then, is God? Is he the "Father of all that is" and as such, also the "Father of Jesus Christ" and "our Father?" Or is he the "Father of the Son," Jesus Christ, and as such, also "our Father" and the fatherly creator of all that is? Our understanding of the "lordship" of God depends on the answer to this question.

The Patriarchal Lord-God

In the patriarchal ordering of society, man (the male) is given all authority in the family: he is the lord and the owner of his wife (or wives) and his children.[1] He is free, while they are not free. As *paterfamilias* he has full rights over his family and its highest authority. Because he begets the children, they belong to him and not to his wife. He is the head of his wife and of the family; the "Fatherland" is governed politically by the ruler of the country, the prince, the *paterpatriae*. The "father of his country" represents the patriarchal type of family relationships on the political plane. Internally he must rule strictly, but benevolently; externally he must show stature and strength. Those who are ruled by him see themselves as his "subjects." He has full rights over them, while they have none over him. But he will not withhold his grace from his obedient "children."

On the religious plane the people are organized ecclesiastically through pastoral rulers and spiritual "fathers." The patriarchal type of family relationships is repeated also in the ecclesiastical structures—from the "children" of the parish to the priests, thence to the bishops, and finally to the "Holy Father." Authority and right come from above; obedience, dependence, and reliance operate below.

In the end, these family, political, and religious pyramids all point to the highest power in heaven, from whom they all receive their authority—to the Lord-God, the Father of All. As lord and owner of the world, God possesses fullness of power, and grants authority to every other power in heaven and on earth. It is for that reason that he must be feared and loved above all else. The patriarchal ordering of the world—God the Father, Holy Father, father of the country, father of the family—is a monotheistic ordering, not a trinitarian one. This father-religion produces in the individual that superego against which the atheistic impulse toward revolt and liberation rises up, has risen up, and always must rise up, because "where the great Lord of the world rules, freedom has no place—not even the freedom of the children of God."[2]

God is only rarely called "Father" in the Old Testament. Where he is, the name is used as a synonym for "Lord" and expresses the relationship of Israel to its God, whom it recognizes as Creator of the world, Lord of history, and God of the covenant, who has chosen Israel (Deut. 32:6; Isa. 63:16; Jer. 31:9). It is not actually intended that God should be sexually determined as male, although Israel was ordered on patriarchal lines: the Decalogue is a male-orientated code. But God-likeness is expressed in both sexes (Gen. 1:27), and where God's pity is spoken of, the metaphor of the mother is used (Isa. 66:13). God as Lord acts in both a "fatherly" and "motherly" way, especially toward Israel, his "first-born son" (Exod. 4:22).

In the New Testament, the patriarchal pattern is found especially in Paul's theology of the "head": "the head of every man is Christ, the head of a woman is her husband, and the head of Christ is God" (1 Cor. 11:3; see also 1 Cor. 3:22–23; Eph. 5:23; Heb. 12:5–10). This teaching presupposes a hierarchical sequence of head-body relationships. Although these are somewhat modified because of Christ's acceptance of the role of servant, they are nevertheless maintained and indeed are strengthened by it. This teaching, too, is monotheistic, not trinitarian. According to it, God-likeness is expressed in the male in a way in which it cannot be found in the female, "since man is the source of the woman, as God is the source and end of all creation."[3]

The Birth of the Son through the Father

The first example of the trinitarian understanding of the Father is to be found in the synoptic saying: "No one knows the Son except the Father, and no one knows the Father except the Son, and anyone to whom the Son chooses to reveal him" (Matt. 11:27). The Johannine theology constitutes a commentary on this passage, in that it stresses the exclusive unity of the Father and the Son: "He who has seen me has seen the Father" (14:9), because "I and the Father are one" (10:30). God the Father is the Father of his Son, Jesus Christ. His fatherhood is determined exclusively by his relationship with the Son. Therefore, his fatherhood becomes known only in the history of the Son, and is experienced only in fellowship with the Son through the Spirit, who is the Spirit of sonship. Thus, whoever wants to understand the trinitarian concept of God as Father must forget the ideas of the patriarchal Father-religion and focus his attention on the life and message of the first-born brother, Jesus Christ. The name "Father" is a theological and indeed trinitarian name, not some general religious, political, or cosmo-logical notion. If God is "our Father" through the Son and for his sake, then he can only be called "Abba, dear Father" (Rom. 8:15; 2 Cor. 3:17) under the inspiration of the Spirit of sonship, who is the Spirit of freedom. Freedom in the Spirit effectively distinguishes the Father of Jesus Christ from the World-patriarch of the Father-religion.

The ambiguity of the Father concept is removed when a clear distinc-tion is made between the *creation of the world* and the *begetting of the Son*. From the act of creation, a father-relationship strictly so called does not arise between God and his creatures. From creation and providence, God is known only as "Lord." It is only in his relationship with his Son that God can literally be called "Father." Therefore, belief in God the Father starts from recognition of the Son, not from God's omnipotence and creation. As Father of the Son, God creates heaven and earth. Through the doctrine of the Trinity, God's name "Father" is indissolubly linked to Jesus the Son. The doctrine of the Trinity does not deify Christ but "christifies" God, because it pulls the Father into the life-story of the Son.

If the Son comes forth from the Father alone, then this coming forth must be thought of as both "procreation" and "birth." However, that means that there must be a fundamental change in the father-concept. A father who both *begets* and *gives birth* to his son is no mere male father. He is a motherly father. He can no longer be defined as single-sexed and male, but becomes bisexual or transsexual. He is the *motherly Father* of his *only-born Son* and at the same time, the *fatherly Father* of his *only-begotten Son*. It was at this very point that the orthodox dogmatic tradition made its most daring affirmations. According to the Council of Toledo of 675, "we must believe that the Son was not made out of nothing, nor out of some substance or other, but from the womb of the Father (*de utero Patris*); that is, that he was begotten or born (*genitus vel natus*) from the Father's own being."[4] Whatever this declara-tion may be supposed to be saying about the gynaecology of the Father, these bisexual affirmations imply a radical denial of patriarchal mono-theism. *Monotheism* was and is the religion of the *patriarchism* just as, we may suppose, *pantheism* ("Mother Earth") was the religion of the earlier *matriarchism*.[5] The Christian doctrine of the Trinity, with its affirmations about the motherly Father, represents a first step toward limiting the use of masculine terminology to express the idea of God, without, however, changing over to matriarchal conceptions. It really points to a fellowship of women and men in which there is no subordination and no privilege. In fellowship with the First-born, there are "no more distinctions between . . . male and female, but all are one," and together heirs of the promise (Gal. 3:28, 29). Only a human fellowship free from sexism and class rule can become like the triune God.

The Unending Pain of the Father

In the older forms of the doctrine of the Trinity, the picture of the loving Father was combined with that of the unmovable Sovereign Lord, because the starting point for the doctrine of God was God's essential inability to suffer. By contrast, more recent studies on the doctrine of the Trinity[6] start from the passion of Christ and reject, along with the picture of the unmovable Sovereign Lord, the axiom of God's impassibility: the deepest ground for the passion of Christ is the *pathos* of God, who for all eternity is love. Thus, the Father cannot remain unaffected by the suffering and death of his Son. This must lead to the reacceptance of the teachings of theopaschitism and patripassianism, which were earlier rejected. Can theological patriarchalism be replaced by a recognition of the "suffering God"? To speak of the "suffering of God" presupposes distinctions within the godhead. Fundamentally, we can only speak of the suffering of God in trinitarian terms. Monotheism does not leave this option open.

When Abraham Heschel was working out his "Theology of the divine Pathos,"[7] in order to show God's passion for Israel and his suffering with Israel, he had to propose a two-poled conception of God: God is free and not subject to anything that may happen, but he is nevertheless, through his *pathos*, committed to Israel in the covenant. He is enthroned in heaven, but he lives with the lowly and the meek. Through his "indwellings" (*shekinah*), the Almighty shares all the sufferings of his people. "God himself divides himself in two. He gives himself away to his people. He suffers with them in their suffering. . . ."[8] The Jewish concept of *theopathy* presupposes this distinction within the godhead. God's omnipotence must then be seen in the context of his power to suffer.

These thoughts are also developed in the Anglican theology[9] of the "passibility of God." The omnipotence that God possesses and that he reveals in his Son is the omnipotence of suffering love. On Golgotha, the eternal being of God is made known. God is love. Love is susceptible to suffering. Love's susceptibility to suffering finds its fulfillment in self-sacrifice. Self-offering is, therefore, the eternal being of God. "In the end it is always the Cross. God—not indeed the Almighty, but God the

Father, with a father's grief and a father's helplessness, in which the power of love is contained. God—wonderful, suffering, crucified."[10]

The Spanish religious philosopher Miguel de Unamuno expresses the conception of the "grief of God" in a striking way.[11] In Christ's agony, the pain of the whole world is laid bare, and at the same time, the "grief of God" is also revealed. The "Christ of Velazquez" not only portrays the agony of Christ, but also throws upon it a reflection of the endless suffering of his Father. God reveals himself as one who suffers. In suffering, he displays his compassion. "He covers all suffering with his own immeasurable suffering." As sufferer, he also calls for our compassion.

Finally, we find in Nikolai a developed trinitarian theology of the "Tragedy in God."[12] He understands the story of human freedom as the Passion Story of God, who must suffer because he wants men to be free. It is a single movement, which originates at the very center of the Trinity and comes to completion on Golgotha: the Passion of God, the tragedy of our freedom.

If we take up this thought and work it out in a trinitarian sense, we can say: in sending his Son into this sinful world, the Father opens himself to the world's fate. With the surrender of the Son to death on the cross, the endless suffering of God begins. On the cross, the Son suffers death, abandoned by the Father. But the Father suffers the death of the Son, and with it his own abandonment of the Son. The suffering of the Father is not identical with the suffering of the Son, but corresponds to it.[13] Our release from pain and our deliverance from suffering spring from the suffering of the whole Trinity: from the death of the Son, the grief of the Father, and the patient endurance of the Spirit. God sets us free to live through his suffering love. It is such love that is divine—not power, predominance, or omnipotence, as in patriarchalism.

The feminine element in the suffering of God has often been seen in the figure of the *Pietà*:[14] the Mother of Sorrows with her dead Son on her lap. But is not the sorrow of Mary the human reflection of, and the beginning of, Christian participation in the grief of the divine Father over the death of his Son?

Lordship and Freedom

As the doctrine of the Trinity replaces monotheism, and as the theology of the Cross replaces the notion of the impassible God, we are led to a new understanding of life with God and in God. "Lordship" cannot be the only image for it. In fellowship with the suffering triune God, we have a deeper experience of freedom. Where God is believed in as "Sovereign Lord," freedom means being *servants of God:* whoever is a servant of the Most High may indeed be totally dependent on God, but he is free in relation to all others. When God is believed in as "Father," then freedom means being *children of God:* those who see themselves as sons or daughters of God are free and equal members of the family. They do not simply pay attention to a Sovereign Lord; their Father pays attention also to them. This means that Christianity is not in fact a father-religion, but a "son's-religion." Finally, there is found a freedom in the Spirit that even goes beyond the son-relationship: it is *friendship with God.* The friend of God does not live any longer "under" God, but with God and in God. He shares in the grief and the joy of God. He has become "one" with God (John 17:21). The revelation of the "suffering God" allows men to understand their sufferings in God and allows them to share in God's sufferings in the world. "Life in God" begins with the recognition of the Crucified One, and involves following him by taking up one's cross. In this recognition and in this way of life, the patriarchal conceptions of the "Universal Father" and all ideas of the "Sovereign Lord-God" become obsolete.

Translated by G. W. S. Knowles

NOTES

1. M. Daly, *Beyond God the Father: Toward a Philosophy of Women's Liberation* (Boston 1973); E. Bornemann *Das Patriarchat. Ursprung und Zukunft unseres Gesellschaftssystems* (Frankfurt 1975).

2. E. Bloch, *Das Prinzip Hoffnung* (Frankfurt 1959) p. 1413.

3. Thomas Aquinas *S. Th.* 1a Q 93, art 4 ad 1: "Sed quantum ad aliquid secundarium imago Dei invenitur in viro secundum quod non invenitur in muliere; nam vir est principium mulieris, sicut Deus est principium et finis totius creatopologieurae."

4. H. Denzinger, *Enchiridion Symbolorum* § 276: "Nec enim de nihilo, neque de aliqua alia substantia, sed de Patris utero, id est, de substantia eius iden Filius genitus vel natus esse credendus est."

5. E. Neumann, *Die grosse Mutter. Eine Phänomenologie der weiblichen Gestaltungen des Unbewussten* (Olten 1974).

6. K. Kitamori, *Theologie des Schmerzes Gottes* (Göttingen 1972); H. Urs von Balthasar, "Mysterium Paschale" in *Mysterium Salutis* III/2 (Einsiedeln 1969); H. Mühlen, *Die Veränderlich-keit Gottes als Horizont einer zukünftigen Christologie* (Münster 1969); J. Moltmann, *The Crucified God* (London 1974); E. Jüngel, *Gott als Geheimnis der Welt* (Tübingen 1977); D. J. Hall, *Lighten our Darkness; Toward an Indigenous Theology of the Cross* (Philadelphia 1976).

7. A. Heschel. *The Prophets* (New York 1962).

8. Fr Rosenzweig, *Der Stern der Erlösung III* (Heidelberg 1954) pp. 192 f.

9. J. K. Mozley, *The Impassibility of God: A Survey of Christian Thought* (Cambridge 1926). Especially worthy of attention is C. E. Rolt, *The World's Redemption* (London 1913). See further K. Woollcombe "The Pain of God," *Scottish Journal of Theology*, 1967, pp. 129–148.

10. C. A. Studdert-Kennedy, *The Hardest Part* (London 1918) p. 14.

11. M. de Unamuno, *Del sentimiento trágico de la vida en los hombres y en los pueblos* (Madrid 1912). On Unamuno see R. Gracia Mateo, *Dialektik als Polemik. Welt, Bewusstesein, Gott bei Miguel de Unamuno* (Frankfurt 1978).

12. N. Berdyaer, *Der Sinn der Geschichte. Versuch einer Philosophie des Menschengeschicks* (Darmastadt 1925). See also P. Evdokomov, *Christus im russischen Denken* (Trier 1977).

13. J. Moltmann, *The Crucified God* (London 1974) p. 242 ff.

14. A. Greeley, *The Mary Myth* (New York 1977) ch. 8.

15

Can There Be an Ecumenical Mariology?

An ecumenical dialogue about Mariology, if it is carried on in all sincerity, with a readiness to understand the deeper roots both of Marian devotion and of the resistance to it, is bound to be difficult. That is why Mariology has been largely excluded from the official ecumenical dialogue. Where Mariological conversations did occur, they often resulted in a mere consensus of specialists, which was of no great importance to the churches represented. If we want to see what an ecumenically compelling Mariology would look like, we must dig deeper and be prepared to face the anti-ecumenical factors at work in Mariology as cultivated by the Church.

Confronted with the grievous history of Church divisions and of the persecution of Christians by Christians, a history graven on the memories of those who suffered from it, it sounds a little naïve when the Bishop of Osnabrück suggests making Mary the "Patroness of Ecumenism" (quite apart from the incongruity of *patron*age in the case of a woman). Looking back into history, we are bound to notice that Marian devotion and its corresponding Mariology have had a divisive rather than a unitive effect: did not the Church's veneration of the "Mother of God" seal the final separation of Christianity from Judaism, for what had the "goddess and her hero" to do with the Jewish mother Miriam (Schalom Ben-Chorin)? The discrepancy between Church teaching and the New Testament is nowhere as great as in Mariology. We need only compare Jesus' apparently historical valediction to his mother (Mark 3:31–35 par) with Church statues of the Madonna and Child. Did not the Church wage war against the Albigensians, Cathari, and Waldensians (reform movements based on a return to the Bible) under the sign of the Virgin? During the political Counter-Reformation, how many evangelical churches were forcibly changed from "Christchurches" to "Mary" churches, the Crucified Savior on the cross behind the altar replaced by the statue of Mary and the Child? What about the counter-revolutionary conservatism of the Roman Catholic Church in its fight against the Enlightenment and autonomy, democracy and modern science, religious freedom and the critique of religion—was not this too under the sign of belief in Mary? The new Roman Catholic Marian dogmas of 1854 and 1950, too, are part of the context of this "anti-Modernism." Many have seen in the Marian appearances of *Fatima* a religious, apocalyptic response to the Bolshevist revolution in Russia. Occasionally, we may see the modern feminist movements revamping the old Mariology, but we are not misled into thinking that the patriarchal and celibate mother-images can now be utilized in the liberation of woman from her humiliation by the masculine world. Mariology, we must say in all honesty and objectivity, has so far been anti- rather than pro-ecumenical. The more the Marian superstructure has been developed, the more it has estranged Christians from Jews, the Church from the New Testament, Evangelical from Catholic Christians, and Christians in general from modern man. But is the Madonna of Church Mariology identical with Miriam, the Jewish mother of Jesus? Can we find Miriam in the Madonna? Or, because of all the splits and divisions that have been perpetrated by the churches in her name, perhaps we *ought* to go back and find out about her. No doubt the ecumenical movement can leave Mariology aside and get on with other and perhaps more important topics. But to do that is to fail to deal with the past. The danger, then, is that the past will eventually repeat itself.

Of course, this is not the time to be developing an "ecumenical Mariology." All the same, we can try to envisage the conditions under which such a thing may come about. By *ecumenical* I mean: (1) the Christian community of the separated churches; (2) the biblical *oikoumene* of Christians and Jews; (3) the secular community formed by Christians together with the whole "inhabited earth"; i.e., first of all with all the poor, for whom the earth is still not habitable. Here, let me make a personal comment: I am conscious of thinking as an Evangelical theologian, as a man, and as a European. That is my starting point; not, I hope, my prejudice.

Negative Conditions for an Ecumenical Mariology

By *negative conditions* we mean those interests and functions in Mariology that hinder ecumenism by not allowing Mary to appear as a figure in the liberating history of the gospel of Christ. I will mention just a few that strike me particularly as an Evangelical theologian. No doubt there are others.

(a) The close connection between *Mariology and celibacy* strikes every-one who finds both equally foreign. Does the celibate consecrate himself to a virginity which he reveres in the divine Virgin? Does she become a wife-substitute, as Ludwig Feuerbach suspected? Does the celibate's own physical mother remain for him the exemplary woman, with the result that, far from him outgrowing his mother attachments, they are religiously reinforced? Is it right for the Church to allow and encourage such inhibitions? Does it not stimulate masculine fantasies in which the woman is the saint or the great sinner, but never a real human person? Since Jesus' call to discipleship, there has always been a free-will celibacy. However, it is part of the community of the new messianic life centered on Jesus: "Whoever does the will of God is my brother, and sister, and mother" (Mark 3:35). It is a limited renunciation for the sake of an unlimited gain. It is not a renunciation requiring religious compensation. Evidently, the messianic community of those who follow Jesus is strong enough to break the power of family origins. Thus, Jesus turns his mother, brother, and sisters away, bids them farewell. This messianic community, however, is open to all believers, including Jesus' mother and family, not because of their blood relationship but because of their faith. That is why Mary and the brothers of Jesus appear in the Easter community (Acts 1:14): as believers. Mary's relationship is more that of a sister. This being so, we are in a better position to see *Jesus' friendship* with the women who accompany him, in the first place with Mary Magdalen (E. Moltmann-Wendel). This open friendship seems to have played a much bigger role in the messianic community than the mother–son relationship that became the focus in later Mariology and stamped its influence on the Church. Does not celibacy make the Church symbolically the mother and the believers the Church's children? What happens to the horizontal relationships essential in every family, brotherly, sisterly, and friendly relationships? Any future ecumenical Mariology should be developed, not in connection with a celibate priestly hierarchy, but with regard to the kind of community intended by Jesus; i.e., a community of faith bound together by open friendship.

(b) Hitherto a *political Mariology* has hindered the development of an ecumenical Mariology. We have already indicated the fateful signifi-cance of traditional Mariology in the Counter-Reformation, anti-Mod-ernist, and counter-revolutionary movements. No doubt what we have here is an emotionally deep-seated and, in part, justified aversion to an increasingly masculine Christianity and political world. But at the same time, we must recognize the Church's fear of the Christian's com-ing of age, of man's moral autonomy, and of the sovereignty of the people—fears that have found their expression in the modern flowering of Marian devotion and the modern Marian dogmas. Probably, however, the real politicizing of Mariology is to be found in *Marian apocalyptic*: Rev. 12 speaks of a "woman clothed with the sun, with the moon under her feet, and on her head a crown of twelve stars." In great pain, she bears a child. But the "red dragon" tries to get hold of the child to devour it, and persecutes both woman and child. There follows the final battle between the dragon and those who have the testimony of Christ. Although this woman is not called Mary, but probably signifies the Israel of God and the Church, this "final drama" has had a deep influence on the Christian Marian imagination: Mary seated on the crescent moon, Mary clothed with the sun, Mary with the twelve-starred crown—this is the apocalyptic Mary. The proto-gospel of Gen. 3:15 was also applied to her, so that pictures and statues show her, and not her Son, treading on the serpent's head. In this way, Mary became the Madonna-guardian of all believers persecuted by the red dragon, the Conqueror (Victrix) in the apocalyptic final battle of the world. Modern Mariology is also to be seen in the context of this apocalyptic interpretation of our time as the "end-time." I hold this apocalyptic Mariology to be just as baneful as the *apocalyptic friend/foe attitude* and the expectation of Armageddon. In any case, dragons can change their colors: they are not always "red," there are others.

(c) Finally, Marian devotion has always been a melting-pot of the most diverse *religious needs and desires.* Because the Gospel of Christ did not grow out of a popular religion but called into being a messianic community from all peoples, the Church in the various countries took up the local folk religion and adapted itself to it. However, through ecclesial symbol and ritual, the Gospel of Christ was to remain the critical standard for religious needs and their satisfaction. This process of adaptation and critical corrective is particularly clear in the history of Mariology. For the most part, the manifold forms of Marian devotion far exceed what is officially acceptable to the Church. Thus, the problem, as such, is whether and how far theology can adopt these religious wishes and wish fulfillments without losing its Christian identity. Mariology must not become the marketplace of depth-psychological speculations. More pointedly: how Christian is Marian popular piety and how Christian is the Church's Mariology? Evangelical theologians have always been at a loss when, in order to justify the new Mariological dogmas, tradition, and, more recently, the *sensus fidelium* were adduced along with and going beyond Scripture. They were afraid that this development spelled the end of truly Christian criteria. On the other hand, one has to recognize that the Protestant attachment to the principle of Scripture was not based solely on faith in "Christ alone." It was also conditioned by the repression of the religious dimension in modern industrial society. This raises the question of the religious relevance of Christian faith. A future ecumenical Mariology will arise in the field of tension between Christology and folk religion. In doing so, as Virgil Elizondo has shown, it will become a "Mariology from below" in which the oppressed people will achieve freedom and dignity in the gospel, the gospel of Christ.

Positive Conditions for an Ecumenical Mariology

Only with great reluctance am I prepared to say what seem to me to be the positive preconditions for an ecumenical Mariology, because ecumenical unity concerning them has yet to be reached, and it is by no means certain.

The Source and Standard for the Church's Mariology Is to Be Found in the Biblical Witness to Miriam, the Mother of Jesus, a Member of the Original Christian Post-Easter Community

Ecclesial Marian devotion and ecclesial Mariology must present the figure of the real Mary without any distortions. In order to see the real Mary, the whole biblical witness must be taken into account. It will not do to construct a history of biblical tradition in order, on the basis of it, to arrive at speculative Mariological extrapolations. This would be merely a retrospective justification of the Church's alienation from its real origin. Thus, it is no good taking Luke's figure of Mary in the Infancy Narratives on the one hand, and then scarcely paying any attention to the disturbing accounts in the Synoptics concerning Mary's encounter with Jesus and her absence from the group of women beneath the cross. Nor is it good to ignore the relationship of Jesus to his mother, as many Evangelical Christologies do. An exemplary study that points the way forward for ecumenical Mariology is the 'Gemeinschaftsstudie von protestantischen und römisch-katholischen Gelehrten': *Maria im Neuen Testament. Eine ökumenische Untersuchung*, eds. R. E. Brown, K. P. Donfried, J. A. Fitzmyer, J. Reumann (Stuttgart 1981).

Mariology Must Serve Christology; It Must Neither Detract from It nor Become Emancipated from It

Like John the Baptist, who is often depicted with her at the foot of the cross, Mary points away from herself and toward her Son; her whole meaning is to be found in this self-forgetting and Christological gesture. A christocentric Mariology would also do justice to the significance of

Christ for Mary, revealing her as the real Miriam. However, this would mean that the other images of Mary, the image of Wisdom (Prov. 8), the image of the Woman of the Apocalypse (Rev. 12), the image of the great Goddess, the Queen of Heaven, or the Eternal Feminine must give way, allowing Mary to be seen once again in the context of the other women around Jesus—among whom Mary Magdalen is particularly prominent. In a christocentric Mariology, Mary is an essential figure in the liberating Gospel of Christ, and not the image of regressive dreams or apocalyptic fears. That is the real meaning of the truism, "No Mary without Christ, no Mariology without Christology."

A Biblically-Based and Christocentric Mariology Will Express the Presence and Activity of the Holy Spirit in the Destiny of Christ and of Christians

According to the gospels, the activity of the Holy Spirit prior to Easter was directed solely to Jesus (John 7:39). It is the Risen One who sends the Spirit to the community. With one exception: according to Luke 1:35, Mary conceives by the Holy Spirit and is filled with the Holy Spirit. She is the first person to play a part in the history of the Holy Spirit, as determined by Christ. Thus, wherever the Holy Spirit is spoken of, Mary, too, will be mentioned, and where Mary is referred to theologically, the Holy Spirit is involved. However, there must be no confusion: it is not Mary, but the Holy Spirit who is the source of life, the Mother of believers, the Wisdom of God, and the indwelling of the divine mystery in creation that will renew the face of the earth. Mary bears witness to the presence of the Holy Spirit. Far from making the divine Trinity into a Quaternity, she is a sign of the Trinity's openness for the unification and the eternal life of the whole creation.

Translated by Graham Harrison

16

The Inviting Unity of the Triune God

I

Is Christianity "a monotheistic form of belief" (Schleiermacher)[1] and indeed, as a monotheistic revealed religion, "the absolute religion" (Hegel)?[2] It is advisable to begin by taking a critical look at this way in which it has become usual recently in Europe to characterize Christianity, and relate it to the history of religion in general. Monotheism has, of course, got a very long history, and it means the worship of the one unique God. However, the modern European concept presumably was first introduced by Henry More and David Hume.[3] It did not denote the specifically Jewish belief. It expressed belief in progress and claimed superiority: Lessing's "Education of the Human Race" goes from polytheism by way of pantheism to "monotheism." Hegel's step-by-step development of consciousness leads from natural religion by way of cultural religion to revealed religion. Pagan "polytheism" is, thus, downgraded to be classed as "primitive religion" and "pantheism" as a religion of the emotions is given a lower rank than rational monotheism. The classification of religions indicated by the concept "monotheism" is in its innocent form the naive absolutism of one's own religious perspective, but in its developed form nothing other than religious imperialism aimed at subjecting "underdeveloped" peoples by liquidating their religions.

Before Christianity is formally classified as a "monotheistic" religion, the contemporary criticism of monotheism must be taken seriously.

Monotheism is not only the worship of a single unique God but also always the recognition of this God's single and unique universal monarchy. There is no monotheism without theocracy. The religions described as "monotheistic"—Judaism, Christianity, and Islam—are theocratic ways of perceiving life and the world. From the other side, imperialistic world conquerors have always tried to find a monotheistic and theocratic basis to legitimize their claims to domination. Hence, the Mongol ruler Genghis Khan declared: "In heaven there is no-one but the one God alone; on earth no-one but the one ruler Genghis Khan, the son of God."[4]

In the face of the one ruler of the universe in heaven, there is for men and women only the attitude of subjection, not that of their own freedom. Therefore, it can be understood that recently in Europe Christian monotheism has called forth atheism as its one alternative: "Either there is a God, and then man is not free; or man is free, and then there is no God."[5] If religious monotheism is combined with absolutism at the level of both Church and State, then only atheism can rescue and safeguard freedom.

Everywhere monotheism is recognizably the religion of patriarchal society: the rule of the Father of all heaven is mirrored by the rule of the father in the family. From this follows the disenfranchisement and enslavement of women. "Monotheism" is only the religious summit of a religious order of domination that forces foreign peoples, women, and nature into subjection and dependence.

What, from a "monotheistic" point of view, is termed "polytheism" and "natural religion" is, in reality, better understood as *spiritism*. It is a highly complex religious system that balances natural and supernatural powers. In shamanism, in the cosmic mysticism of China, and in Hinduism are to be found the treasures of ancient ecological wisdom. In contrast to this, monotheism's domination and exploitation of nature must be labeled primitive. Even in those polytheistic religions that derive their life from a pantheistic foundation, the maternal mystery of nature is preserved. From this point of view, monotheism with its masculine bias can hardly be regarded as a higher religious or even moral development for mankind.

If the Christian belief in God is not to share the distress of monotheism and be destroyed, then the unity of the triune God should no longer simply be termed "monotheistic" but should be more precisely defined with reference to the freedom of men and women, the peace of nations, and the presence of the spirit in all natural things.

II

Ancient Israel is usually made responsible for the emergence and formation of strict monotheism. However, with reference to the modern concept of "monotheism," this is not correct. What people have said since the Enlightenment is that Israel was the first to overcome polytheism and introduce the ethical worship of one God. Israel was the first nation to understand its national divine father as the "united God" and, thus, lay the foundation for religious universalism. The *shema Yisrael* still sounds today like the original form of monotheism: "Hear, O Israel: The Lord our God is one Lord; and you shall love the Lord your God with all your heart, and with all your soul, and with all your might" (Deut. 6:4–5). It could be said that polytheism scatters people's attention among many different gods and powers, whereas this Jewish monotheism concentrates it on the one God, and thus, focuses man on a person. The powers of nature then lose their divinity and are seen as merely earthly natural powers. Acknowledgment of the transcendent God makes the immanent world the profane world of mankind.

But if we look more closely at this confession of Israel, we discover that God is acknowledged not as "One God" but as "One Lord." As the first commandment shows, his dominion is concerned with the liberation of the people from servitude in Egypt to life in freedom in alliance with this God. What is acknowledged is not the one God's transcendence of this world, but the act of liberation immanent in the world on the part of the unique Lord. The exodus from slavery is the one reason for having "no other gods beside him," as the second commandment states. Because the experience of the exodus was constitutive for Israel and is re-enacted at every Passover, the acknowledgment of the Lord is exclusive. It does not suffer any other Lord. However, this does not mean that this God must in himself be a numerical or monadic unity. On the contrary: the God of the Exodus and of the Covenant is at one and the same time transcendent and immanent with regard to the world. He has nothing to do with the metaphysical one that stands in opposition to the physical many. Nor has he anything to do with that moral transcendence that is contrasted with man's immanent fulfillment of his duty as a source of responsibility. Rather, he dwells among the people he has chosen. Hence, recent Jewish thinkers have corrected the Enlightenment thesis of "Mosaic monotheism" and presented a more differentiated picture of the unity of the God of Israel.

This is how Franz Rosenzweig interprets the *shema Yisrael:* "The *shekinah*, God's settlement and dwelling among men, is thought of as a division that takes place within God himself. God himself divides himself from himself, he gives himself away to his people, he shares in suffering its sufferings, he goes with it into the misery of exile, he shares in its wanderings . . ." In this surrender by God of himself to Israel, there is "a divine suffering." God, who "shares in suffering" Israel's fate, makes himself "in need of redemption." If Israel's sufferings are overcome, then God's suffering with Israel ceases. If Israel attains its freedom, then the God dwelling in Israel attains his blessedness, in other words himself. The division in God is overcome and transcended. Then God will be *one* God. This reunion of God's *shekinah* dwelling in Israel with God himself is anticipated in every acknowledgment of God as the "one Lord." "Acknowledging God's unity"—the Jew calls this uniting God. This unity exists to the extent that it comes into being, it is unity in formation, and this becoming is entrusted to man's soul and hands.[6]

The God of the Exodus, the God who dwells among the people of his Covenant, is a God who differentiates himself and identifies himself with himself. In this process of differentiation, his "unity" is not an exclusive but an inclusive unity, in other words a unity uniting Israel with itself. Prayer and acknowledgment of the one Lord must, therefore, be conceived and used as active factors of this divine unity that unites with God.

Abraham Heschel, too, has clearly distinguished Israel's history of God from metaphysical and political monotheism.[7] His starting point is not the sovereign impassibility of the ruler of the world but the passionate feeling of the God of Israel. In his creative emotion with its readiness to suffer, God goes out of himself and enters into his creation. He becomes the companion in suffering of his people. He dwells in heaven and at the same time with the poor and those without rights. Heschel, thus, presents the God of Israel as a "bipolar God" and uses for this the idea of the spirit of God (*ruah*) who renews the face of the earth (Psalm 104:30) and creates for man a pure heart and a new spirit (Psalm 51:10). It is in his creative emotion that God's inner differentiations arise: as creator, he continues to transcend the world, but in his spirit, he is involved in his creation and "is in all things" (Wisdom 12:1). Even more important is the way God distinguishes and reveals himself in his name "Lord": compare Exodus 6:3 and Isaiah 51:15 with 1 Corinthians 8:6. "Yet for us there is one God, the Father, . . . and one Lord, Jesus Christ." One cannot, therefore, define God's unity exclusively by means of elimination and delimination in such a way that what is ultimately indivisible counts as the one that defines everything, but it must be understood as a unity that differentiates itself, goes out from itself, invites the other to join it, and unites it with itself.

III

On the basis of the history of God to which the New Testament bears witness, Christianity is indeed the *Trinitarian* confession of the Father, the Son, and the Holy Spirit. However, in its own history, especially in the West, it has given a one-sided emphasis to the unity of the triune

God. In its arguments against the polytheism of the various nations, Christianity presented itself as the superior universal religion of the one God.[8] When Christianity became involved with the Roman empire and seized the opportunity to become the imperial religion, it placed the universal monarchy of the one God in the foreground, and from this, the Christian emperor could derive the legitimation of his sovereignty and the multinational Christian imperium its inner unity. While the Nicene creed of 325 still described the unity of the Son with the Father as a unity of substance, *homoousios,* and thus, stressed the hypostatic difference between the Father and the Son, the Athanasian creed, of Western origin, already put in the foreground the thesis "God is one." God's unity, thus, does not merely consist in the united divine substance of the Father, the Son, and the Spirit, but in the one identical divine subjectivity in which he acts externally. Augustine's famous distinction between God's works needing to be inwardly divided but externally undivided (*ad intra divisa, ad extra indivisa*) has given rise to the idea that the triune God may within himself be differentiated in a trinitarian way, but that he appears to the outside world monotheistically as one in action and manifestation. The doctrine of the trinity is, in this case, nothing other than "Christian monotheism."[9] However, if we call the Christian acknowledgment of God "trinitarian monotheism," then we cling firmly to the pyramidal structure of monotheism, and only introduce a trinitarian differentiation at the very top.

The unity of the triune God is, then, seen in the monarchy of God. This was admittedly stressed by the Greek Fathers, too, but they did not equate the nature of the triune God with his lordship over the world, because the latter consisted in the economy of salvation, while it was the doxology that first acknowledged and praised the eternal nature of the triune God. However, in the West, the essential unity of the triune God was seen in his lordship and equated with it. God is one, that is, he is one lord, one person, one subject, one divine I—this was still Karl Barth's interpretation.[10] If this is the right starting point, then the three divine persons of the Father, the Son, and the Spirit can only be seen as modes of being "in" which the one God exists. The unity of the triune God then resides in the sovereignty of his lordship. Therefore, the root of the doctrine of the trinity is to be found in the proposition, "God reveals himself as the Lord."[11]

However, this monotheistic proposition does not appear in the New Testament in this form. According to the New Testament's professions of faith, Jesus is the Lord, and God is the Father of our Lord Jesus Christ (Rom. 15:6; 1 Cor. 1:3; 2 Cor. 11:31; Eph. 3:14; etc.). All the New Testament's professions of faith start from the trinitarian difference between God the Father of Jesus and Jesus the Lord. The Father, who out of unconditional love, sends his own son Jesus and sacrifices him for the redemption of the world has raised him up from the dead and established him as Lord of his kingdom. The Son will exercise his liberating and redeeming lordship (Rom. 14:8–9) until the final consummation and will then hand the kingdom over to the Father (1 Cor. 15:24). The trinitarian difference between God the Father and the Lord Jesus Christ opens up the history of salvation and is directed at that perfect union of which it can be said that in it "God is all in all" (1 Cor. 15:28). Without this trinitarian difference between God the Father and the Lord Jesus Christ, the history of salvation cannot be understood as the taking up of all creation into the redeeming community of God.

At least since the start of the Romanization of Christianity, there has been an equation of "Father" and "Lord" in the concept of God—an equation with serious consequences. According to Lactantius, the one God is Lord and Father at one and the same time: "We must all love him, because he is the Father, but also fear him, because he is the Lord."[12] The double structure of fearing and loving God corresponds to the "two persons" in God, his role as Lord and as Father. Men and women are, therefore, always God's servants and children at one and the same time. This Romanization of the image of God also involved transferring the Roman *patria potestas* to God: God holds the *potestas vitae necisque*, the power of life and death. Once masculine domination in the family, in the State, and in the Church was legitimized by this image of God, monarchical forms of lordship arose. According to whether there was more emphasis on God's role as father or on his role as lord, there was more emphasis on the political patriarchalism of the "Father of the Country" or the political absolution of the ruler. However, in this dominant Father of All, we can no longer recognize the Father of Jesus Christ whom Jesus himself addressed so trustingly and tenderly as *Abba*. In the father-like Lord of Heaven, we can no longer find Jesus, "the friend of publicans and sinners."[13]

If we wish to return from these historical deformations of the Christian image of God to the original biblical confession of faith, then we must define the unity of the triune God, not in a monotheistic, but in a trinitarian way. The history of Jesus with the God whom he called "my father" in the Spirit that was experienced as the Holy Spirit—the history to which the New Testament bears witness—is a history that takes place between different subjects, as is shown by the story of Gethsemane. Father, Son, and Spirit are distinct subjects with will and reason who communicate with each other in prayer and response, are turned towards each other in love, and are only "one" together. While Paul and the synoptics mean by God the Father of Jesus Christ and clearly subordinate Jesus the Son, in St. John's gospel, we find a developed trinitarian language: "I and the Father are one," says the Johannine Jesus. He distinguishes between "I" and "you" and points to a unity that is to be found not only in mutual recognition and shared will but also in mutual in-dwelling: "I am in the Father and the Father in me" (John 14:11, 17:21, and elsewhere). "With the Father the Son" may not form a single entity, but he is one with him, which is expressed by means of the plural "we" and "us." If we wish to translate this intimate and unique unity of the Father and the Son into trinitarian terms, then the best means is the concept of perichoresis. The divine persons exist not only with and for each other but also *in each other*: the Son in the Father, the Father in the Son, the Spirit in the Father and in the Son. Thanks to their eternal love, the divine persons exist so intimately in each other that they constitute themselves in their unique, incomparable, and perfect unity. This perichoretic concept of the unity of the triune God is the trinitarian concept of unity. It should be noted that this trinitarian unity is to be grasped equally originally with the persons of the trinity. Their unity is not a secondary "community" of the persons, nor are the persons secondary "modes of being" of the one God. The perichoretic concept of the unity of the trinity links God's threeness and oneness together without reducing the one to the other. The dangers of modalism and of tritheism are equally excluded.

If we can best grasp the biblically attested history of the Father, the Son, and the Spirit with the concept of perichoresis, then the concept of the unity of the triune God needs to be developed not only in a trinitarian, but also in a soteriological manner. It is precisely this that is expressed by the "high-priestly prayer" of the Johannine Jesus: "That they may all be one; even as thou, Father, art in me, and I in thee, that they also may be in us, so that the world may believe that thou hast sent me" (John 17:21). The community of Jesus' friends is meant to correspond to the perichoretic community of the Father and the Son. It is not the persons of the trinity and their relations, but their perichoretic community that has its effect and is reproduced in the community of Jesus. However, this community does not only correspond to the triune God, but also exists "in him" by the power of the Holy Spirit. The perichoretic unity of the triune God is, therefore, an open, inviting unity that unites with itself. It is not confined to God in order to define him exclusively as the one over against the many, but is inclusively open for all creation, whose misery consists in isolation from the living God and whose salvation is, thus, to be found in being graciously taken up into the community of God. The perichoretic concept of the unity of the Father, the Son, and the Holy Spirit would not correspond to the history of salvation attested in the Bible if it were not understood soteriologically as an integrative concept of unity. Because of the gracious love that flows out in abundance the trinity is "open" to those who are lost. It is open for all created beings who are loved, found, and accepted. The triune God does not stand transcendentally outside the world. "It is far better to say that the relationship of the divine persons to each other is so wide that the entire world finds room there."[14]

The Christian acknowledgment of the triune God is originally a baptismal confession of faith. It expresses and constitutes the community of the triune God. It is the new community of human beings, Jews or pagans, Greeks or barbarians, lords or slaves, men and women in Christ (Rom. 10:12, Gal. 3:28), a community in which they are "of one heart and soul" and "have everything in common" so that "there is not a needy person among them" (Acts 4:32–34). That is the life of the trinity and the inviting picture of the triune God on earth.

IV

As opposed to the deformations of life by monotheism, which were mentioned at the start and which have rightly been criticized, trinitarian belief and the inviting trinitarian life of love press for the following changes.

The one-sided patterns of domination and subjection are replaced by forms of community based on free agreement. At the grassroots, the Church consists of and in such communities and exists through them. This also means the democratization of the process of decision in political and economic life. It can also lead to the decentralization of political and economic power, to the extent that better systems of communication are built up to link together into a single network the individual communities in which one can keep track of what is going on.

Man's patriarchal privileges and the deformation of woman they bring about are overcome. The trinitarian community is a community of brothers and sisters and can become the model of a human community.

The trinitarian community is experienced in the Holy Spirit. The fellowship of the Holy Spirit binds men and women together. The Spirit is, thus, also easily called the communal spirit or the communal divinity. However, the community of the spirit does not only embrace man's liberation and redemption, but from the start, determines the community of creation (Psalm 104). By means of the indwelling spirit of creation, all creatures are related to each other in such a way that they exist for each other, with each other, and in each other. The mystery of creation is the perichoresis of creatures in the in-dwelling of the divine spirit. A universal cosmic "sympathy" keeps creation alive. "Thou sparest all things, for they are thine, O Lord who lovest the living. For thy immortal spirit is in all things" (Wisdom 11:26–12:1). The trinitarian confession of faith leads to the discovery of God's spirit in all things, and the life of the trinity leads men and women back into the community of creation, because from being the masters and exploiters of nature, they become once again members of that all-embracing community.

If we bring these remarks together, we can finally understand the Christian doctrine of the trinity as a critical counterbalance and apply it as follows.

By the link between God the Father and the fate of Jesus, monarchical patriarchalism has been made impossible. God the Father is Jesus' "Abba," and only he who sees this Son sees the Father.

By the link between Jesus, the Son of Man, and God, whom he called "Abba," his dear Father, that atheistic humanism is made impossible that offers the man Jesus sympathy but rejects every God, including Jesus' God.

By the link between the Spirit and the Father of Jesus Christ, as well as with the figure of the Son, polytheistic spiritism is made impossible— the outlook that sees many spirits in nature and values them according to their power.

However, by means of the doctrine of the trinity, the elements of truth are in this way set free and united in the religion of the Father, in the religion of the Son, and in the religion of the Spirit.

Translated by Robert Nowell

NOTES

1. F. Schleiermacher, *Glaubenslehre*, 2nd edition, § 11.

2. G. W. F. Hegel, *Philosophie der Religion*, part 3.

3. See *Historisches Wörterbuch der Philosophie* s.v. "Monotheismus," vol. VI pp. 142–146.

4. M. de Ferdinandy, *Tschingis Khan* (Hamburg 1958) p. 153.

5. Jean-Paul Sartre, *1st der Existentialismus ein Humanismus?* (1946).

6. F. Rosenzweig, *Der Stern der Erlösung* (Heidelberg 1954) part 3, book 2, pp. 192 ff. See also S. Ben-Chorin, *Jüdischer Glaube* (Tübingen 1975) I:"Monotheismus als Ausschliesslichkeit Gottes," pp. 31 ff.

7. A. Heschel, *The Prophets* (New York 1962) pp. 252 ff.

8. For a more detailed treatment of this point, see J. Moltmann, *The Trinity of the Kingdom of God* (London 1981).

9. Karl Barth *Kirchliche Dogmatik* I/I (Zürich 1932) pp. 371, 374.

10. *Ibid.*, pp. 368 ff.

11. *Ibid.*, pp. 320 ff.

12. Lactantius, *Vom Zorne Gottes* (*De ira Dei*), ed. H. Kraft and A. Wlosok (Darmstadt 1974) p. 77.

13. J. Moltmann "Ich glaube an Gott den Vater. Patriarchalische oder nicht-patriarchalische Rede von Gott," in *Evangelische Theologie* 43 (1983) 397 ff. In this article I have presented the historical connections in greater detail.

14. Adrienne von Speyr quoted by B. Albrecht, *Eine Theologie des Katholischen, Einführung in das Werk Adrienne von Speyrs* (Einsiedeln 1973) I, p. 126.

17

Peace, the Fruit of Justice

The Church: Product and Instrument of Divine Peace[1]

Does political peace have a theological dimension? Does religious peace have a political dimension?

Many churches are still uncertain whether the Church should take part in debates about "secular peace," or restrict itself, its preaching, and pastoral efforts to "peace with God" and the "spiritual peace" of individuals.[2] If the Church concerns itself with political matters, then, those of another political opinion maintain, it reduces peace with God to a political level and "shalomizes" the peace from above. If the Church does not concern itself thus, those who are committed and politically active say, then its silence makes it party to the force that produces unfreedom, for whoever remains silent in the face of evil is an accomplice of evil (Martin Luther King). To avoid such unprofitable contention, I begin with the event that makes the Church *Church*, and that decides each person's Christian existence: the justifying and peace-giving action of God in Jesus Christ. Paul sums up the Christian message of divine justice thus: "Jesus, our Lord . . . was put to death for our trespasses and raised for our justification" (Rom. 4:25). In Colossians, the same news is presented as a reconciling message of divine peace: "For in him [Jesus Christ] all the fulness of God was pleased to dwell, and through him to reconcile to himself all things, whether on earth or in heaven, making peace by the blood of his cross" (1:19–20). Everything that is the Church, and similarly, everything that ordains Christian existence, is indebted to this justifying, reconciling, and peace-giving divine action through Jesus Christ. What was done for us on the Cross on Golgotha, and in his resurrection from the dead, was the work of God and precedes everything which the Church does and says. The Church is the fruit of God's expiatory suffering and is the creation of God's justifying action. In both together, it is the work of God's will to peace. Because God creates justice, Christ is. Because God establishes peace there is a Church. Therefore, Jesus Christ's Church has to be a Church of peace. Accordingly, all divine service in the Church of Christ begins with a salute of peace, and the Church's blessing is pronounced with the peace of God, which passes all understanding.

However, every gift gives rise to an appropriate task. The Church of Christ is the work of divine justification and peace giving, and is also and just as seriously the instrument of that divine action. The justification of the sinner gives rise to the sanctification of the justified, so that they may do the work of justice in the world. The reconciliation of those troubled by lack of peace prompts the mission of the reconciled as peacegivers in this world without peace. No other response from Christians to the justifying word of God would be appropriate to the dynamic spirit of that divine word. Those reconciled to God become immediately and inalienably the peacegivers of their world. To be sure, the creative activity of God and the responsive activity of human beings are not on the same level, for God is God and humans are humans. However, we cannot separate the two levels. People owe their peace to the action of God, but God assigns everything to new human activity. God justifies in order to sanctify. God summons in order to send. God gives peace that there may be peacegivers. Anyone who remains personally content with the peace of God in itself, and does not become a peacegiver, has not experienced the inward thrust of divine peace and does not know the divine Spirit.[3]

As the work and instrument of divine peace, the Church exists in various societies and at various social levels, and therefore, in the thick of economic, social, and political conflicts. These conflicts extend deep into the Church itself. Every Christian experiences them, is affected by them, and accordingly has to inquire into his or her own peace-giving potential in his or her own particular context. Political theology refines awareness of the political context in which churches and Christians actually exist. Of course, some may behave as if that had nothing to do with the Church or the believing spirit of Christians, but such conscious repression helps no one. The more effectively a church acknowledges its social, political, and cultural environment, the more faithfully it can carry out its divine commission, and the more effective an instrument of divine peace it can become. The declarations of the Latin American Catholic bishops' conferences at Medellin in 1968 and at Puebla in 1978 are exemplary in this respect. The fact that we in the First World do not achieve anything of the same order demonstrates, I think, the new "Babylonian captivity" of the Church, which is only non-Babylonian in that the Church does not experience it as captivity because of the privileges it enjoys in western society. However, a Church that accepts such privileges and accordingly says nothing about the injustice perpetrated by society is not a Church that acknowledges Christ alone and only Christ as its Lord. The task of political theology is not some kind of "politicization of the Church," but the necessary christianization of existence and of the functions of the Church in modern societies.

The major overall conflicts of the world today are reflected in life's many small conflicts. They may be summed up in the paradox that we live in one world that is nevertheless divided.

(1) The development of the scientifico-technological civilization of modern times has produced the noisome injustice of the Third World. By that I mean both the poor people of the Third World nations and the growing poverty in the First World industrial nations.

(2) The same modern civilization has produced for its supposed security the "system of nuclear deterrence," which enables the terrible end of this world to become a reality at any time. The system of deterrence threatens an opponent with universal destruction and, therefore, represents the hitherto most inclusive form of deadly violence and organized lack of peace.

(3) This modern civilization buys its technological successes by means of a progressive, reckless destruction of nature. Every year many varieties of plants and animals vanish for ever. The atmosphere is irreparably destroyed. Forests are defoliated. Deserts spread. The so-called ecological crisis of modern industrial societies is only a euphemism for the ecological death of nature and the ecological suicide of the human race. An atomic war is apocalypse now; the destruction of nature is an amortized apocalypse. The Chernobyl disaster of 1986 was a warning of both developments. The overall situation in which the Church, which has intimately experienced the experience of divine peace, is summoned to establish peace was tellingly characterized by Mikhail Gorbachev when he said: "The human race has lost its immortality." The human race, as such, is under deathly threat from human beings. It could die out.

The major churches today agree: (1) war can no longer be a political option; (2) the spirit of the logic and practice of the nuclear deterrence system must be rejected; and (3) a just peace can be the only legitimate goal of politics.

Hope and Practice of Peace

The great saving word in the Old Testament is *shalom.* Because it is so inclusive it is difficult to define. It means the blessed joy of a successful life. It means the sanctification of life in (the reality) of all its relations. It means a just life of which it may be said: "See, it is very good and no more is needed." It is the fullness of life in the presence of the living God. It is the fullness of life in the mutual love of human beings. It is the fullness of life in the community of creation with all other creatures. Characteristically, *shalom* is neither divided nor limited. Here it is impossible to distinguish salvation from well-being, the peace of God and secular peace, the soul and politics. *Shalom* tends to universality.[4]

That is why, even in the Old Testament, *shalom* became the prophetic word of promise of the future divine salvation for the entire creation. As long as violence and unjust suffering are features of the earth, there is no *shalom*. As long as death reigns, God's *shalom* is still a long way off. Whatever of shalom Israel experienced historically as a nation, and whatever the individual believer experiences of *shalom*, is merely, therefore, a premonition and an indication of the universal *shalom* to come. In every individual fulfillment of the divine promise of *shalom*, there is the experience of the still unfulfilled promise of *shalom* for everyone. Therefore, every historical taste of *shalom* awakens longing for the future of *shalom* fulfilled. Israel found *shalom* in its covenant with God. However, this covenant made Israel a "light for the nations." In regard to Israel, God is interested not so much in Israel as such but in universal righteousness and the peace of nations. Israel is nothing more than the promise made flesh of *shalom* for the nations and for the whole of creation. The messianic promises of the prophet Isaiah show this clearly. The Messiah and his people bring "everlasting peace" (Isa. 9:6) into the world, because they "bring justice" (Isa. 11:4) for the poor and wretched.

Christians recognized this promised Messiah in Jesus, because through him and in his community, they experienced the salvation, the *shalom*, of God. In Jesus' proclamation of the kingdom of God to the poor, justice is accorded to those who suffer injustice. In Jesus' proclamation of the kingdom of God, the sick receive health and the dying life. In his proclamation, outcasts and aliens are accorded community. Through his surrender to death on the cross and in his resurrection from the dead, eternal life is made apparent: a life in the full *shalom* of God, because it has vanquished death. Christians live from the fulfillment of the divine promise of *shalom* through Jesus and in Jesus. However, because this promise is fulfilled only in him, but not visibly in the world, *shalom* already exists in faith but also simultaneously in the future in hope. Christ is the unique commencement of the universal *shalom* of God in this world and in our history.

In communion with Jesus the Messiah, human beings experience the presence of God's *shalom* in the Spirit. That is, the experiences of turning from death to life, of rebirth into hope, of the recreation of love, and of revolt against violence and indifference. In the experience of the creative Spirit, what was thought to be impossible becomes possible, the weak are made strong, those deprived of justice receive it, the rejected are loved, and peace becomes possible.

Experiences of the prophetic and messianic anticipations of the universal *shalom* of God in Israel and in the Church afford the following prospects for the action of peace:

(1) Peace is not a condition but a process, not a possession but a way.

(2) Peace is not the absence of power, but the presence of justice. In peace research, we distinguish now between a negative and a positive concept of peace.

The negative definition maintains that peace is nonwar; that is, absence of the open and of the collective use of force. To define the negative notion of peace more specifically, peace is the absence of force, of need, of unfreedom, and of fear. This negative understanding of peace obtains when statesmen opine that in the last 20 years, nuclear deterrent systems have "preserved the peace." Of course, this claim is quite untenable, and moreover, peace here is confused with armistice. Nothing is said about the cost of the deterrent. The greater the cost of ensuring that there is peace, however, the less justification there is for calling what is thereby assured, peace. Although it is very easy to agree on a negative definition of peace, it is quite unsatisfactory.[5]

The positive definition, however, defines peace as a state of social justice, democratic conflict solving, and international cooperation. Many people think this is utopian, but the negative notion of peace does not work without positive elements.

The Christian concept of peace unites both definitions: peace is the absence of force, suffering, and injustice, and the presence of justice, freedom, and a life in communion with God, other people, and nature. The service of peace, then, means resistance to force and war, and is a service to justice and to life.

Peace researchers differentiate between peace as a state and peace as a process.

Anyone defining peace as a state must either reduce expectations of peace to such an extent that they fit a historical condition, or wait here for peace in history, but in vain. While people continue to enrich themselves at others' expense, while people continue to oppress others, and while people continue to be afraid of others, there is no peace. Peace as a state is a utopia, and the worst utopia of this kind is that of the status quo. Only those who have a good life-style think they live in peace. They ignore those who have to live impoverished lives.

Therefore, it is better to see peace as a historical process, with instances of progress, and with setbacks. On the road to peace, we have to reduce violence, armaments, and structural force, and we have to build community and reciprocal trust. On the road to peace, we are concerned with the diminution of economic exploitation and to establish a just universal economic system. On the road to peace, we are interested in removing unfreedom and in ensuring the democratic participation of the people in political decisions.

In the Christian interpretation, historical peace is a multiple process of anticipation of that universal peace that the coming kingdom of God will fulfill. Here and now, already, Christians live by virtue of the peace of the kingdom which is to come, and wherever possible introduce that peace into this violent world. Christians are not oriented to "the beyond," as some would say, but introduce the beyond into the here-and-now. When it is lived authentically, Christian faith is not the "opium of the people" but the power that enables the people to be liberated.

Peace, the Fruit of Justice

The other great saving word in the Old Testament is *zedaka,* justice. "In the Old Testament there is no concept which is so very important for all human relations as that of *zedaka*."[6] It is the yardstick not only for the relationship between people and God, but for their relations with one another and for their relations with the rest of creation. *Zedaka* does not mean—as in the Graeco-Roman world from which we derive our notions of justice, *justitia,* behavior appropriate to a predetermined absolute ethical standard—but living loyalty to community. The God of the Exodus and of the Sinaitic covenant is the faithful God. His truth is that he remains loyal to his promise, and thereby makes it trustworthy and reliable. Accordingly, Psalm 143:1 prays: "In thy faithfulness answer me, in thy righteousness." By his covenant, God enters into a community together with the nation of his choice. His righteousness is that he maintains this covenant. The righteousness of the people is that, for its part, it maintains the covenant and its law. If the nation becomes disloyal and godless, then God's loyalty to his covenant becomes apparent as grace, which makes the unrighteous righteous by recalling them to the covenant. Hence, Psalm 32:1 says: "Behold, a king will reign in righteousness." The great feast of reconciliation is the major feast in Israel. It celebrates divine justice as reconciling grace. "The notion of a punitive *zedaka* has no support—it would be a *contradictio in adjecto*" (G. von Rad, *op cit.* p. 375). God's justice is always saving, always brings justice, and always establishes righteousness. In his righteousness, God does not merely confirm what is just and what is unjust, but proffers justice to those without it and shows the doers of violence the injustice of their ways. Through his justice God creates peace, substantial peace.

There is no peace in oppression. Where injustice and violence rule, there is no peace, although everything is quiet and no one dare protest. Those are false prophets who then cry "Peace, peace!," when what actually prevails is not peace but only death. It is not the Church of Christ, but the religion of the anti-Christ that preaches "reconciliation" for the sake of such a peace in any society in which justice is trampled down, as the "Kairos Document" of critical and prophetic Christians in South Africa rightly says.[7] In the Old and New Testaments, it is theologically clear that justice has precedence over peace, because justice creates peace, but peace does not bring about justice. Therefore, the peace activity of the Church and of Christians has to be directed to justice. Whoever brings justice to the wretched serves peace, even if he or she is delivered up to the anger of the rich. Whoever takes up the cause of the despised serves peace, even if he or she delivers himself or herself up to the hatred of the self-righteous. The WCC Conference in Vancouver in 1983 correctly placed the convenant for justice in first place before the covenant for peace and for the life of creation.

I would like to relate the biblical tradition of divine *zedaka*, and the *zedaka* of human beings and creation to our notions of justice, in order then to direct righteous activity to the establishment of *shalom* in our world.

An earlier idea of European legal culture defined justice as "*justitia distributiva*." "*Suum cuique*" is the watchword: to each his or her own. This nimble formula unites legal equality ("to each . . .") with the actual difference of people ("his or her own"). Not the same to each, but to each according to his or her means. This idea of justice is, however, largely related to property and work. Every human being has the right to life, food, and freedom, as is appropriate to specifically human nature.

The individually and communally relevant idea of justice extends beyond this materially directed concept. It consists in the acknowledgment of the other in his or her otherness, and in acceptance of the other in his or her specificity for supplementation of one's own self. Reciprocal acknowledgment and acceptance produce a just community. This undoubtedly corresponds to the Christian idea of justice as justification: "Welcome one another, therefore, as Christ has welcomed you, for the glory of God" (Rom. 15:7). This individually related notion of justice is also the concept of justice at the basis of modern societal ideas of covenant and contract.

Finally, justice may not be formulated ideally. Instead, we have to inquire into actual justice in a world of violence and injustice. In such situations, justice pre-eminently assumes the form of siding with the powerless and with victims of violence. This partisan acknowledgment is to be found unmistakably throughout the Old and New Testaments. "The Lord lifts up those who are bowed down; the Lord loves the righteous . . . the Lord lifts up the downtrodden, he casts the wicked to the ground" (Ps. 146/147). Just as unequivocally, it gives rise to the commission: Execute "justice for the fatherless and the widow" (Deut. 10:18). That is the divine law of mercy, the sympathetic option for the poor, which Jesus so emphatically showed us. "Mercy" does not mean being soft-hearted, as it were, but that those deprived of justice receive what is due to them. The weak have a right to the protection of mercy, and the strong are duty-bound to be merciful. "Mercy" is not mere gentle benevolence, but feeling commitment to the rights of the other. Therefore, it is not something outside the order of justice but itself productive of justice. Like the acknowledgment of the other, the exercise of mercy toward the weak is the basis of all orders of justice that serve the cause of peace. "Peace is the fruit of justice . . ." I would like to illustrate this principle in terms of two choices: that of love of one's enemy and that of the nonviolent suppression of force.

Anyone who gets into an argument and takes part in conflict is subject to the law of retribution: an eye for an eye, a tooth for a tooth. Whoever relates to the enemy in accordance with this law is in a dilemma from which there is no exit. He or she must become the enemy's enemy, hating the hater, molded by the enemy. If evil is met with evil, then one evil always follows on the other and is justified by the other evil. That is fatal. Liberation is possible only if there is no thinking of enemy as enemy. The love Jesus puts in the place of retribution is love of one's enemies (Matt. 5:43ff.).

Love of an enemy is not retributory, but accommodating and creative love. Whoever repays evil with good does not merely react but creates something new, no longer allowing the enemy to prescribe the rules of the game. Love of one's enemy demands a great deal of sovereignty. The more liberated from fear one is, the greater the success of love of one's enemy. Love of an enemy, however, can never mean subjection to the enemy, but must intend the intelligent and creative suppression of enmity. It is a kind of love that seeks to subvert enmity (P. Lapide). Love of an enemy does not ask, How can I protect myself from this enemy? but, How can I free the enemy from his inimical attitude? Love of one'e enemy makes the enemy conscious of his or her own responsibility. Therefore, love of one's enemy cannot be condemned as mere piety but as a true ethic of responsibility. Love of one's enemy applies not only in private life where it is especially problematical, but in political life, where we do not ensure that we have peace by exterminating all our enemies, but only by ensuring that we overcome enmities and assume responsibility for our common security. The politics of love of one's enemy demands thinking along with and for the others. The question is not how western Europe can protect itself from the "Russian threat," but how we can construct a common order for peace in Europe between West and East. That presumes the demilitarization and democratization of our thinking.[8]

Love of one's enemy gives rise to nonviolent suppression of force. That sounds paradoxical, but is not so. Nonviolence does not mean depoliticization, because a distinction has to be made between "force" and "power."[9] "Power" is the justified, legitimate, and legal use of force. In this sense, the modern state possesses the so-called "monopoly of force" in our society. By "force" I understand the unjust and unjustifiable use of power. We speak, thus, of "naked force" or "brutality." In our societies, Christianity has been unable to get rid of barbaric violence. However, it has made it necessary to justify every use of force, especially a state's use of force. Justice also restricts the use of force by a state, not only internally in respect of citizens of the state in question, but externally in regard to other states and to humankind as a whole. Threatening the human race with a nuclear holocaust is an act of force that cannot be justified in any way. The first form of suppression of force is the association of all exercise of power with justice. There follows the duty to resist all unjust uses of power, whether illegal or illegitimate, or directed against human rights. Nonviolence does not exclude a power struggle, if that struggle is concerned to keep power in line with justice. Anyone who resists actively or passively under a public rule of violence is only doing his or her duty as a citizen, and supporting the restoration of justice or the obtaining of justice for all. That person is justified in using all instruments of power, but may not use brutality, because that would compromise his or her own goals. Hence, the promotion of disarmament until all nations are incapable of attacking one another.

The power of nations that suffer from the rule of violence is not terror but solidarity. General solidarity deprives violent rulers of all appearance of justice and takes the fright out of their threats. In our own times, we have a number of instances of peoples overcoming military dictatorships in nonviolent ways: Greece, Argentina, the Philippines. The rule of violence is weakly grounded when it is isolated and deprived both of trust and of fear. The nonviolent suppression of force is certainly possible. Of course, it can demand martyrdom. We think of Gandhi and of Martin Luther King. We think above all of Jesus himself. When we think of him, then we also discover that not only active behavior has liberating power and leads to "success," but that suffering, too, has a liberating because reconciling power and can become a "blessing" to many. "The blood of the martyrs is the seed of the Church" was how it went in the ancient Roman empire. That is true in a somewhat different sense of the seed of peace in justice, which a number of small groups sow today.

Are We Capable of Peace?

How can Christians, communities, and the churches organize their commitment to peace through justice?

I assume that peace is the flesh of justice, and for that reason, justice is the soul of peace. If that is the case, then the Church must be seen as the body of divine peace and testify to peace through its own existence, not merely through pastoral letters and political demonstrations.

The Church exists in various social forms. Here I list in descending order: (1) the universal Church; (2) the national Church; (3) the local parish; and (4) the voluntary group and movement. The service of peace must take various forms on these different levels. I think it is reasonable to make distinctions here, so that there is no mutual overloading.

I begin down below with the voluntary group.

Commitment to peace always demands a personal commitment to nonviolent action and personal readiness for sacrifice. Hence, peace groups everywhere and the Third-World groups for social justice. In such cases, concerned people come together voluntarily and work at an actual task they acknowledge and undertake in common as their own task. They develop their own readiness to participate in demonstrations and in social action. Together with this readiness for public action, a special form of spirituality comes into being. Dietrich Bonhoeffer called this new way of life "resistance and submission." Taizé calls it "contemplation and struggle." "Mysticism and liberation" is the watchword of the basic communities in Latin America. These peace groups come together regionally and internationally through networks, and in this way, construct a form of ecumenism from below. However, these are groups and movements and networks of like-minded people. Thus, the Catholic peace movement, Pax Christi, has difficulties with the German Catholic hierarchy. The basic communities in Latin America are not to the liking of all bishops. The Christian peace movement in the Reformed Church in Germany is looked on with considerable misgiving. The reason is not only that the representatives of institutions fear the uncontrollable spontaneity of these groups and movements, but that the local parishes consist not of like-minded but of differently minded people. The "Union of Catholic Soldiers" in Germany issues polemics against Pax Christi, and the Protestant forces' chaplains attack the Reformed peace movement in our Church. What, then, is to be expected from the local parish? And what required?

The local parish is the product of the proclamation of the gospel and of baptism. It usually assembles on Sunday morning for divine service. People assemble who think differently about peace and justice. They do not come together in order to meet politically like-minded people in the same church. Therefore, the local church parish can hardly become a peace group. I think that its witness to peace is to be found on another level. Hitherto, the local parish was largely a religious community and a community for divine service in the ritual sense. If, however, it has regard to the whole gospel of Christ, it will be transformed into a living community. The more closely Christians in the local parish live together, the more aware they become of the social, economic, and political conflicts in which they exist, and inquire into justice and peace in these conflicts. The more they recognize that divine salvation intends the entire restoration or sanctification of creaturely health, the more aware they will become of their own duties for the healing of the social and political sicknesses of the society in which they live. In addition to divine service, the parish assembly then becomes important, too, for the working groups report to it, and local tasks are discussed there. It is also the place where the peace groups can contribute their experiences to the local parish, so that local parishes can get going with the learning process of peace.

The local or national churches are neither local communities or parishes nor peace movements. Theirs is a regional context—that of the area covered by the church. They have to face the conflicts that prevail in such areas, and in regional peace conferences try to replace mutual assured destruction with mutual trust; that is, the "European churches' conference" for a divided Europe. Its political counterpart is the KSZE conferences: conferences for the construction of "trust-conducive measures" and reciprocal security partnerships between West- and East-European nations.

Finally, the universal Church to date has been visible only on a denominational level: in Rome, in Geneva, and in the international organizations of the various denominations. It will be perceptible only when that all-Christian "convocation for peace" is in preparation at which Christianity as a whole testifies before a mortally threatened human universe with the justice of God, the peace of nations, and the life of creation.

The watchword for all organizational forms of the Church is "Think globally—act locally!" To make that possible, communication in the churches must be improved. The pastoral letters, encyclicals, handouts, and memoranda on peace we have met with to date have for the most part descended by one-way channels. They have seldom reached the basis and are scarcely taken seriously. Moreover, the reports on the experiences of the basis are hardly ever read and considered "up above." It would seem to be the duty of church leaders to receive the experiences and questions from below and to transmit them further. Only when the churches at all levels, in national and local churches, local parishes, and communities and peace groups, start a common learning process for justice and peace, can they really begin to speak with the one voice that will enable them to be heard.

Translated by J. G. Cumming

NOTES

1. In this article, I consciously adopt some ideas and formulations from the paper given by Dr. H. Falcke of Erfurt GDR, on "Theology of Peace in the One, Divided World" at the session of the *Gesellschaft für Evangelische Theologie* in February 1987, to show that Christians in East and West can speak with one voice on this matter. Falcke's paper is to be published by Christian Kaiser Verlag of Munich in spring 1988, in a symposium on "Peace Theology—Liberation Theology."

2. Cf. in this respect, the symposia *Aktion Sühnezeichewn-Friedensdienste.* (eds.), *Christen im Streit um den Frieden* (Freiburg 1982); German Bishops' Conference (eds.) *Hirtenworte zu Krieg und Frieden* (Cologne 1983).

3. As against the "Armageddon theology" of such cynical apocalypticists as Hal Lindsey, *The Late Great Planet Earth* (Grand Rapids 1970), *id., The 1980s: Countdown to Armageddon* (King of Prussia, PA, 1980).

4. N. Lohfink, *Unsere grossen Wörter. Das alte Testament zu Themen dieser Jahre* (Freiburg 1977).

5. E. Eppler, *Die tödliche Utopie der Sicherheit* (Hamburg 1983).

6. G. von Rad, *Theologie des Alten Testaments.* I (Munich 2nd ed. 1957) p. 368.

7. *Challenge to the Church. A Theological Comment on the Political Crisis in South Africa. The 'Kairos Document'* (Braamfontein 1985).

8. This requirement was also put before the participants in the international forum "For a world without nuclear weapons, for the survival of Humankind," Moscow, February 1987, by General Secretary Gorbachev: *Für die Unsterblichkeit der menschlichen Zivilisation* (Beienrode 1987).

9. See in greater detail, J. Moltmann, *Politische Theologie—Politische Ethik* (Munich-Mainz 1984) pp. 124ff.

18

Revolution, Religion, and the Future

The Modern Era: A New Beginning and Its Contradictions

The Paris events of 1789 were hailed in the various states of Germany with messianic enthusiasm by some, while they were hated by others with an apocalyptic terror. However, both groups immediately recognized that the French Revolution meant the dawn of "a new epoch in the history of the world," as Goethe put it on 20 September 1792, after the cannonade of Valmy. The *ancien régime* collapsed, in France first of all, later in the different German states as well; and a new democratic era began, first in France, and from 1848 in Germany, too. This was the age of the bourgeois world, and it lasted until the Bolshevik revolution in Russia, in 1917.

The other side of the political revolution, however, was the industrial one that followed. The world of the great industrial areas came into being, the world of new mass cities, the proletariat, European economic imperialism and the exploitation of nature through human domination. In the twentieth century, Europe's political hegemony destroyed itself in two world wars. But the scientific and technological civilization it had created spread inexorably, and became global.

However, today, all over the world, this civilization finds itself entangled in at least three deadly contradictions.

(1) It has produced the misery of the Third World.

(2) It is driving the earth toward ecological catastrophe through its progressive destruction of nature.

(3) It is threatening its own survival through the system of nuclear deterrents, by which it aims to secure its own safety.

In the period leading up to March 1848, German philosophers and poets imagined that with the French Revolution a new time had dawned. Two hundred years later this "new time" has turned into something

very like the "end-time" of humanity, an era in which at any moment
the end of the human race can be brought about by human beings
themselves. So, if we look back to 1789 from the perspective of 1989,
what we see is not unequivocal. It is ambiguous. We are left with mixed
feelings. The revolution was never completed. But what form will the
completion take?

French Practice and German Theory

Two hundred years ago, the Germans looked on fascinated at the
events in France. However, looking on was, in fact, all that they did.
They did not achieve anything comparable themselves. Consequently,
the political revolution in France was answered in Germany by an
intellectual one. One of the first people to spark this was Kant, with
his transcendental philosophy of subjectivity. The great philosophical
school of German idealism—Kant, Fichte, and Hegel—may, therefore,
be interpreted as the German theory of the French Revolution,[1] so
powerful was the impact of events. However, in Germany, revolutionary
theory was where things stopped. The theory did not lead on to praxis. It
was Karl Marx who for the first time brought Hegel's theory of revolution
down to earth and made it practical through and through.

Let us examine the events of those early days. When the first news
from Paris arrived in Germany, devout Protestants in Württemberg who
were waiting for the coming of the kingdom of God, sent an emissary
to Paris to find out for certain what was happening. He never returned.
However, "the revolutionary wish to bring about the kingdom of God is
the salient point of all progressive education, and the beginning of
modern history," declared Friedrich Schlegel. This is important for the
German Enlightenment. It was eschatologically orientated. "The philosophers have their millenarianism too," wrote Kant.[2] In 1791, the theological students at Tübingen university were carried away by the spirit of
liberty: Hegel, Schelling, and Hölderlin planted a Jacobin cap on the
maypole and danced round it to the sound of the Marseillaise. Terrified,
the Duke of Württemberg exhorted them to hear reason. In 1798, talking
about the French Revolution, Kant wrote: "A phenomenon like this can
never again be forgotten, because it reveals a disposition and a capacity
in human nature for betterment, a capacity which no politician could
have thought out for himself from the previous course of events." Drawing on Thomist sacramental theology, he interpreted the revolution as
a "historical sign" of humanity: it is a sign of remembrance, a sign of
hope, and a sign of the presence in the human race of a trend toward
the good. That is to say, men and women had emigrated from a self-

inflicted tutelage toward the independent and public use of their own reason.[3]

Hegel described the same phenomenon more emphatically: "Never as long as the sun had shone in the firmament and the planets had revolved round it, had it been perceived that man stands on his head—that his existence centers in his ideas—and that it is there that he forms reality. Anaxagoras was the first to say that the *nous* [the intellect] governs the world; but only now has man come to recognize that thought should govern spiritual reality. And this was indeed a glorious sunrise."[4]

Fichte related his philosophical system even more directly to the French Revolution: "My system is freedom's first system. Just as that nation is striking off mankind's outward fetters, so my system strikes off the fetters of things in themselves, of outward influence, and as its first principle sets up man as an independent being."[5]

The Idealist philosophers saw the ideas of the Enlightenment at work in the French Revolution: *human rights* and human dignity, *democracy* as the constitution of liberty, and *reason* as the means whereby to build a free and humane world. All in all, the French Revolution meant the humane emancipation of human beings from their multifarious dependencies and alienations. They recognized in the political revolution the dawn of "the age of history." Ever since 1789, "revolution [has become] the identifying mark of our age in world history," said Julius Friedrich Stahl. The future is no longer determined by the past. Traditions no longer legitimize the orders of state and society. The world of men and women has ceased to take its bearings from the cosmic orders of nature. Through the industrial revolution, people have been put in a position to construct their own world according to their own wishes and ideas. Through the political revolution, political rule has ceased to be legitimized by religion; its legitimation is now popular sovereignty. Through both revolutions, human beings have become the determining subjects of their own history, and modern society and the modern state must be rationally organized for this purpose.

But if people become the masters of their own history, they can also dig their own graves. As freedom grows, danger grows with it. To keep this danger at bay, men and women seek for a transcendent support. If this human history of humanity is not to end in chaos, it must take its bearings from a history that is wider, more comprehensive—the divine history of the absolute mind (Hegel), the natural history of evolution (Darwin), or the objective laws of dialectical materialism (Marx and Engels). Although the great thinkers of the nineteenth century thought in terms of the great paradigm "History," nearly all of them were aware that history is merely another name for crisis, and that crisis is simply another word for revolution. History is a ceaseless crisis, and crisis is the "permanent revolution."[6] Consequently, every mental and political effort was made to discover the historical laws of revolution, to master the social laws of society, and to enforce particular blueprints for the future. Life in history is life in permanent crisis and perpetual new decision. The goal of the new social sciences of Saint-Simon and Auguste Comte was therefore "*terminer la révolution*"—to end the revolution. The popular revolutionary movement can be mastered by sociological knowledge and sociological techniques.[7] So "to end history" by way of the transition from the revolutionary era to an era made possible by bureaucracy—an epoch "*post-historie*"—was on the agenda from 1789 onward, together with revolution itself: from the theocracy of earlier times by way of modern democracy to postmodern technocracy.

Antirevolutionary Apocalyptic in Religion

When the ideals of the French Revolution were betrayed in the Jacobin terror, and when Napoleon, on France's behalf, made his bid for world supremacy, the initial German jubilation over French liberty soon switched over into an apocalyptic "terror of the negative" over this "fury of extinction" (Hegel's phrase).[8] It was the Christian churches, above all, that saw the Antichrist on the way and that—in the fall of Europe as it had been—conjured up the final struggle of Gog and Magog. *The anti-revolutionary option* came into being in the Catholic and Protestant churches—an option that has endured to the present day. The churches saw a future for religion and Christendom only in "the Holy Alliance" of Austria, Prussia, and Russia against Napoleon. Later on, they developed emphatically antirevolutionary, conservative political ecclesiologies. In the different German states, the Protestant churches hallowed as a religious patriotism the national consciousness that had grown up during the war of liberation against Napoleon (1813): "For God, king, and country."

Let us look at the testimonies of the time. "All revolutions are contrary to the kingdom of God," proclaimed the German revivalist theologian Gottfried Menken.[9] In 1831, August Vilmar, a conservative theologian who is still influential even today, termed the revolution "the abominable monster from the abyss": the revolutionary spirit is the denial of all the higher divine order, and turns people into beasts who merely follow their instincts. The revolution and its children—democracy, emancipation, equality before the law, rationalism, and liberalism—are signs of the approaching end of the world. The Antichrist is raising his head, and those who belong to him know "neither God nor prince, neither order nor law, and they are hence proceeding with all their might to destroy Christianity."[10]

Julius Friedrich Stahl, the influential Protestant theologian and Prussian churchman and politician, interpreted the signs of revolution with the same apocalyptic solemnity: because the French Revolution is anti-Christian, only Christianity is in a position to heal the nations from "the sickness of revolution." With this revolution, we have entered upon "the apocalyptic era": the principle of popular sovereignty as the absolute "principle of evil." This revolution cannot, therefore, be fought with compromises, nor can it be overcome through a political "constitutional act." The only power capable of overcoming revolution is Christianity.

Abraham Kuyper interpreted the storm signals of revolution in exactly the same way. Kuyper was a Reformed theologian, the leader of the Dutch Antirevolutionary Party and for years prime minister of the Netherlands. For him, the quintessence of the French Revolution was the anarchist slogan "*ni Dieu—ni maître*" (neither God nor master). He saw this popular sovereignty as the denial of all divine and divinely appointed authority in state and family. Thus for him, atheism led logically to anarchy and the destruction of morals. "Modernism" and "Christianity" must fight one another to the end. The struggle between them is itself already the beginning of the end of the world. Kuyper lauded "Calvinism" as "the only defence for the Protestant nations that can stand its ground against the modernism that is invading them and flooding over them," because in Calvinism men and women humbly bow the knee before God, but raise their heads proudly toward their fellow men. In modernism, on the other hand, people clench their fists toward God and humiliate themselves before their fellow men. *Reformation against Revolution* is his most influential book.[11] Kuyper's spirit is still alive today in the Boer religion of South Africa, the only difference being that there modernism has been replaced by Communism, and the Bolshevik revolution has taken the place of its French predecessor.

The political apocalyptic of the religious right in the United States (e.g. Jerry Falwell)[12] also goes back to the basic antirevolutionary, apocalyptic option taken up by the churches in the nineteenth century: the French Revolution was the beginning of the end of the world, the Bolshevik revolution leads right into it, and a nuclear "Armageddon" will bring about the end itself in the near future. Absurd though these notions about the end-time may seem, they are dangerous to the highest degree, and even today show something of the long-term effects of the French Revolution on its opponents.

Religion, Revolution, and the Covenant for Life

The vision of hope for "liberty, equality, and fraternity" can be betrayed and repressed, but "it can never again be forgotten," now that it has taken root in the hearts of the oppressed. Anyone who declares that this liberty is a human right can never deny it to anyone. Thus, this vision of hope still exerts its influence today, and beyond our own time, in the struggle of oppressed peoples to liberate themselves from European imperialism and in the struggle for freedom of the poor and those who are without rights in all the different societies. The cultural movement for the liberation of women from patriarchy and male industrialism, and the ecological movement for the liberation of nature from human exploitation and annihilation, show how influential these ideas still are, and how far they still cast ever new ripples.

But the antirevolutionary reaction still makes itself felt too, in *the authoritarian principle* "God, king (or governmental power), and country (or family)." In many countries today, the ruling classes are building up authoritarian regimes, which they legitimize through the ideology of "national security." They are misusing religion by turning it into an ally against the revolution of the people, making out that this revolution is something Godless and anarchical. What they hope for is not a world of justice and peace for everybody, but the decisive apocalyptic battle between Catholicism and socialism (Donoso Cortes) or between Christ and Antichrist (Julius Friedrich Stahl), or between the "free world" and the "realm of evil." Because in the *ancien régime* the churches allied themselves with feudalism, the revolutionary liberty of the people was bound to be justified and fought for only in anticlerical and atheistic terms. Moreover, because the popular political revolution and the proletarian revolution of the workers were atheistic, the churches and their theologians were forced into the conservative camp. The rise of democracy in politics, the development of liberalism and socialism in economics, the growth of scientific and technological rationalism, and the awareness of freedom among ever new classes of people—all these things, therefore, came up against the suspicion of the clerics and the incomprehension of the theologians.

It was only when the bourgeois age was drawing to a close in Western Europe, in the middle of the twentieth century, that churches and theologians hesitantly began to adopt a positive attitude toward the developments of the modern mind and spirit that had grown up out of the French Revolution. Vatican II is the great signal for the "actualization" of the gospel of freedom in and through the Catholic church. The ecumenical movement is the corresponding sign in the non-Roman Catholic churches. Political theology, the theology of revolution and liberation theology, feminist theology, and ecological theology are all new working drafts in our generation designed to overcome the fateful and fundamental antirevolutionary, conservative, and apocalyptic option in Christianity; and their purpose is no longer merely *to react* to the development of the modern mind and spirit, but *to run ahead of it,* carrying the light of hope.[13]

This is all the more important, because developments in the modern world have led to such enormous contradictions that today the future of humanity itself is called in question. Faith in progress has given way to fear of the future. Consequently, faith in God must save hope for humanity and liberate it from both hybris and resignation, for perseverence. The real ways out of the danger are neither escapism into the "postmodern age," nor the gentle seduction of the New Age. Humanity cannot be saved either by capitalism, or by socialism as it really exists, because both of them deepen the social and ecological perils of this world and are not solutions; they are part of the problem. But a new historic alliance between socialists and Christians, a positive mediation between reason and religion, faith in God and human freedom, would be the presupposition for resolving the conflict between revolution and religion that has existed ever since 1789.

The unsolved and unsolvable problems of the revolutionary hope for humanity is not liberty. It is not even equality. It is the mediation of the two through the *solidarity,* which at the time of the French Revolution was called, so biblically and so humanistically, "fraternity"— brotherhood; although this equally means the sisterhood of women, and the sister and brotherhood of women and men.

Which form of human community protects and effects both liberty and equality, the self-fulfillment of individuals and the mutual recognition and acceptance of people who are different? I believe that this can only be brought about by a *cooperative reform* of modern society "from below." The theological and political concept that is relevant here is the concept of *covenant.* This concept molds the form of God's people in the Old Testament and in the New. It has also put its impress on the constitutional history of the modern democracies based on popular sovereignty. In the covenant, men and women are both free and dependable. Their covenant is the realization of their mutuality, both in their need and in their abilities. Political covenants in the form of alliances also give effect to international dependencies, even between different social systems. Finally, only a new covenant between human culture and the life of the earth will be able to ensure the survival of both. The covenant of free and equal men and women, drawn from all the different nations, cultures, and religions, can "complete" the French Revolution, because it will fulfill its hope.

Translated by Margaret Kohl

NOTES

1. J. Ritter, *Hegel und die französische Revolution* (Cologne 1957).

2. I. Kant, *Das Ende aller Dinge*, (1794), *Werke*, ed. W. Weischedel (Darmstadt 1964) VI, pp. 175ff.

3. I. Kant, *Der Streit der Fakultäten* (1798), *Werke*, op. cit. VI, p. 361.

4. G. W. F. Hegel, *Vorlesungen über die Philosophie der Weltgeschichte, Werke,* ed. H. Glockner (Stuttgart 1927–40) XI, p. 557 (ET *Lectures on the Philosophy of History*, trans. J. Sibree (Dover and New York, 1956).

5. J. G. Fichte, *Briefwechsel*, ed. H. Schulz (Leipzig 1925) I, pp. 349f.

6. R. Koselleck, *Kritik und Krise. Ein Beitrag zur Pathogenese der bügerlichen Welt* (Frankfurt 1959).

7. J. L. Talmon, *Political Messianism. The Romantic Phase* (New York 1960).

8. G. W. F. Hegel, *Phänomenologie des Geistes* (1807), *Werke, op. cit.* III. "Die absolute Freiheit und der Schrecken" (ET *The Phenomenology of Mind*, trans. J. B. Baillie, New York 1967; *Hegel's Phenomenology of Spirit*, trans. A. V. Miller, Oxford, 1977).

9. *Cf.* R. Strunk, *Politische Ekklesiologie im Zeitalter der Revolution* (Munich and Mainz, 1971) pp. 102ff.; J. Moltmann, *The Church in the Power of the Spirit*, trans. Margaret Kohl (London and New York 1977) pp. 41ff.

10. A. Vilmar, *Kirche und Welt* (Gütersloh 1872).

11. Kuyper's book was based on the Stone lectures, given in Princeton, NJ, and was first published under the title *Calvinism* (New York 1899; reprinted Grand Rapids 1931).

12. G. Fackre, *The Religious Right and Christian Faith* (Grand Rapids 1982).

13. *Cf.* J. Moltmann, *Was ist heute Theologie? Zwei Beiträge zu ihrer Vergegenwärtigung,* Questions disputatae 114 (Freiburg 1988).

19

Has Modern Society Any Future?

The Contradictions and Conflicts of Modern Society

Modern society is a child of the industrial revolution. Today we are in fact going through the third industrial revolution: the mechanization of production was followed by its electrification, and nowadays we have its computerization. The change in methods of production demands mobility and flexibility from the men and women concerned. It requires of them the ability to realize new potentialities and the strength to overcome the contradictions and conflicts they suffer in the process. Socially and politically, modern industrial society is inevitably a society of permanent reform. It is only if it is prepared for transformation that this society can reduce the risks it has created for itself and can fulfill its own potentialities.

But for every social reform we need a historical vision—the vision of a future worth living for. This vision is more vital than ever at times when technological change involves many people in huge social conflicts and economic risks. "Where there is no vision the people perish" (Prov. 29:18). The person who simply wants to extend his present into the future will neglect the new possibilities the future offers him. By suppressing these possibilities, he is suppressing the future itself. Today a simple prolongation of what already exists no longer produces any future worth living for. It is only through conversion and reform that we shall be able to save for the future the things we think are worth keeping.

Has modern society any future?

Many people who are suffering from the contradictions in our society, and who recognize them for what they are, have serious doubts. Many people who are suffering from the contradictions without recognizing them are despairing, in dumb apathy. Generally speaking, we may say that in the wealthy societies on earth there has never been so much disorientation, resignation and cynicism, and self-hate and aggression toward society's institutions as there is in Western industrial societies today. There has never been so much misery and so much mass death in the poorer societies as there is today in the countries of the Third World.[1] Let me list a few of these contradictions:

We are not only living in class societies. We are living in "two-thirds societies" as well. That means societies in which two-thirds of the population are pushing the other third down below the poverty line and degrading them into "surplus people," although the means are available for providing every member of society with a life in freedom and justice. The sufferers are children, old people, the handicapped, the untrained, and many of the minorities. In West Germany, for example, we have an unemployment rate of 8–10 percent, and according to official government statements, have settled down "to living with this structural unemployment" in the future too, although according to Article 23 of the General Declaration on Human Rights "every person has the right to work." Ten percent of our population are deprived not only of the chance to earn a decent living, but also of the self-respect given by work and wages, and the community shared with other people. The fact that many of the Western industrial societies have produced a "new poor" in the last 10 years is not an unavoidable fate. It is the result of neglects in the field of social policy. The fact that a generation of young people is growing up whom threatening unemployment attests daily that they are not needed, is a scandal. We know that there is a connection between unemployment, attacks on property, and prison sentences. In the United States, 50 percent of the people in prison were unemployed at the time they committed their crime. In West Germany, burglaries have increased by 60 percent since 1979. In these young people, our society is reaching its end, and their despairing answer is "no future."

The person who has hope for the future saves in the present and invests for the time ahead. The person who has no hope and no desire for the future enjoys the present and piles up debts, which have to be paid by his children, or by somebody else, at some later point. A society's hope and its hopelessness can be read very clearly from its investment and its debts. Our Western societies are by no means only the creditor nations for the increasingly indebted countries of the Third World. They themselves are heaping up huge mountains of debt in their national budgets, the United States most of all. In so doing, we are laying an appalling burden of debt on our children and making life hard for them. This is "no-future" politics.[2]

Modern societies have invented and developed the system of nuclear deterrence to protect themselves from one another. Out of their fear of mutual destruction they expend more and more on security, from atomic bombs to Strategic Defense Initiatives. "Mutually assured destruction" is supposed to guarantee security. However, the more that is spent on this "security," the less the thing "secured" is worth saving. Nuclear deterrence does not threaten potential opponents alone. It threatens the whole of humanity and all higher forms of life on earth with annihilation. It holds the threat of global mass murder. Humanity as a whole has become mortal, and the destruction or survival of humanity is going to be decided simply by the two or three major political and military systems. Up to now, we have not experienced nuclear terrorism, but it is already possible. With Hiroshima and Nagasaki in 1945, the potential end of humanity began. The end of our human future is possible at any time.

Not the least, modern industrial society has produced more wealth than any other society before it. However, it produces this wealth for human beings, at the expense of nature. No earlier society irrevocably destroyed so much of the natural environment as has this one. The "ecological crisis" into which our societies have brought nature and human beings is probably already an "ecological catastrophe," at least for weaker forms of life.[3] People who know are living with the tormenting anxiety that nature could deteriorate to such a degree that humanity could join the dinosaurs as an extinct form of life. What makes this idea so disturbing is the suspicion that the decision may have already been irrevocably made, because we can no longer retrieve the poisons that are rising into the ozone layer and seeping into the ground. If this is so, the fate of humanity would already be sealed, before the symptoms of extinction show themselves. In this case, we should indeed have no future, but only a present, which in the foreseeable future will become the past.

Have Christians a "vision of hope" for this world, or is established Christianity fused with our society to such a degree that we just about share its impasses and risks, but no longer have any message of hope of our own to offer our contemporaries? In a pluralistic society, the Church of Christ has certainly no right to speak for everyone, Christians and non-Christians alike. However, everyone in this society has the right to hear what Christians have to say as Christians—which means, on the basis of their particular faith and their all-comprehensive hope.

The Christian Experience of God and the Christian Hope for the Future

When Christians think about the future of this mortally threatened society, they begin with the experience that makes them Christians.

But what does make people Christians? It is the justifying, peace-giving activity of God in and for us unjust and peaceless people. "Christ was put to death for our trespasses and raised for our justification," says Paul (Rom. 4:25). The Epistle to the Colossians (1:19–20) says the same thing about peace: " . . . through him [Christ] to reconcile to himself all things, whether on earth or in heaven, making peace by the blood of his cross." Everything that defines what being a Christian means goes back to this justifying, reconciling, and peace-giving act of God's in Christ. It is the experience of grace, of acceptance by God, the experience that men and women are raised up in community with one another, men and women who have given themselves up because they can no longer see any future ahead of them.

But every gift involves a charge. When unjust men and women are justified, the consequence is that they are sent out to work for more social justice. When peaceless men and women are reconciled, the consequence is that they are sent out to make peace in the conflicts of this society. There can be no other response for Christians to their experience of God. Of course, the creative acts of God and the responsive acts of men and women are not on the same level, for God is God, and human beings are human beings. But God himself has joined the two levels, and no one must put them asunder. Men and women owe their righteousness wholly to God; and God finds the righteous dealings of men and women wholly important. When God justifies, he puts into the heart of the person justified the hunger and thirst for justice and righteousness. Christians experience the political and social conflicts of this society in their own persons. The more they believe in God's righteousness and justice, the more painfully they suffer from the injustice they see. If there were no God, we could perhaps come to terms with violence and injustice, because "that's the way things are." But if there is a God, and if God is just, then we can no longer come to terms with these things. Then we can never get used to injustice, but will refute and resist it with all our strength. If God exists, then justice exists, and a judgment no one can escape.

If the peace of God is experienced in faith, then hope awakens for peace on earth, faith responds with thoughts, words, and works to the divine justice and righteousness that has been experienced, and hope expects the new just world. Faith accepts peace with God, but hope anticipates the new world of peace. Faith finds the consolation of God in all suffering, but hope looks to the future of a new creation in which there will be no more mourning, crying, or pain. To put it simply: anyone who believes in God hopes for this earth and does not despair. He looks beyond the horizon of apocalyptic terrors to God's new world, and what he does will be attuned to that world.

In ecumenical discussion, ever since the Assembly at Uppsala in 1968, we have called this life in hope "life in anticipation." Because the anxieties and fears are even greater today, I believe that the message of Uppsala is a topical one, and more important than ever. "We ask you, trusting in God's renewing power, to participate in the anticipation of God's kingdom, showing now something of that new creation which Christ will on his day perfect . . . *God makes new*. Christ wants his Church to foreshadow a renewed human community." People do not live solely from traditions. They live in anticipations too. In apprehension and in hope, we anticipate the future and adapt ourselves to it in the present. The people who today despair and say "no future" are anticipating the end and destroying the lives of other people. However, Christians anticipate the future of the new creation, the kingdom of justice and freedom, not because they are optimists but because they trust the faithfulness of God. Of course, we shall not realize the kingdom of righteousness and justice in the world. However, we cannot dispense ourselves from preserving this world for God's future, because we can also annihilate it. There is no salvation without this earth.

Creating Justice in Society

Let us now look at the life of men and women in their essential relationships from the aspect of God's righteousness and justice, for it is righteousness and justice that bring peace and create future.

I proceed in the following sequence:

(a) People in community
(b) Community in generations
(c) Generations in the natural environment
(d) Church of the whole creation

People in Community

Modern industrial society has produced the public individualism in which everyone wants freedom for himself, and no one bothers too much about anyone else. The principle of competition means that the "good performers" are rewarded, and the weak are punished. If, in addition, opportunities for living, occupations, and jobs are deliberately kept scarce on principle, the result is a struggle of "every man for himself," for then there is never enough for everyone. The consequence is a society of climbers, in which more and more people get pushed onto the fringe, or off the ladder. The ideology of "there isn't enough for everyone" makes people lonely, isolates them, and robs them of their relationships to other people; and the end is social death.

If people in our society are going to be able to live in a more humane way again, we shall have to build up communities from below, and recognize that human beings can develop their personhood only in relationships and groups. The alternative to poverty is not property. The alternative to poverty *and* property is community. The principle of life is "mutual help." Peter Kropotkin already showed that this was true in both the animal and the human world, contrary to Darwin's view. In communities, we become rich: rich in friends, in neighbors and colleagues, in brothers and sisters on whom we can rely in case of need. Together, as a community, we can help ourselves in most of our difficulties. Together, in solidarity, we are strong, and able to shape our own destinies. But if we are divided, we can be controlled, according to the old Roman maxim: divide and rule! Thus, community is the real protection for personal freedom.

Everywhere modern society has become centralistic. It has created huge industrial and administrative centers in the great cities, and in this way, it has impoverished the local communities and drained the country. The build-up of a new humane society will, therefore, have to begin with these local communities, which can be surveyed and experienced; and many of the functions and assignments that have been given over to the central authorities will have to be passed back to these local communities. In the age of the modern media, decentralization is not a technical problem. Society is humane and alive in independent local communities.

The unemployment problem has to be seen in the same context. Work is one of the fundamental needs of human life. It makes it possible for people to live in the material sense, but it does more than that. It creates social recognition and personal self-respect. It forms the person. "The right to work" is, therefore, not merely a material right. It is a profoundly personal one. The way we work and the way the chances to work are distributed determines not merely our personal destiny, but our common future at the same time.[4]

If we are to work for justice in the various sectors of this field, the following points, at least, are important: (1) the just distribution of job opportunities for women and men through shorter working hours and the creation of new jobs; (2) fair wages and humanely designed places of employment; (3) generous opportunities for training and further training; (4) instead of earlier retirement, the introduction of sabbatical years during a person's working life; and (5) the social recognition of the work people perform without remuneration, above all housework and work on behalf of children and old people in the family.

We need a new definition of work. To put it very generally, work is active participation in the processes of society, not merely in its production process. All honest work within the social process must be given public recognition—through money among other things.

Community in Generations

We have apparently become accustomed to seeing human life horizontally: all human beings living at a particular time. But a glance anywhere in the Old Testament shows us that earlier civilizations viewed human life in longitudinal sections, people in the sequence of the generations. It is true that men and women are not merely social beings; they are generation beings too. They are created in generations. They live with one another and for one another in generations. Thus, human life stands and falls with the preservation, or the breach, of the generation contract, which is unwritten but underlies the whole of life. This generation contract says that parents look after their children when they are small and need help, and that children care for their parents when they grow old and are in need of help. However, the generation contract does not apply merely to families. It applies to all the people in the different generations who live together in a society. Because everyone lives in the sequence of the generations and owes his life to it, everyone also has the duty to look after the older and the younger generation. Shared humanity is also lived in the community of the generations who look after one another—not merely in the partnership between men and women, but in the solidarity of old and young as well.

Now, there is not merely personal and collective egoism. There is also the egoism of the present generation toward the generations to come. Human community in the succession of the generations can endure only if there is a just distribution of the opportunities for living between the present generations and the coming ones.

Today the generation contract is threatening to break down, and this threat is a potentially deadly one. In this generation, we are in the process of using up most of the earth's existing crude oil. We are leaving appalling mountains of debt in the public budgets of local authorities, cities, and nations, which will have to be paid off by coming generations. We are depositing toxic industrial waste in the earth, which our children will have to dig up again and dispose of. Nuclear power stations are producing atomic waste which, in view of its decay time, will have to be stored until the years 3000, 5000, and longer. Not the least, compared with other societies with which we are familiar, in the future there are going to be more old people in our societies and fewer young ones. The pensions the young people are going to have to pay for the old will increase. To put it briefly: the present generation is making life hard for the generation to come.

If we want to bring justice into the sequence of the generations, we shall have to set up the cost-utility accounts more honestly, where the property we have succeeded in acquiring is concerned. It is an impossible state of affairs if we use up the profits now, leaving the costs to be paid by future generations. The West German constitution states that property involves "social obligation." Anyone who acquires and owns property assumes social responsibility. However, property belongs to the succession of the generations as well, and, therefore, also involves the obligation to pass it on to the generations still to come. All regulations about property must be embedded in the generation contract, for property can in justice only be used in a way that takes the coming generations into consideration. In earlier agricultural societies, it was a matter of course that inherited land should be passed on intact to one's children. Among the American Indians, seven coming generations have to be considered in every grave decision about migration and settlement. In modern industrial societies, this justice between the generations with regard to heritable property must be deliberately created, because it no longer counts as a matter of course, and because many people no longer see how these things hang together.

Human generations constitute the community of human beings in time, and the community of human beings in time belongs to the sequence of the generations. This community in time is a truly humane community if there is justice between the generations and if the generation contract is observed. In our present situation, the rights of children and the rights of the coming generations to live must be observed particularly scrupulously, because children are the weakest links in the chain of the generations, while the coming generations do not yet have any voice at all, and will, therefore, be the first victims of present injustice.[5]

Generations in the Natural Environment

The next obvious sphere to which life belongs is the natural environment, and the relation between human civilization and nature. Human beings are not only social beings and generation beings. They are natural beings as well. They belong to nature and are dependent upon nature. Human civilizations can only develop in equilibrium with the cosmic conditions of the earth's organism, which provide their framework. If civilization destroys these, human civilization itself dies. Before modern times, the agrarian societies realized this, and in their animist religions, they reverenced the cosmos and respected the earthly conditions that are the framework for the earth. It was only modern industrial societies that detached themselves from nature's laws and rhythms for the first time. These societies were built up exclusively according to the desires and notions of human beings. Modern scientific and technological civilization is the first civilization that merely subjugates nature, exploiting it as "raw material." Science and technology would make nature "the slave of man," prophesied Francis Bacon, while René Descartes extolled the fact that science and technology were going to make the human being "*maître et possesseur de la nature.*" However, nature protests against her rape by modern industrial society, through her silent death or through counter-revolutions such as AIDS, algae, and so forth. In a collapse of this kind, human beings will die out. The earth will survive without them.

In the long run, societies that are aligned in a one-sided way toward growth and expansion are not viable, because they make immoderate demands on the human and natural foundation on which they rest, destroying it and ruining themselves in the process.

Only the comprehensive conversion of our life-style and our industrial production methods can avert the ecological death of humanity. We need an ecological reform of our society, of production, consumption, and transport. This would be technically quite possible, if there were a political will behind it. All human property, especially major industrial property and transport layouts, must be tested for their "environmental compatibility." Anything that places a burden on the natural environment, or destroys it, must be decommissioned, or must not be built at all. There must be an end to the production of consumer goods whose waste products are nondegradable—for example, plastic and certain chemical products. The waste-producing life-style in the prosperous countries must be exposed as "unnatural" and "unhealthy" and must be reformed in favor of a more natural and healthier way of living. The ecological justice on which a viable symbiosis of humanity and nature is based will be just as important in the future as economic justice and the justice between generations.

Again, the ecological reform of our society will begin in small, surveyable local groups. It is only "aliens" who do not bother about the destruction of their environment. The people who have to live there preserve it and keep their surroundings livable. That is why citizen action groups are quite rightly formed to protest against the major projects of outside, multinational concerns that destroy nature.

Moreover, and not least, attention must be drawn to the human problem involved in the increasingly risky technologies. Nuclear power technology and genetic engineering require infallible human beings, because they react extremely adversely to human error. Are these dangerous technologies controllable at all by faulty and corruptible human beings? The Windscale/Sellafield, Harrisburg, and Chernobyl catastrophes, as well as the diverse international corruption scandals in the

German nuclear industry, say that the answer is "no." At some point, the trial-and-error method comes up against its limits. We cannot afford any further major errors, neither a "worst case" in nuclear power stations, nor a nuclear war, nor a serious accident in genetic engineering laboratories. But this means that we cannot afford any more experience in these sectors. We only live once. A major nuclear accident or a nuclear war will only happen once, and afterward there will be no one left whom the experience can make wise. This means that either human beings must withdraw from these deadly technologies and look for other, more humane sources of energy, or we shall have to get rid of—or genetically reconstruct—the human beings about whom it was hitherto possible to say so tolerantly that "to err is human." In genetic engineering, too, we are beginning to see the end of the experiment. Bacteria produced by means of genetic engineering cannot be retrieved once they have been let loose. An act of this kind will happen only once and irrevocably. It is no longer possible to be wise after any such event. We are setting developments afoot that are getting out of control. We are making free decisions through which we lose our own freedom. If these decisions are final, irrevocable, and unrepeatable, then we are not dealing with experiments anymore, for there is then no more potential scope. Then truth and error can no longer be distinguished. This is the point of no return: all or nothing. That means that we are coming to the end of time, and into the presence of what was traditionally called doomsday.

A Church of the Whole Creation

Let us come back to the inner attitude of men and women. What we need above all is a new respect for nature, and a new reverence for the life of other created things. Here I see the great task for the religions of the world, and above all the Christian Church; for it was the Western "religion of modern times" that freed the way for the secularization of nature. At the end of our civilization's long history, the ancient view about the harmony between the forces of nature has been destroyed—destroyed by modern monotheism on the one hand, and by scientific mechanism on the other. Modern monotheism has robbed nature of its divine mystery and has "broken its spell," as Max Weber said. It has made her the material for human conquest. If we are to arrive at a new respect for nature and a new reverence for the life of other created beings, "the religion of modern times" will have to be fundamentally reformed. We shall no longer be able to separate God and nature, but shall have to perceive God in nature and nature in God. We shall have to integrate human beings once more into the all-embracing community of creation, from which we have detached ourselves. We shall have to understand once more that nature and we ourselves are God's creation, and in the name of God's creation we shall resist humanity's destruction of nature. We shall no longer wish to know nature in order to dominate it, but will desire to know it so as to participate in it. We shall concede nonhuman nature a say in the ecological reform of our society and shall observe the rights of our fellow creatures, both animals and plants. We shall rediscover and learn to respect in nature the Wisdom of God about which Proverbs 8 says: "He who finds me finds life; but he who sins against me injures his own soul; all who hate me love death." In the ecological reformation of "the religion of modern times" I see the greatest task for the Church of Christ today. The precondition for an ecological reform of modern industrial society is a spiritual and cultural conversion, which has its roots in a new religious experience of the reality of God and nature. The Church must become the temple for the whole creation.

Has modern society any future? Its future is conversion. Will humanity survive the crises we have described? We cannot know, and we must not know. If we knew that humanity is not going to survive, we should not do anything more for our children but would say "after us, the deluge." If we knew that humanity is going to survive, we should not do anything either, and by doing nothing we should miss our chance for conversion. Because we cannot know whether humanity is going to survive or not, we have to act today as if the future of the whole of humanity were dependent on us—and yet at the same time trust wholly that God is faithful to his creation and will not let it go.

Translated by Margaret Kohl

NOTES

1. Because many problems in the Third World have their causes in conflicts and contradictions in the First, I am only entering into the latter here.

2. Evidence in R. North, *Wer bezahlt die Rechnung? Die wirklichen Kosten des Wohlstands* (Wuppertal 1988).

3. *Cf.* R. Lester Brown *et al.*, *The State of the World: A Worldwatch Institute Report on Progress toward a Sustainable Society* (New York 1987).

4. Thus also *Economic Justice for All: Catholic Social Doctrine and the US Economy: Pastoral Letter of the Catholic Bishops' Conference of the USA*. National Conference of Catholic Bishops, 1986. This is a good declaration on economic and social justice, but the perspective "ecological justice" is unfortunately lacking. However, without this, there can be no permanent economic and social justice either.

5. *Cf.* also *Our Common Future. The Brundtland Report of the World Commission on Environment and Development* (London 1987).

20

Human Rights, the Rights of Humanity, and the Rights of Nature

The Existence of Human Rights

In many civilizations, growing insight into the fundamental rights and duties of human beings went hand in hand with an awareness of the "humanity" of human beings. Wherever there came to be a concept of "the human being" as such, the rights of human beings, simply as human beings, were formulated too. These ideas are not exclusively Christian or European, although it was during the era of the Western Enlightenment that the formulations of human rights made their way into North American and European constitutions, and it is through these constitutions that human rights have acquired world-wide recognition today. Like other universal ideas—mathematics, for instance—human rights have meanwhile become independent of the particular European history in which they developed, and now seem plausible and convincing simply on their own account, whenever people become aware that they are not merely Americans or Russians, black or white, men or women, Christians or Jews, but that they are first and foremost human beings. This means that there can be no copyright claims to human rights, neither Jewish and Christian, nor enlightened and humanist.

Today the nations are entering upon a common world history because they endanger one another mutually and mortally through the nuclear threat and because they share the equally mortal danger of the ecological crises. The more this movement toward a shared future proceeds, the more important human rights are becoming, as part of a worldwide human society capable of averting these dangers. Human rights are, therefore, increasingly going to provide the universally valid, ethical framework for the evaluation and legitimation of "human" policies, a framework on which there can be a general consensus. The recognition and the implementation of human rights for people everywhere will decide whether this divided and dangerous world is going to be replaced by a humane worldwide community that is in harmony with the cosmic conditions of life on earth, or whether human beings are going to destroy both themselves and the earth. Because the situation is so extremely dangerous, it must be established that human rights have an authority overriding all the particular interests of nations, groups, religions, and cultures. Today, particularist religious claims to absolute truth and the ruthless enforcement of particularist political interests are threatening the very existence of humanity itself.[1]

However, the existing formulations of human rights still are not enough. We must work toward their expansion if human rights themselves are not to become a destructive factor in our world. It seems to me that human rights have to be extended in two directions: (1) the fundamental rights of humanity must be formulated; and (2) human rights have to be harmonized with the protective rights of the earth and other living things, and have to become a part of these.

The declarations of human rights, which are in force in the United Nations today, can be found, first, in the Universal Declaration of Human Rights of 1948 and, second, in the 1966 International Covenants on Human Rights (on Economic, Social and Cultural Rights, on Civil and Political Rights, the Optional Protocol). They certainly have very little binding force in international law, for the preamble says merely that human rights are a joint ideal to be attained by all peoples and nations. At the same time, since about 1970, civil rights movements in many countries have shown that these declarations have an astonishing power, and in the Conferences on Security and Cooperation in Europe (the first of which was held in Helsinki in 1975) their influence has increasingly come to prevail in international law in Western and Eastern Europe.[2]

Right down to the end of the Second World War, it was internationally accepted that the question of how a country treated its own citizens was a matter solely for its own sovereign decision. This is no longer the case. Although many states still reject "interference in their internal affairs," the way a country treats its citizens is according to law a matter for all the other countries, too, because today everyone falls under international law insofar as this protects human rights.

The categories and groupings of human rights already emerge from their history. Following the crimes of the Fascist dictatorships and after the Second World War, the North Atlantic states drew up charters of individual human rights, over against the state and the forces of society.

In their struggle against capitalism and class rule, the socialist states have emphasized economic and social rights. The people of the Third World, in the misery to which they have been reduced, are today demanding the right to existence, the right to live and survive. We can, therefore, distinguish the following groups: (1) protective rights—the rights to life, liberty, and security; (2) freedom rights—the right to freedom of religion, opinion, and assembly; (3) social rights—the right to work, to sufficient food, to a home, and so forth; and (4) rights of participation—the right to codetermination in political and economic life.[3]

The roots of these different human rights and the bond linking them is what Article I calls "human dignity." Human rights exist in the plural, but there is only a single human dignity. Human dignity is one and indivisible. It does not exist to a greater or lesser degree, but only wholly or not at all. Human dignity means the quality of being human, however the various religions and philosophies may define this. At all events, human dignity makes it illegitimate to subject human beings to acts that fundamentally call in question their quality as what Kant called "determining subjects." Because human dignity is one and indivisible, human rights are a single whole too, and cannot be added to, or subtracted from, at will.

However, to base human rights on human dignity also shows the limitations and perils of their inherent anthropocentricism.[4] Human rights must be harmonized with the rights of nature—the earth from which, with which, and in which human beings live. Human dignity is not something that separates human beings from all other living things. It is merely a special example of the dignity of all the living—the dignity of all God's creatures, to put it in Christian terms. Human dignity cannot be fulfilled through human rights at the cost of nature and other living things, but only in harmony with them and for their benefit. Unless human rights come to be integrated into the fundamental rights of nature, these rights cannot claim universality. On the contrary, they themselves will become factors in the destruction of nature, and will then also ultimately lead, paradoxically enough, to humanity's self destruction.

In the ecumenical discussions after the Second World War, we can see interesting shifts of emphasis. From 1948 (the Assembly of the World Council of Churches in Amsterdam) up to about 1960, discussion centered on the question of religious liberty—until people realized that religious liberty can be implemented only in the context of other individual human rights. The Conferences on Security and Cooperation in Europe, as well as conditions in Turkey, show that it is still important to demand both today. Step-by-step, religious liberty, together with individual human rights, is also being recognized in the countries with state ideologies and state religions.

Since about 1960, questions about human rights in the social and economic sectors have come to the fore. Racism, colonialism, dictatorship, and class rule are being attacked as serious infringements of human rights. The right to personal freedom cannot be protected in a world of flagrant political injustice and economic inequality. Only economic and social rights put people in a position to implement freedom for themselves. The ecumenical consultation in St. Pölten, Austria, in 1971, was a milestone in the history of discussions between the Christian churches about human rights, because here representatives of the people of the Third World talked and were listened to. Today, in the industrial countries, the ecological discussion is at the center of interest. It sets human rights imperatively in the framework of the conditions in which the earth itself lives, and in the framework of the cosmos, which sustains life.

At the end of the 1970s, the major churches then issued their own declarations on human rights. In 1976, the World Alliance of Reformed Churches made a statement on the theological foundation of human rights, in 1977 came the declaration of the Lutheran World Federation on theological perspectives on human rights, and in 1976 a working paper was issued by the papal commission *Iustitia et Pax* on "The Church and Human Rights." Unfortunately, there has, as yet, been no joint Christian declaration on this topic.

If I am right, only the declaration of the World Alliance of Reformed Churches has taken up a stance on the problems facing us today with regard to human rights and the rights of nature, although the Alliance, too, has failed to expand the actual framework in which human rights have to stand if they are really to be universal and supportive of life.

I now attempt a systematic survey, seeing human rights as a spiral that presses in the direction of universality, one group of human rights pointing forward to the next:

(1) no individual human rights without social rights

(2) no human rights without humanity's right to protection from mass annihilation and genetic change, and the right to survive in the succession of the generations

(3) no economic human rights without ecological duties toward the rights of nature

(4) no human rights without the rights of the earth

Individual and Social Human Rights

"We hold these truths to be self-evident, that all men are created equal, that they are endowed by their Creator with certain inalienable rights," says the U.S. Declaration of Independence. If this means all human beings, irrespective of sex, race, religion, health, etc., then it means every single person. Every human being is a person, and as a person is equipped with "inalienable rights." The U.S. Constitution and the constitutions of the French Revolution, with their maxims about the liberty and equality of all human beings, also, of course, already posed the fundamental problems of modern constitutional states: how to mediate between individual rights to liberty and the protective rights of society in the sphere of social security and economic provision. This is where the political conflict between the liberal democracies and socialism arises.

In the "prophetic" religions, Judaism, Christianity, and Islam, the liberty and equality of all human beings is based on belief in creation, about which the U.S. Declaration of Independence also speaks. Human beings—all human beings, every human being—enjoy their dignity because they are made in the image of God.[5] Men and women are intended to live in this relation to God. It gives their existence its inalienable transcendent dimension of depth. In the relationship to the transcendent God, people become persons whose dignity must not be infringed. In claiming to be human institutions, the institutions of the law, the state, and industry become duty bound to respect this personal dignity of all human beings. They would destroy themselves if they were to treat human beings as objects, things, marketable goods, underdogs, or working tools. They would lose their legitimation.

In the lordship myths of many peoples, it is only the ruler who is venerated as "God's image on earth," "the Son of Heaven," and "the Son of God." The ruler is "the shadow of God and human beings are the shadow of the ruler," says the Babylonian rulers' code. However, according to Jewish, Christian, and Islamic faith in creation, it is not any ruler who is created as God's image on earth. It is the human being—all human beings and every human being. This means that all men and women are kings or queens, and that no one must dominate anyone else. The *Sachsenspiegel*, or "Saxon Mirror" (a thirteenth-century private codification of laws) already said this (*Landrecht* Book 3, Art. 42): "God has created and formed human beings in his own image and has redeemed them through his own anguish, the one like the other . . . According to my view," says the author, "I am unable to understand why anyone should be [the property] of another."

In the political history of Europe, belief that everyone was created in the image of God, and respect for the liberty and equality of all, led to the democratization (in principle) of all rule exercised by one human being over others. Every exercise of power has to be legitimated toward other human beings. Ruler and ruled must at all times together and to the same degree be recognizably "human beings." This means that all citizens are equal before the law, to which even rulers are subject. A democratic way of arriving at political decisions, the temporal limitation of the commission to rule, the control of rule through the separation of powers and through popular representation, the binding of government to the constitutional charge and, not least, a large measure of popular self-determination and communal self-administration: all these things have become political ways of respecting the fact that every human being is created in God's image and that all human beings enjoy a common dignity.

However, the movement for freedom in European and North American history was one-sided in stressing only individual rights over against political rule, and neglecting people's rights to social equality and their economic security. It was the fault of Western liberalism to overlook the social dimension of liberty, which is to be found in the solidarity of human beings with one another. This was also an error in religious history in the West, from Augustine onward; it is not the individual, bodiless soul that is God's image; it is the human being together with other human beings, because God created human beings "male and female," according to the biblical story of creation.

Although individual and social rights have different intellectual roots and have still never been gathered together in a single document, individual and social rights belong logically together, and whenever they are implemented they involve one another. Human sociality has, in principle, the same dignity as human personhood. The person is not there "before" the community, nor is the community "before" the person. Persons and communities necessitate and condition one another mutually, and complement one another, in the same way as human individuation and socialization. Consequently, no preference can in principle be given to individual rather than to social rights, although this is always what is assumed in the Western world. The rights of persons can be realized only in a just society, and a just society can be realized only on the basis of personal rights. The freedom of persons can be developed only in a free society, and a free society grows up only out of the freedom of persons. There can be no "free choice of work" without "a right to work." The "right to work" presupposes "the free choice of work," if human beings are to live as free men and women.

It is pointless and absurd when the democratic West and the socialist East bewail the violation of individual rights on the one hand or the infringement of social rights on the other. It is much better for both sides, and more helpful for humanity generally, if the two sides learn from one another and find a balance between their ideas about the freedom and equality of human beings.

Human Rights and the Rights of the Human Race

Human rights have hitherto been formulated only in the context of persons and societies, but not yet with a view to humanity itself, although the concept "human being" logically includes the concept "humanity." Has humanity as a whole rights and duties too? This has not been very much thought about, because people always presupposed that the life and existence of humanity was a matter of course—divinely willed and a fact of nature.

However, ever since 1945, with Hiroshima, it has become increasingly evident that the human race is mortal and that its time has a time-limit. This has been made clear through the super powers' commitment to the nuclear deterrent system, and through the production of chemical and biological means of mass annihilation. Humanity's very existence is under deadly threat through the "crimes against humanity," which are possible at any time through the unleashing of wars with atomic, biological, and chemical weapons.[6] Yet, humanity should survive and wants to survive. This fundamental affirmation of human life is implied in every declaration on human rights. It is now time for us also to formulate and recognize publicly humanity's right to existence and survival, for this is something human beings can deny. There are even specific situations in which the rights of humanity have unconditional priority over the particular rights of certain classes, races, and religion, and when all special interests, however justifiable they may be, have to be subordinated to humanity's right to exist. Even the "class struggle" as a way of bringing about the liberation of the oppressed makes sense only if it belongs within the framework of the survival of humanity.[7] Even the absolutist claim of particular human religions must be subordinated to the right of humanity to exist and to survive, because that claim could otherwise lead to the suicide of the human race.

Because the threat to humanity proceeds from the power of the state, which is in possession of atomic, biological, and chemical weapons, the limitations of state power must be more closely defined in the context of humanity as a whole. To threaten potential enemies with the methods of mass annihilation that can lead to the extinction of the human race goes beyond the right of any country that claims to be "humane." The different countries do not merely have a duty toward their own citizens. They have a duty toward humanity as a whole, as well. They do not merely have to respect the human rights of their own citizens. They have to respect the rights of the citizens of other countries, too, for human rights are indivisible. National foreign policies based on rivalry with other countries and systems must give way to a "worldwide domestic policy," which is committed to the survival of humanity, a policy that will serve the mutual promotion of life and the security of all. This means that international human solidarity in the ending of mutual threats has to take priority over loyalty toward our own nation, race, class, or religion. Individual states and communities of states have human duties toward the right of the human race to live and survive.

If human dignity forbids us to infringe anyone's "quality as determining subject" or to destroy it permanently, this applies not merely to individuals but also to coming generations and the human race as a whole. Modern genetic engineering and the new reproduction medicine have made it possible not only to cure hereditary diseases, but actually to breed different human beings through eugenics.[8] Prenatal diagnostics enable the evolution through selection of new human generations. Manipulations of the germ cells can fundamentally alter the genome of the human race. Of course, therapeutic interventions are permissible as long as they conduce to healing. But manipulations designed to breed living things that lack the human quality of being "determining subjects," and manipulations designed to breed so-called supermen, destroy the essence of human beings and, therefore, human dignity as well. If by protecting human dignity, the state has also taken on the duty of protecting every human life, then it has the additional duty of protecting the humanity of human life in this and coming generations; otherwise, it would lose its legitimation. The "optimizing" genetic intervention in the species human being (or whatever name may be given to "advantageous" genetic interference with the human species) belongs just as much to the new category of crimes against humanity as the annihilation of what are supposed to be the "unfit" and the destruction of races declared to be inferior. There is a new racist application of evolutionary theory and eugenics to the future of the human race that annihilates its dignity and humanity. The genetic self-destruction of humanity is a new and increasing danger, which stands side by side with the continuing nuclear threat.

"Humanity" is not merely made up of all the people living in the cross section of any single time. It also means people in the longitudinal section of all the times, in the sequence of human generations. At any single time in any single area, there are always different generations living together and looking after one another: parents caring for their children, the young for the old. Because the human race exists in the temporal sequence of the generations, up to now a natural "contract between generations" has ensured the survival of the human race—a contract that, because it is natural, was considered a matter of course. The law of inheritance conferred a degree of justice between the generations, so that there came to be a certain equalization of the chances in life enjoyed by those living earlier and those living later. Today, this unwritten contract between generations is threatening to break down, and this breakdown can have deadly consequences for the human race. In the industrial nations, we are in process of using up in a single generation the greater part of the nonregenerative sources of energy (oil, coal, wood, and so forth), and in our public budgets, we are leaving the generations to come horrific mountains of debt they will one day have to pay off. We are using up the profits of industrial production in our own time and are pushing off the costs on to times in the future. We are producing huge rubbish dumps coming generations will have to dispose of, although we know quite well that it is very difficult to dispose of chemical waste, and nuclear waste cannot be disposed of at all, but will have to be kept under surveillance until the year 3000 or 10,000, according to the decay time of the material.[9]

However, the human race can survive only if the contract between generations creates justice between the generations in which humanity exists in time. Because today the contract can be irrevocably broken, it must be formulated and publicly codified. In our present situation, we have to pay particular attention to the rights of children and the right to live of coming generations, because children are the weakest links in the generation chain, while coming generations have as yet no voice at all and are, therefore, the first victims of the collective egoism of generations today.

Economic Rights and Ecological Duties

Human dignity also means actually being able to lead a life of human dignity. This involves certain minimum presuppositions, socially and economically—protection from hunger and sickness, for example, and the right to work and to personal property. Recently, the protection of the natural environment has also come to be counted among the minimum guarantees of personal human dignity. We can think about and develop economic rights and political rights to liberty in an analogous way. In the political sphere, it contravenes the dignity of human beings to be made mere objects of state power; and in the same way, it is inconsistent with human dignity if people are degraded economically to mere working tools and pure purchasing power. If they are to live out their "quality as determining subjects" in the economic sector, too, human beings must be given a just share in work, property, food, protection, and social security. The concentration of capital goods and other means of production, as well as foodstuffs, in the hands of a few, and the suppression and exploitation of the many, is a severe violation of human dignity. A worldwide economic situation that allows millions to die of hunger is unworthy of humanity and is, in Christian terms, an infringement of God's glory, which is to be found in human beings, as his image.

If it is all human beings, not any special races or classes, who enjoy the dignity of being created in God's image, so that they are "free and equal," this must lead to a democratization of economic life that will correspond to political democratization. The trade union movements and workers' rights to codetermination in factories and commercial enterprises are steps in this direction. However, the worldwide democratization of economic life is proving particularly difficult, because here the interests of capital are in alliance with the interests of the nations of the First World. Yet, it can be shown that unless there is more justice through a democratization of the worldwide economy, there is going to be an economic and ecological catastrophe for humanity generally, because the growing exploitation and indebtedness of countries in the Third World is compelling people there to cut down their rain forests and to exploit their fields and pastures until they turn into dust bowls and deserts, and this means destroying large areas of what provides the foundation for the life of humanity as a whole.

The fundamental economic rights of each and every human being are bound up with particular fundamental ecological duties. The body of basic economic rights cannot be increased *ad infinitum*, in the wake of a rapidly increasing population and the growing demands of particular nations, because, as everyone knows, ecological limits are set to economic growth on this earth. The human struggle to survive cannot be pursued at nature's expense, because the ecological collapse of nature would mean the end of all human life on earth. Economic rights must, therefore, be harmonized with the cosmic conditions of the nature of the earth where human beings live and increase. This means that ecological justice between human civilization and nature must match economic justice between the people in a society, between human societies, and between the generations of the human race. However, up to now, the only correspondences have been ecological and economic injustice: the exploitation of human workers was precisely matched by the exploitation of natural resources. The exploitative relationship of human beings to nature will cease only when the exploitative relationship of human beings to one another ends and is reversed. This is not merely a moral judgment. It is a counsel of wisdom as well, for today the technical means of exploitation have been increased to the point when they can totally destroy the natural foundations of human life. It is, therefore, stupid for the sake of short-term profits to annihilate the foundations on which one's own life is based in the long run—stupid because suicidal.

Many people, therefore, see the protection of nature from destruction by human beings as being one of the minimum guarantees of individual human dignity. However, then we can speak only of the individual's right to an unharmed environment, in the way that we can talk about the individual's right to freedom from bodily harm. In this case, nature is perceived only as "environment," existing for the sake of human beings themselves. However, this viewpoint is sufficient to preserve nature from the aggression of human beings. Nature must be protected from human beings for her own sake, which means for the sake of her own dignity. The very same modern anthropocentrism is inherent in earlier formulations of human rights and human dignity has also led to the narrow and dangerous view of nature as "human environment." The protection of nature with its plant and animal species, the protection of the conditions of life on earth, and the protection of earth's equilibriums must be assigned a status in modern state constitutions and international agreements that corresponds to the status assigned to human dignity.[10] Does nature, and do other living things, have a dignity analogous to the dignity of human beings?

The Rights of the Earth and the Dignity of Its Living Communities

If the world is seen merely under the aspects of private law, it evidently consists only of "persons" and "things," just as, according to the modern view of the world (held since Descartes), there are only subjects and objects. Are animals really only "things" in relation to the human persons who can possess and use them? Are they not living beings, capable of feeling pain, and human beings' fellow creatures? Do they not, then, have rights of their own and a certain subjectivity human beings should respect?

Ever since the beginning of modern Western civilization, we have become accustomed to viewing nature as the environment *for us*; it is related to ourselves. We look at all other natural beings with an eye solely to their utility value. Only human beings are there "for their own sake." Everything else is supposed to be there "for the sake of human beings." This modern anthropocentrism has robbed nature of its soul and made human beings unembodied subjects. Premodern views of the world, the views held in antiquity, saw the whole world as "ensouled." Aristotle still talked about the soul of plants, the soul of animals and the soul of human beings, as well as the soul of the world, all these souls being differentiated and yet related, in a single complex. The Old Testament talks the same language (Gen. 1.30; Isa. 11). Postmodern views of the world, on the other hand, assume that human beings are a unity of body and soul, their bodily needs and the relations to other natural living things prompting the development of the notion of a cosmic community, of which human beings are an integral part.

Both these attitudes indicate that the modern cleavage between person and thing, subject and object, does justice neither to the natural community or symbiosis in which and from which human beings live on earth, nor to the bodily existence of human beings themselves. If this cleavage is rigorously forced through with modern methods, nature's symbioses will be destroyed and human bodilyness with them. Ultimately speaking, modern anthropocentrism is deadly for human beings themselves.[11] Of course, we can hardly go back to the cosmocentrism of ancient times in the way we see the world and life, even if some modern thinkers see this as a way out of the deadlocks of the modern world, because anthropocentrism is the very basis of modern industrial society; whereas, cosmocentrism was the foundation of the agrarian society of the preindustrial age. However, modern anthropocentrism can be fitted into the conditions for life on earth and into the symbiosis, or community, of all living things in a way that is not a nostalgic and "alternative" flight from industrial society, but which will reform it until it becomes ecologically endurable for the earth, and is integrated into the early fellowship of the living.

However, a community of life shared with all other living beings on this earth will remain a dream if it is not realized in a community of all the living based on law. An earthly community of this kind would have to open the human community based on law for the rights of other living things and the rights of the earth, fitting the human community into the universal laws of life which apply to the whole earth. This means respecting the earth, plants, and animals for themselves, before weighing up their utility value for human beings. Just as human dignity provides the source for human rights, so the dignity of creation is the source of the natural rights of other living things and the earth. A general declaration on animal rights that corresponds to the General Declaration of Human Rights of 1948, harmonizes with it and, where necessary, corrects it, ought to be part of modern state constitutions and international agreements. A draft of a declaration of this kind has existed since 1977.[12]

An animal is not a person in the human sense, but it is not a "thing" or a product either. It is a living being, with rights of its own, and it needs the protection of public law. Respect for this fact means putting an end to industrial, hormone-controlled meat production, and going over to a way of keeping animals that will be in accordance with the requirements of their species. It will also mean reducing as far as possible the millions of animals used in animal experimentation and replacing them by other techniques, such as simulators. In the United States, at least 17 million animals are "expended" in laboratory experiments every year; in Europe, one million were used in the chemical center in Basel alone. More and more people are quite rightly asking: "Do the practical benefits of animal experimentation outweigh the moral costs?" (*Newsweek*, 16 January 1989). The moral costs are undoubtedly evident in the growing indifference toward other life, whether it be animals, embryos, or other people, an indifference the backlash of which is inescapably felt in our own lives. In view of the deadlocks of the industrial societies, with their hostility to nature, we must rediscover the position and role of human beings in the warp and weft of life on earth, and go on to make human rights part of the wider, comprehensive rights of nature, if we want to survive.

As I see it, this requirement is self-evident. However, it poses a serious question to the religions that have provided the foundations for modern Western civilization. Has the Jewish and Christian tradition not conceded human beings God-like privileges towards all other living things ever since the biblical accounts of creation? Are not human beings alone God's image on earth, and destined to rule over the earth and its other living things? Did this anthropology not provide the basis for developing human rights, especially in the West? This is, indeed, the way we have to see the matter, for this is what has been maintained for centuries by churches and theologians. Yet, it is not the whole truth, because the special destiny of human beings applies only *within* the community of all creatures, which they are intended to respect, as Psalm 104 makes clear. We can talk about the special dignity of human beings on the presupposition that the dignity of all other beings as creatures is recognized—not otherwise. As images of the Creator, human beings love all their fellow-creatures with the Creator's love. If they do not, they are not the image of the Creator and Lover of the living. They are his caricature. That is why the special rights to life and existence enjoyed by human beings are valid only as long as these human beings respect the rights of the earth and other living things.

According to the biblical traditions, there is a community based on law that goes beyond the human community of law—a community of the earth and human beings rooted in the special rights of God the Creator to what he has created. We find this in the enactments about the sabbath: the weekly sabbaths and the regular sabbatical years are given to human beings and the animals belonging to the human household. But "the sabbath of the earth" is assigned a special, emphasized importance (Lev. 25 and 26). According to Ex. 23, Israel is to leave the land uncultivated every seventh year, and is not to harvest it "so that the poor of your people may eat." According to Lev. 25, an ecological purpose is added to this social one. "So that the land may keep its great sabbath to the Lord." In the seventh year, the earth is to lie fallow, so it can renew itself. This is the earth's right. The person who keeps "the sabbath of the earth" will live in peace, but anyone who disregards it will be visited by drought and hunger for having destroyed the earth's fertility. According to the ancient biblical story, God gives Israel up to Babylonian captivity for seventy years "until the land—God's earth— had enjoyed its sabbaths" (II Chron. 36.20f.). Today, the earth's right to regeneration is largely disregarded. Chemical fertilizers and pesticides force the earth into a permanent, unnatural fertility. Irreversible erosion is the consequence, and human famines become unavoidable. Anyone who disregards the rights of the earth is mortally threatening coming generations and the survival of humanity.

The World Religions in the Forum of Human Rights[13]

Because present life and the future survival of humanity depend on the observance of human rights, the rights of humanity and the rights of nature, the world religions will also have to subordinate themselves to the world's preservation. In all the different religions, there is nothing higher than truth. Today, the religions will really only become "world" religions when they begin to integrate themselves into the conditions of life and the growing community of law of this single world, and are prepared to surrender their particularist claims to absoluteness in favor of universalism. The religions must learn to respect religious liberty as a human right, and in this framework, to behave tolerantly toward one another and to be ready for dialogue. This also means that they have to subordinate their own legal codes—the Torah and the Sermon on the Mount, the laws of the church and the Shari'a, the ethics of Hinduism and Confucianism, and so forth—to the minimum demands of the rights of men and women, humanity and nature. If contradictions were to be maintained, this would make the religious communities the enemies of the human race.

On the other hand, the further development of the rights of men and women and of humanity is dependent on creative contributions by the various religious world views. Up to now, formulations of human rights have been based on the tradition of modern Western humanism, which in turn grew up in the context of the Jewish–Christian religion. As we have seen, this culture is strongly anthropocentric in emphasis. Judaism, Christianity, and Islam have, therefore, been called "historical religions" over against the Asian and African "nature religions." It is true that they are concerned with human hope and historical progress whereas the nature religions cultivate the wisdom of equilibrium and adjustment. They have, therefore, also been called "prophetic religions" and "book religions," compared with the directly sensory spirituality of the Indian and Chinese religions, which have close ties with nature. However we may describe these very general differences, where the ecological problem of modern society is concerned, the balance between progress and equilibrium, the harmony between human history and nature, and the unity of person and nature are of vital importance. Today, the inter-religious dialogue will have to direct its attention toward these vital human questions if it is to be of practical value for both the Western and the Eastern religions, and for humanity.

Translated by Margaret Kohl

NOTES

1. Cf. J. Moltmann, *Creating a Just Future*, London and Philadelphia 1989. Also L. S. Rouner (ed.), *Human Rights and the World's Religions*, Boston University Studies in Philosophy and Religion IX, Notre Dame, Ind. 1988.

2. Cf. W. Heidelmeyer (ed.), *Die Menschenrechte. Erklärungen, Verfassungsartikel, Internationale Abkommen*, Paderborn 1972.

3. Cf. W. Huber and H. E. Tödt, *Menschenrechte Perspektiven einer menschlichen Welt*, Stuttgart 1977; J. M. Lochman (ed.), *Gottes Recht und Menschenrechte Studien und Empfehlungen des Reformierten Weltbundes*, Neukirchen 1976; text and preparatory papers in A. O. Miller (ed.), *A Christian Declaration on Human Rights*, Grand Rapids 1977.

4. The modern concept of "human dignity" comes from Renaissance humanism. Cf. Pico de la Mirandola, *Oratio de dignitate hominis* (1486), Zürich 1988. It is linked with the anthropocentrism of modern anthropology: "I have set thee at the center of the world . . ." (10) However, as long as the special dignity of human beings is defined by separating them from animals and by excluding other living things, the concept serves human domination over nature and becomes the energy of life. This anthropocentrism, which is so hostile to nature, can be overcome only if human dignity is theologically defined: it is based on the fact that men and women are the image of God. It then stems from the relationship in which God puts himself to human beings, and can do without demarcations and exclusions.

5. On the *imago Dei* doctrine cf. L. Scheffczyk (ed.), *Der Mensch als Bild Gottes*, Wege der Forschung CXXIV, Darmstadt 1969; J. Moltmann, *God in Creation*, London and New York 1985, Chap. IX, "God's Image in Creation: Human Beings," 215ff.

6. As far as I am aware, it was the Assembly of the World Council of Churches in Vancouver in 1983 that first talked about "crimes against humanity," meaning crimes against the whole human race.

7. M. Gorbachev, *For the Sake of Preserving Human Civilization*, Moscow 1987. Lenin already said that "Situations may arise in which the concern of

the whole of mankind has to be given precedence before the class interests of the proletariat."

8. This is recommended by P. Singer, *Practical Ethics*, Cambridge 1979. For a contrary view cf. C. Altner, *Leben auf. Bestellung? Das gefäahrliche Dilemma der Gentechnologie*, Freiburg 1988.

9. Cf. *Our Common Future. The Brundtland Report of the World Commission on Environment and Development*, London 1987. On the question of the contract between generations, cf. P. Saladin and C. A. Zenger, *Rechte künftiger Generationen*, Basel 1988.

10. G. M. Teutsch, *Lexikon der Umweltehik*, Göttingen 1985.

11. A. Auer, *Umweltpolitik. Ein theologischer Beitrag zur ökologischen Diskussion*, Düsseldorf 1984, however, believes that it is possible to maintain an anthropocentrism that is ecologically tolerable (203ff.). The alternative is not a cosmocentrism such as K. M. Meyer-Abich recommends in *Wege zum Frieden mit der Natur. Praktische Naturphilosophie für die Unweltpolitik*, Munich 1986. The answer is rather to decentralize human culture and to incorporate it harmoniously into a single web with nature.

12. The German law on the protection of animals in the version of 18 August 1986 (BGBL I 1320) introduces the concept of the "fellow-creature": "The purpose of this law is to protect the life and well-being of animals out of human responsibility for the animal as a fellow-creature. No one is permitted to cause an animal pain, suffering, or damage without reasonable grounds." Cf. A. Lorz, *Tierschutzgesetz, Kommentar,* Munich[3] 1987. This presupposes the theological framework of Creator, creature, and fellow-creature in a community of creation, and is probably unprecedented in a secular statute.

13. Cf. L. S. Rouner (ed.), *Human Rights and the World's Religions* (n. 1).

21

Fundamentalism and Modernity

In the title, we have described fundamentalism as an "ecumenical challenge." The answers from the various religions, which we have collected in this issue only partly justify this theme, because religions or religious movements others regard as fundamentalist often do not understand themselves in this way. Fundamentalism arose in nineteenth-century American Protestantism as a reaction to Protestant liberalism and is, therefore, a well-known and worldwide problem in Protestantism. The mere transference of the term to Catholic traditionalism and its late antimodernism lessen the term's expressive power, because this is a different religious tradition, albeit in the same cultural sphere. If we speak of fundamentalism in the Orthodox church, the terminology becomes even more unclear, because one can discover comparable phenomena only with the aid of analogies. At any rate, there is the same Christian foundation, and even Orthodoxy must come to terms with a culture which is called "modern." The transference of the designation fundamentalism to other religions of the book makes the term completely uncertain and vague. However, the old Protestant expression has long since become a sociological and psychological category in everyday speech, used in an attempt to understand comparable movements from otherwise incomparable religions and world-views. Therefore, we must accept the emigration and extension of the word *fundamentalism* from its Protestant origin as it has taken place. We cannot reverse history here.

What is nowadays thus termed fundamentalism is a secondary phenomenon: the primary religious, interreligious and a-religious challenge is not fundamentalism but the modern world. Fundamentalism seems to be a typically religious reaction to the challenges of the modern world, but not itself to be a challenge. That raises the following questions.

Is fundamentalism an antimodern phenomenon, or in being antimodern, is it a modern phenomenon? What is the difference between modernism and fundamentalism, and where are they similar or do they stand on the same basis? How does fundamentalism view the modern world and how does the modern world view fundamentalism? Is fundamentalism part of what Adorno and Horkheimer call the "dialectic of the Enlightenment" and its internal contradictions, or does it point to the world of postmodernity? Can the modern world get rid of fundamentalism? Is it nothing but what Martin Marty has called obstinate "oppositionalism" or is it preserving in a desperate way a trust in the earth and time that is being ideologically and technologically destroyed by modernity, as G. Müller-Fahrenholz argues?

Fundamentalism in Conflict with the Modern World

The original fundamentalism did not challenge the principles of the modern world independently and directly, but always only their influences on its own faith community. Therefore, the picture that fundamentalists have of the "modern world" can only be discovered indirectly from their polemic against liberalism, secularism, and modernism. Fundamentalists do not react to the crises of the modern world but to the crises the modern world produces in their faith community and their basic certainties.

The certainty of faith is based on the firm foundation of divine authority. In the "religions of the book," this is the divine authority of the primal document of revelation: like God himself, God's word is free of error and infallible. For Protestant fundamentalists, this was and is the Bible; for Muslim fundamentalists the Qur'an is "an unfalsified, pure, divine revelation which is exalted above all errors" (Elshahed). The historical and empirical sciences of the modern world are acknowledged to the degree that they coincide with Bible or Qur'an, but rejected to the degree that they put this timeless authority in question. Creationists who reject the theory of evolution have founded their own "scientific" institute to demonstrate scientifically that the world was created 6000 years ago. That shows that no blind antimodernism nor even any mere "oppositionalism" predominates here. Rather, fundamentalists are concerned with the infallible and unqualified rule of their "fundamentals" over scientific methods and results. Only in cases of conflict is it said that the white wall is black if the divine authority claims this to be so, or that Jesus cannot have had any brothers and sisters because the dogma of his ever-virgin mother rules this out. For Muslims, too, its unfalsified purity and freedom from error is the basis for the "universal claim" of the Qur'an, not just over all human beings but also over all realms of life. Therefore, Elshahed says that the commandments and prohibitions of the Qur'an have a "rational basis," without giving rational evidence, because this is not a question of accord with autonomous human reason, but rather the total claim of the Qur'anic revelation over human reason. The primal document of divine revelation cannot be subjected to human exegesis, but conversely, human exegesis must be subjected to the primal document of divine revelation. Fundamentalism excludes any rational insight into the historical conditioning of its origin and its hermeneutical difference from the changed historical conditions of the present. The content of truth in the primal document of revelation is timeless and need not constantly be interpreted and presented anew, but simply preserved unfalsified. A fundamentalism of revelation does not argue, but asserts. It does not call for insight, but subjection. It is not concerned with a hermeneutical problem but with a power struggle: either God's Word or the "spirit of the age." Nor is fundamentalism any retreat or defensive phenomenon, but an attack on the modern world in order to conquer it. It fits into the various contemporary theopolitical strategies for the "re-evangelization" of Europe or the "re-Islamicization" of the Arab world. It is clear that even the most serious mistakes of scientific technological civilization do not justify any surrender of human reason and its rational insights. This faith in authority is not just irrational but also antirational.

The great enemy of any fundamentalism is called liberalism/pluralism. What is meant is the rise of modern human subjectivity and its individual freedoms: freedom of faith, freedom of conscience, and freedom of religion. These individual freedoms from religious ties became the foundation of the modern democracies in the fight for human rights and civil rights. No free world without religious freedom. By "freedom of religion" is not meant the corporate rights of the various religious communities, but the individual right of persons "to worship in the church of your choice," i.e., the right to make one's own decision over faith and the right to change this decision, the right to individual entry into and departure from religious communities. Whether a religious community recognizes "freedom of religion" is always demonstrated by the way in which it deals with its dissidents and apostates. The individual freedoms of modern human subjectivity are a foundation of the modern world. Science, technology, transport, and culture are dependent on them. If they are disputed or abandoned, then this modern civilization is destroyed. However, these freedoms not only enrich but are felt by many people to go too far and to be a burden. Such people find it difficult to make their own independent decisions on religious and ethical questions. So, not only in politics but presumably even more strongly in religion, there is the "escape from freedom," the term used by Erich Fromm in his description of the "authoritarian personality," above all of Germans. The escape from freedom makes possible dictatorships of religious welfare and disseminates the fundamentalist "certainties" of a religious kindergarten mentality. Through the "escape from freedom," one's own decision is handed over to a higher authority and, thus, freedom from responsibility is purchased. However, there is no authority that can decide for a person what this person has to be personally responsible for. The extension of fundamentalist lack of responsibility at a time of growing risks from human power heightens these risks and is itself one of their sources.

In Christianity, individual coming of age in religion led to the secularization of the state, education, and the sciences. Religion was no longer regarded as an affair of the state—*cuius regio, eius reliigio*—but as a "private matter." Protestantism encouraged this secularization most because it was the first to stand up for the individual human freedoms I have mentioned. Therefore, it also experienced the first reactions, in pietism and later in fundamentalism. Catholicism was confronted with secularization only as a result of the French Revolution. It reacted with restoration, antimodernism, and most recently the Lefebvre movement. In the Islamic world, Turkey under Kemal Ataturk adopted Western secularization and the separation of religion and politics. However, the fundamentalist movements are re-Islamicizing politics, schools, and culture, in order to restore the totalitarianism of the Qur'an: "According to the Islamic view of the world, public and private life cannot be separated and thus secularized" (Elshahed). Common to all these fundamentalist reactions to the modern secularization of culture is the attempt to restore the unitary religious state, whether this is the "Christian West," "the first nation under God," or the "Islamic state," and to do so by religious imperialism, because these unitary religious states have a missionary and messianic foundation. But that creates political religions that provide religious motivations for political and military decisions to make them absolute and free of doubt.

Permanent modernization is of the essence of the modern world. Since its beginnings, development, progress, innovation, and a linear orientation on the future have been built into the macroproject of scientific technological civilization. However, that requires that supposed certainties will constantly be made uncertain and traditional identities given up. Elshahed passes a typically fundamentalist verdict: "Wherever Western modernity gets a footing, human beings lose their identity, culture, values, and norms. Material values take the place of morality and social coherence." Jerry Falwell of the "moral majority" or Archbishop Lefebvre would put it in just the same way. The capacity to appropriate the past and turn it into something new (cf. G. Müller-Fahrenholz) is blocked off as "modernist." How can this development best be brought about? By understanding time in terms of apocalyptic catastrophes and by the expectation of an imminent end to the world. If the end of the world is to be expected in this generation, belief in progress and a concern for innovation are absurd. Improvements in the situation of the world and investment in the future only delay the end, which is coming anyway, and must come in order to destroy the perverse modern world system and rescue the fundamentalists who resist it. The result is the apocalyptic fatalism of the masses on the one hand and neoliberalism in economics on the other: short-term profits, the incurring of debts and no investments. "After us the flood." Fundamentalism can also make itself a factor in ending "this world," in the apocalyptic Armageddon politics of amassing nuclear armaments for the "last battle," as under President Ronald Reagan in the U.S.A., or in Saddam Hussein's rhetoric of the final battle, when he attempted to talk into existence "the mother of all battles" in Kuwait. The heightening of the friend–foe relationship in the horrific modern world to a final apocalyptic battle between Christ and the Antichrist or between the true Islam and the "Satan" U.S.A., the West, apostasy and blasphemy, are part of the phenomenon of modern fundamentalism. Fundamentalism is, in fact, supposed and claimed to be an "experience of the end of the world" (G. Müller-Fahrenholz). However, what we have here are not just apocalyptically exaggerated anxieties but a perverse wish for death and a macabre will for the end. Nothing is so disastrous as the expectation of disaster. Anxiety about catastrophes brings on catastrophes, because it anticipates catastrophe and does not prevent it.

If we attempt to bring these four dimensions of fundamentalism under a single heading, we can say that fundamentalist identity is an identity that has been threatened, made anxious and uncertain, and, therefore, reacts aggressively. It is an identity that is uncertain of itself, but defines itself by delineating and denying real or supposed enemies. For a long time Christian and Islamic fundamentalism were anti-Communist. The worst thing that can happen to such a negative identity is the loss of the "enemy" over against which one has defined oneself. So, since the collapse of Soviet Marxism, anti-Communist fundamentalism has found itself in deep crisis over its orientation. Who is the enemy now? Because these people cannot define themselves without an enemy, the "enemy" has to be found. For some, it is the liberalism and materialism of the "Western world," for others the economic supremacy of Japan; and for both, with some probability, whether in Islam or in Christianity. Only when the need for an enemy as part of self-discovery ends can there be peace and mutual recognition between the religions, and especially between Christianity and Islam.

Fundamentalism in the Contradictions of the Modern World

The certainty of victory for the belief in progress, the expectation of soon being able to overcome unmodern fundamentalism, has been lost in the increasingly manifest contradictions of the modern world. Fundamentalism is finding more of an echo and more adherents, above all in the modern world. Why? The catastrophes of the modern world are showing many people that something is wrong with this world itself. After two world wars, after Hiroshima and Chernobyl, after increasing destruction of the environment and growing impoverishment of the masses in the submodern Third World, it makes sense to take fundamentalism seriously, not only as "oppositionalism" but also in its unique categories.

Over against the linear conceptions of time characteristic of the belief in progress, fundamentalism puts the whole of life in the category of eternity and investigates the "timeless truths" of faith and the "absolute commandments" of morality. In so doing, it sets itself diametrically against any time that is lost and to be gained. Its own apocalyptic corresponds only to the end of time the West's technological and military belief in progress has brought about, whether in a possible nuclear inferno or in the ecological destruction of the world. The great alternative to belief in progress and anxiety about apocalyptic catastrophes is the category of eternity, which relativizes the difference in times modernism has made absolute. The modern pressure toward contemporaneity also becomes relative in the category of eternity. Its place is taken by "absolute values," which must be put forward unconditioned and unconditionally. Not least in the category of eternity, the hermeneutical differences over the book of revelation become unimportant, because less attention is paid to the nature of the witness than to the content of what is witnessed to. Before the self-revelation of God there is only one time: the present. One can call this position precritical, but one can also argue that it is postcritical, a position Karl Barth advocated particularly impressively. In the category of eternity, neither the time of the book of revelation is made absolute, as tends to happen with fundamentalists, nor one's own present, as tends to happen with historical relativists. In the category of eternity, the different ties become "contemporaneous," as Kierkegaard put it. That does not exclude historical-critical research but presupposes it; however, it distinguishes the hermeneutical mediation between times from the mediation of eternity in time.

The modern world presupposes the free responsibility of a subject come of age. But who in the modern world can achieve such subjectivity? Only the educated middle class that has arrived, not the poor, uneducated people. The modern world is not a universe but a divided and split world. The First World has produced the Third World, in which the masses are not treated as subjects and persons, but as objects and what Gustavo Gutiérrez has called "unpersons." In this submodernity today a "fundamentalism of the poor" is coming into being, spontaneously and without organization, through the rapid expansion of charismatic groups and Pentecostalist movements. Experiences of the Spirit and a fundamentalist orientation on the Bible are turning passive objects into subjects and communicating a sense of personal worth to "unpersons." The Bible is the Word of God, and all who read it and can hear have direct access to God without the supervision of church, state, and the educated classes. There is also this "fundamentalism of the poor" in the rich class societies of the First World.

Finally, the secularization of culture and the privatization of faith have manifestly silenced faith and left culture to other forces. We need not want to return to unitary and totalitarian religious states, simply because we lament the lack of religious ties in modern society. Liberation theologians and political theologians also want the return of faith to politics: not, however, by the standards of the Christian empire but by those of the Sermon on the Mount. Fundamentalist millennial politics and political theology as discipleship of Christ can both be found today in politics, but unfortunately usually on opposite sides of demonstrations. If fundamentalists are fighting for the reintroduction of school prayers and penalties for abortion, liberation theologians are fighting for the ending of exploitation and the overcoming of premature deaths among the poor from famine. If charismatic fundamentalists stress miraculous healings of the sick, political theologians stress the liberation of the oppressed from violence. Common to both is a concern to be politically active as a result of their faith, and a recognition of the material components of salvation and its relevance for this world. Even where the two fight each other, there are striking parallels. On the left wing of the evangelicals and the socially involved Pentecostalists, there is already a series of new alliances with liberation theologians and political theologians: in Latin America in the popular movement, in Europe in the peace movement. Opposition to the contradictions of the modern world unites them.

We shall have to live with fundamentalism—against us, alongside us, and even in us. The liberation of fundamentalists for openness to the future of God and the world remains a task for theology and the church.

Translated by John Bowden

22

End of Utopia—End of History?

Since the undramatic, banal collapse of socialism in the former Eastern bloc in 1989/1990 one has been able to read something in any of the better newspapers about "the end of utopia." Both old conservatives and neoconservatives are thus triumphing over their opponents of the Left.

In 1991 Joachim Fest, the editor of the famous German newspaper *Frankfurter Allgemeine Zeitung,* wrote a book on this new trend in Germany entitled *A Dream Destroyed: The End of the Utopian Era.* It began with the astonishing assertion that with the "end of socialism" not only this one utopia but all utopias generally had "died the death," and, therefore, people had to live "in the future without the great tam-tam of utopias." The "price of modernity" is now said to be "life without utopia." If one asks in amazement how it can be that the death of socialism as put into practice should also be the death of utopian socialism—which was fought against by all the Marxists after Marx—one is told that not only has utopian socialism died but also democracy with its French Revolution dream of "freedom, equality, and brotherhood." Not only this utopia or that but a whole "utopian age" is now said to have come to an end. The French Revolution was the first solemn attempt to translate utopian ideas into political practice, and socialism was the last. "To the degree that only the most extreme eschatological seriousness underlies them, all these dreams of a new order, whether orientated on the past or on the 'goal of history,' inevitably issue in terror, whatever their original impulse may have been" (p. 57).

Joachim Fest overlooked the fact that with his prophesied "end of the utopian age" he was also announcing the death of the "American dream" of the "self-evident truth" that all human beings are created free and equal, as the Declaration of Independence puts it. He forgot that the 1948 Universal Declaration of Human Rights is an ideal, as the preamble said, which the United Nations so desperately attempts to put into practice. It was composed after the experiences of inhuman dictatorships with the resolve to create a new and peaceful world order. It was the experiences of political terror that brought into life this universally recognized utopia of justice. In the same way as this utopia sets out to protect the freedom of all men and women, so the social utopias set out to protect the equality of all men and women. In the same way as those utopias of justice represent the hopes of the humiliated and hurt, so the social utopias represent the hopes of the weary and heavy-laden. Since the American and French Revolutions, the two have belonged together: there can be no equality without freedom, no freedom without equality. All human beings are born "free and equal." In the postwar conflict between East and West, in the end the freedom of the West proved superior to the equality of the East. But for that very reason, in the postcommunist period the task will be equality in the form of social and economic justice, in and between the societies on this earth.

So who are the subjects of the visions of a free and just life? They are the oppressed people and the hungry masses. As long as these exist, there will also be utopian projects for overcoming humiliation and exploitation. As long as there is such misery there is also hope for a future different from the sufferings of the present. Hope is the lifeforce of the victims of the present systems of the world. Because they cannot have a fair share in the present they long for an alternative future. Of course, specific ideas about this hope change, because they relate to the concrete experience of the misery of oppression, the death of children, and the devastation of the natural basis of life. Utopias come and go, but hope remains.

Who wants an "end of utopia," and who is served by the dark "end of the utopian age?" The answer is obvious. Those who dominate and enjoy the present want to extend their present into the future and are afraid of any alternative future. They want to suppress the "underside of their history" from public awareness. So they declare that their system is the "end of history," to which, as modern cynicism has it, there is "no alternative."

Francis Fukuyama has become the prophet of this new political and economic apocalyptic. He is a member of the planning staff in the State Department in Washington, the spokesman of American neoconservatives and as a later pupil of Alexandre Kojève, a right-wing Hegelian. According to his famous article "The End of History?" in *The National Interest*, 16, 1989, 3–18, the triumph of the West consists in the fact that all the great alternative systems to "liberal democracy and global marketing," all the things like Fascism, nationalism, and socialism, are exhausted. No further alternatives can be recognized. So we are at the beginning of a time without alternatives, which Kojève with his arbitrary interpretation of Hegel called "the end of history, posthistory." For Fukuyama, as for all other prophets of posthistory like Cournot, de Man, Seidenberg, Gehlen and so on, this is no promise of happiness: "The end of history will be a very sad time . . . In the posthistoric period there will be neither art nor philosophy, just the perpetual caretaking of the museum of human history." He developed this later view in his book *The End of History* (New York 1991), in which he gave a more differentiated account. His interpretation of the age was in tune with the mood of the age. Even the sober *Herald Tribune* in 1990 broke out into eschatological jubilation: "After some millennia of trying out various systems we are now ending this millennium in the certainty that in pluralistic capitalist democracy we have found what we were looking for. There can still be endless improvements to the system and approaches to perfection in postmodernity, but there are no longer any alternatives to the fundamentals of the system."

The notion that human history has reached its end when there are no longer any alternatives to the present political and economic system is a false conclusion that Hegel himself did not draw. All human life-systems have been and are changed when their intrinsic contradictions become intolerable. Who bears the cost for the "global marketing" of all things? What does the world market look like from below when seen through the eyes of the millions of unemployed, with the eyes of people in the Third World, with the eyes of the nature that is being marketed? The protest of human beings who have been made superfluous and of the earth that has been raped will not leave the world in its present state. Anyone who proclaims "the end of history" over it wills the downfall of the world, for, as Erich Fried remarked, "anyone who wants the world to remain as it is does not want it to remain." If this world is to survive, we need utopian visions that lead people out of the misery they are experiencing. "Where there is no vision, the people perish." Their creative source is the unconditional *Yes*, which is spoken by the hope of life. The hope for the kingdom of God and God's righteousness that Christian faith arouses and keeps alive is a great affirmation of life.

Table of Original Publications

1. Metz, "The Future in the Memory of Suffering," in Johannes B. Metz, ed., *The God Question* (*Concilium* vol. 6, no. 8 [1972]). A version of this essay later appeared in Johann Baptist Metz, *Faith in History and Society* (New York: Seabury, 1980).

2. Metz, "Messianic or 'Bourgeois' Religion?" in *Concilium* #125 (1979). A version of this essay later appeared in Johann Baptist Metz, *The Emergent Church* (New York: Crossroad, 1981).

3. Metz, "Theology in the Modern Age," in Claude Geffré, Gustavo Gutiérrez, Virgil Elizondo, eds., *Different Theologies, Common Responsibility* (*Concilium* #171 [1984]).

4. Metz, "Facing the Jews: Christian Theology after Auschwitz," in Elisabeth Schüssler Fiorenza and David Tracy, eds., *The Holocaust as Interruption* (*Concilium* #175 [1984]).

5. Metz, "Theology in the Struggle for History and Society," in Marc H. Ellis and Otto Maduro, eds., *The Future of Liberation Theology: Essays in Honor of Gustavo Gutiérrez* (Maryknoll, N.Y.: Orbis Books, 1989).

6. Metz, "Unity and Diversity: Problems and Prospects for Inculturation," in Johann-Baptist Metz and Edward Schillebeeckx, eds., *World Catechism or Inculturation?* (*Concilium* #204 [1989]).

7. Metz, "1492—Through the Eyes of a European Theologian," in Leonardo Boff and Virgil Elizondo, eds., *1492–1992: The Voice of the Victims* (*Concilium* 1990/6).

8. Metz, "Freedom in Solidarity," in Norbert Greinacher and Norbert Mette, eds., *The New Europe: A Challenge for Christians* (*Concilium* 1992/2).

9. Metz, "Time without a Finale," in Hermann Häring and Johann-Baptist Metz, eds., *Reincarnation or Resurrection?* (*Concilium* 1993/5).

10. Moltmann, "The 'Crucified God': God and the Trinity Today," in Johannes B. Metz, ed., *The God Question* (*Concilium* vol. 6, no. 8 [1972]).

11. Moltmann, "The Liberating Feast," in Herman Schmidt and David Power, eds., *Politics and Liturgy* (*Concilium* vol. 2., no. 10 [1974]).

12. Moltmann, "Messianic Hope in Christianity," in Hans Küng and Walter Kasper, eds., *Christians and Jews* (*Concilium* #98 [1974]). A version of this essay later appeared in Jürgen Moltmann, *The Experiment Hope* (Philadelphia: Fortress Press, 1975).

13. Moltmann, "The Confession of Jesus Christ," in Hans Küng and Jürgen Moltmann, eds., *An Ecumenical Confession of Faith?* (*Concilium* #118 [1978]).

14. Moltmann, "The Motherly Father," in Johann-Baptist Metz and Edward Schillebeeckx, eds., *God as Father* (*Concilium* #143 [1981]).

15. Moltmann, "Can There Be an Ecumenical Mariology?" in Hans Küng and Jürgen Moltmann, eds., *Mary in the Churches* (*Concilium* #168 [1983]).

16. Moltmann, "The Inviting Unity of the Triune God," in Claude Geffré and Jean-Pierre Jossua, eds., *Monotheism* (*Concilium* #177 [1985]).

17. Moltmann, "Peace, the Fruit of Justice," in Hans Küng and Jürgen Moltmann, eds., *A Council for Peace* (*Concilium* #195 [1988]).

18. Moltmann, "Revolution, Religion, and the Future," in Claude Geffré and Jean-Pierre Jossua, eds., *1789: The French Revolution and the Church* (*Concilium* #201 [1989]).

19. Moltmann, "Has Modern Society Any Future?" in Concilium Foundation, *Threshold of the Third Millennium* (*Concilium* 1990/1).

20. Moltmann, "Human Rights, the Rights of Humanity and the Rights of Nature," in Hans Küng and Jürgen Moltmann, eds., *The Ethics of World Religions and Human Rights* (*Concilium* 1990/2).

21. Moltmann, "Fundamentalism and Modernity," in Hans Küng and Jürgen Moltmann, eds., *Fundamentalism as an Ecumenical Challenge* (*Concilium* 1992/3).

22. Moltmann, "End of Utopia—End of History?" in Norbert Greinacher and Norbert Mette, eds., *Christianity and Cultures* (*Concilium* 1994/2).